Take CHARGE of the Classroom

Take CHARGE of the Classroom

Disrupting Outdated Behavior Management Models

Aaron Daffern

Library of Congress Control Number: 2021913697

Copyright © 2021 David Aaron Daffern

All rights reserved. This book or any portion thereof may not be reproduced or used in any manner whatsoever without the express written permission of the author except for the use of brief quotations in a book review or scholarly journal.

First Printing: 2021

ISBN-13: 978-0-9990241-7-1

Aaron Daffern Consulting
River Oaks, TX
www.AaronDaffern.com

Dedication

I wish I this book when I first started teaching. In fact, I still needed it when I left the classroom for administration 11 years later.

This is for all the educators out there doing the best they can while wishing that they could do better.

Contents

Introduction 1
    Take CHARGE model 6
    How to read this book 9
    Metaphors 12
Confidence 21
    1 – 1 Introduction (Confidence) 23
    1 – 2 Purpose (Confidence) 29
    1 – 3 Positivity (Confidence) 49
    1 – 4 Protection (Confidence) 71
    1 – 5 Conclusion (Confidence) 93
Heart 99
    2 – 1 Introduction (Heart) 101
    2 – 2 Relationships (Heart) 107
    2 – 3 Respect (Heart) 129
    2 – 4 Release (Heart) 151
    2 – 5 Conclusion (Heart) 173

Anticipate 179
- 3 – 1 Introduction (Anticipate) 181
- 3 – 2 Procedures (Anticipate) 187
- 3 – 3 Productivity (Anticipate) 209
- 3 – 4 Planning (Anticipate) 229
- 3 – 5 Conclusion (Anticipate) 249

Reinforce 255
- 4 – 1 Introduction (Reinforce) 257
- 4 – 2 Attention (Reinforce) 263
- 4 – 3 Action (Reinforce) 285
- 4 – 4 Attitude (Reinforce) 307
- 4 – 5 Conclusion (Reinforce) 327

Grow 335
- 5 – 1 Introduction (Grow) 337
- 5 – 2 Interpersonal (Grow) 343
- 5 – 3 Intrapersonal (Grow) 363
- 5 – 4 Intellectual (Grow) 383
- 5 – 5 Conclusion (Grow) 405

Engage 411
- 6 – 1 Introduction (Engage) 413
- 6 – 2 Motivation (Engage) 419
- 6 – 3 Memory (Engage) 439
- 6 – 4 Making meaning (Engage) 459
- 6 – 5 Conclusion (Engage) 481

Appendix 487
Bibliography 495

INTRODUCTION

I'm writing this introduction in January of 2021. The preceding year is one that will be remembered for generations as a turning point in history. We are still in the slow beginning phases of the COVID-19 vaccine rollout. Joe Biden has just entered office as the 46th president. Educators, students, and parents are wondering when (if) schools will get back to normal.

When will we have 100% face-to-face instruction?

When can we finally log off of Zoom?

I'm not going to try to predict when any of those things will happen. Maybe things will never go back to normal.

We might just need to embrace the term *new normal* (sigh).

I distinctly remember when COVID-19 first became real for me. I was chatting with an assistant superintendent of Dallas Independent School District (DISD) the Friday before spring break. The date was March 13, 2020 and some neighboring districts had already declared that they would extend their break for a week or two to try to figure out what the fuss was all about. DISD hadn't officially said anything yet so we were both prognosticating before leaving for break.

Combining our vast intellects, our prediction was that we would get an extra week of spring break for a deep cleaning of schools.

That was our best guess before the world suddenly broke. Thus, I've learned not to even try to figure out when we'll emerge from the shadow of COVID-19.

So, while schools and teachers struggle to simultaneously teach face-to-face and virtually, with infections numbers rising all over the place, I can't see into the future to see when (if ever) we'll get back to normal teaching practices. While my initial idea for this book dates all the way back to 2018, its journey has grown into something larger than I could have ever foreseen.

More than anything, I believe that the ideas in this book contain the one thing that every teacher and child needs for today and tomorrow.

Hope.

We cannot predict what teaching will look like next year or even next week. Perhaps we'll always have a virtual component to instruction. We might not ever find a way to close Pandora's technology box.

While there are wonderful teachers and educators out there innovating and hustling as hard as they can to make face-to-face and virtual teaching work, there are many more that will never recover from 2020.

It shattered the will of too many educators.

It created learning gaps that we'll have to deal with for the next ten to twenty years.

It exposed schools and teachers that had been barely getting by and left their inadequacies on display for all.

Introduction

So how do we recover? How do we get back to normal, whatever that normal might be?

The hope I'm sharing in this book is all about taking charge of the classroom.

This is not about exerting your will over students. Rigidly controlling them or following around them mercilessly with testing, tracking, and data binders is not the answer. The simple truth is, learning is done *by* students, not *to* students. Yet too many teachers either don't understand that the full weight of learning should fall on the students or, more likely, don't know how to properly set them up for success.

Let me paint a picture for you. Think about what you're going to read with two simple questions in mind: Does this describe your classroom? If not, would you like it to?

As you walk into the room, you see students in groups or pairs engaged in various activities. They aren't working silently but are instead talking and laughing in a subdued but energetic manner. You look over the shoulder of a pair of students, wondering what could be so interesting. You see a problem that they are collaborating on. The students are not only working to answer the question, they are discussing which representation would best prove their work. After a short debate, they decide to use two representations, one for each of them.

You move on to a group of three students and ask what they are working on. One student pipes up and articulately responds with a learning statement spoken in the first person. Thinking that she might just be reading off a posted objective, you ask follow up questions to see if she really understands what she's doing and why. Her answers, and the rigor of the task, show that the students are not only fully aware of what they are learning but are also able to give descriptions of how far along they are on the learning continuum.

Looking up, you try to spot the teacher. Sitting at the back table with two students, you notice the teacher working with manipulatives on some type of intervention lesson. That winds down and, as you watch, the two students get up, push in their chairs, and move to join their classmates in the activities they are already engaged in. The teacher silently gets up, glances at a list on her clipboard, and kneels down next to a few other students. They join her at the back table and a new small group lesson begins.

The simple truth is, learning is done by students, not to students.

As you take one final look around the room, you see an environment rich in print and content. Students are actively working on tasks, many of which seem self-selected, and do not need behavioral directions or verbal cues. You theorize that if, for some strange reason, the teacher were to leave the classroom, everything would continue without missing a beat.

That vision is not some distant utopia. It can happen in a virtual, face-to-face, or blended classroom. If you desperately want the previous scenario to be a description of your classroom, then you are in the right place.

What you read can happen in low-income or high-income schools. The curriculum doesn't matter, the state of your technology is irrelevant, and

INTRODUCTION

even the quality of your school leadership has a relatively low impact.

This book is written for you, a teacher on her own that desperately wants to take charge of her classroom. You're tired of waiting for school or district leadership to implement a viable behavior management program. You've given up hope of ever having the newest touch screen TV or a class set of iPads. The curriculum your district supplies has more holes in it than a slice of Swiss cheese. You're teaching virtual and in-class students all at the same time.

What can you do on your own by simply closing your classroom door and doing what's best for you and your students?

That's where hope comes in.

We know how to create this idyllic scene in classrooms across the country. The answer, unfortunately, is not simple. Neither is it one-dimensional. In fact, strands from multiple disciplines and fields must be woven together into a larger tapestry before a clear solution emerges.

The central themes of taking charge of your classroom emerge from research, experiences, best practices, and good old common sense. It's not a program or a kit that you can order from Teachers Pay Teachers. It's not a separate curriculum that will compete with whatever mandate or initiative that your district happens to be pushing at the moment.

Instead, taking charge is a framework, a series of principles that are loose enough for personalization and can be applied in any context, grade level, and zip code. Yet it's structured enough that it doesn't take a doctoral student to figure out how to make it work in your classroom tomorrow.

If that sounds appealing, then keep reading, my friends.

Take CHARGE model

This book is not written for teacher preparation programs at the university level, though aspiring teachers would do well to take these principles to heart. Neither is it written for peer-reviewed research journals or as part of a doctoral dissertation.

It's written for you, the professional educator. You, the one working over 60 hours a week trying to keep your personal life from collapsing while not leaving any of your students behind.

To that end, I'll let you know up front that the writing style is meant for those that aren't too interested in having every other sentence interrupted by random names and dates in parentheses. I'm purposefully keeping the citations sparse in most sections and each citation applies not only to the sentence it's found in but also to its surrounding context. This book is written to be read as a narrative with minimal interruptions.

That does not mean, however, that this book is simply pulled from my imagination. No, the foundation of this book and the Take CHARGE model rests on the shoulders of educators and researchers that are much smarter than me.

I draw from the growing wealth of knowledge found in the field of social-emotional learning and how it applies to classroom wellness. For decades educators have used basic classroom management principles that focus on procedures, which also influenced my thinking.

For too long we've ignored the importance of race and cultural literacy. Work from that field is included, as is neuroscience, what we know about the physical structures of the brain, and its implications for teaching and learning. Even parenting books hold some truths for us since educators often act as *de facto* parental figures for students.

INTRODUCTION

Finally, behavioral therapists and psychologists have developed treatments and principles that have proven to curb or eliminate maladaptive behaviors. Truths from that field are woven together with research on memory and growing executive skills.

True solutions do not come from focusing on a single source or theory but weaving together threads from multiple sources, all of which contribute to a tapestry that gives us hope.

Hope for a better future for our students. Hope for rekindling the joy of teaching. Hope for humanity.

To that end, taking charge of the classroom can be thought of in six large sections or strands.

<u>C</u>onfidence – Taking charge begins within educators themselves, not with students or environments. Teachers learn to enter the classroom confidently when they are grounded in their purpose, choose positivity, and understand that their primary role is to protect students. Learning brains are safe brains.

<u>H</u>eart – The heart of teaching is students, not content. Relationships form the basis of everything else that happens in the classroom. These relationships are strengthened when teachers respect students, both their potential and the cultural strengths they bring with them, rather than holding a deficit view. Finally, the heart of teaching is releasing control, honoring students' autonomy and building their agency.

<u>A</u>nticipate – Veteran classroom teachers, if asked for classroom management advice, will typically say, "Procedures, procedures, procedures." They know that one (but not the only) key to successful classrooms is the implementation and maintenance of procedures. Additionally, good teachers maximize productivity to reduce down-time and take care to plan their lessons carefully. By doing these things, they

can anticipate problems and usually avoid them altogether.

<u>R</u>einforce – This truth will be the hardest for some teachers to hear but is the one that will most likely get them over the final behavioral hurdle. What you focus on in the classroom, you get more of. By constantly nagging students and chiding them for minor infractions, you only guarantee that you'll get more of the same. Behavioral therapy has proven that the most efficient and long-lasting way to change behavior is to reinforce positive actions and ignore negative ones. By using the power of their attention, teachers can increase actions and attitudes that meet their expectations without shaming students for their poor choices.

The heart of teaching is students, not content.

<u>G</u>row – Trying to stop poor behaviors is not the same as teaching students good ones. In the grow strand, teachers explicitly teach and help students grow interpersonal, intrapersonal, and intellectual skills to help them succeed. While teachers do want students to stop calling out or hitting others, that merely inhibits poor behaviors. More than that, they can teach their students about resilience, growth mindsets, and curiosity, to name just a few beneficial traits.

<u>E</u>ngage – The most well-behaved class will be primed for learning but not guaranteed to achieve unless academics are addressed. After implementing the first five parts of the Take CHARGE model, the final step is to fully engage students with powerful teaching practices. First, students are motivated by a combination of five facets and instruction that leverages these will be far more captivating. Second, students make meaning by processing new information and tying it to prior knowledge,

Introduction

not sitting and getting. Finally, new work on memory and retrieval practice shows simple tips for greatly improving retention and achievement.

How to read this book

Seems like a silly idea – front to back, right?

Not necessarily.

If you are reading this book for the first time, or are in need of behavioral solutions you can implement tomorrow, I would recommend reading this book using the *immediate impact sequence*. Instead of moving through the book from beginning to end, it runs through the six parts of the Take CHARGE model in three separate waves.

In each wave you'll learn new components for each of the six major sections. The sequence is designed to help you construct an overall picture before diving into the details by skipping the introduction and conclusion of each section and getting right to the good stuff. The sequence is listed below and you'll also find a tip at the end of subsection directing you where to go next.

Immediate impact sequence

- 2 – 2 Relationships (Heart)
- 3 – 2 Procedures (Anticipate)
- 4 – 2 Attention (Reinforce)
- 1 – 4 Protection (Confidence)
- 6 – 2 Motivation (Engage)
- 5 – 3 Intrapersonal (Grow)
- 2 – 3 Respect (Heart)
- 3 – 3 Productivity (Anticipate)
- 4 – 3 Action (Reinforce)

- 1 – 3 Positivity (Confidence)
- 6 – 3 Memory (Engage)
- 5 – 2 Interpersonal (Grow)
- 2 – 4 Release (Heart)
- 3 – 4 Planning (Anticipate)
- 4 – 4 Attitude (Reinforce)
- 1 – 2 Purpose (Confidence)
- 6 – 4 Making meaning (Engage)
- 5 – 4 Intellectual (Grow)

Action boxes

Reading is all well and good, but how do you know if you're actually making a difference?

I'm glad you asked.

At the mid-point and conclusion of each subsection you will find action boxes. The first part gives you two action steps you can take to immediately implement what you just read.

The second part of each action box describes what to look for and notice if you want to find evidence of implementation. Third, reflection is an integral part to any learning process. The two questions that are provided can be used for self-reflection or as part of a book study.

Finally, if you are using the *immediate impact sequence* you will find a tip at the bottom of the action box at the end of subsection letting you know what part of the book to read next. An example, from the end of subsection 2 -2 Relationships (Heart), can be found on the opposite page.

INTRODUCTION

What can you do tomorrow?

Plan random acts of kindness. Think about how you can integrate noncontingent reinforcement into your daily interactions with a student. Choose a student with whom you have few positive interactions and decide on an initial interval, from five to ten minutes. Stay consistent. When your notification or reminder dings, have a short positive interaction with the student (e.g., smile, gentle touch, kind word). Note how the relationship improves.

What does this look like in the classroom?

The teacher develops and maintains **connection rituals**, which can include:

- Greeting students at the door with a smile and handshake;
- Classroom rituals (e.g., walk-and-talks); and
- Using humor (sharing jokes, puns, or comics) with students.

How can you reflect on your learning?

Which connection rituals have you found to be successful?

_____

_____

How can you use noncontingent reinforcement to increase positive relationships in your classroom?

_____

_____

Immediate impact: Go to 3 – 2 Procedures (Anticipate) – pg. 187

The Look Fors in the middle of the action boxes are split into three types, one for each major subsection of the Take CHARGE model. One type, like the one on the previous page, looks at teacher behaviors and their effects on students and the classroom environments. If you read using the *immediate impact sequence*, each set of Look Fors during your first time through looks at teacher behaviors.

The second type of Look For, evident in the second time through the *immediate impact sequence*, shifts the focus to student impact. As you increase the effectiveness of your teacher moves, the spotlight shifts from what you are doing to what the students are doing.

The third type, seen during the final time through the Take CHARGE model using the *immediate impact sequence*, examines classroom tasks and responsibilities. Taking charge of your classroom doesn't just improve your behaviors but impacts students and accelerates learning through rigorous tasks and student responsibility.

You can find a list of all the Look Fors in the appendix.

If you plan to follow the *immediate impact sequence*, go ahead and follow the tip below to get started. If you want to read the book in order, please keep reading the next section.

Immediate impact: Go to 2 – 2 Relationships (Heart) – pg. 107

Metaphors

Now, before jumping into the deep-end, I have a confession to make. I've never met a metaphor I didn't like.

In fact, I'm a big fan of metaphors and think that apt images have the power to take vastly intricate ideas and make them easier to think about.

So, this book doesn't use one big metaphor. Or even two.

INTRODUCTION

What you'll find are three big metaphors that overlap and (hopefully) work together to help make this book both understandable and digestible.

Iceberg model

The first metaphor that aims to help you understand how to take charge is that of an iceberg. As you imagine an iceberg, you can probably picture how this representation is typically used. While what is above the surface of the ocean might seem large, the proportion of the iceberg hidden beneath the waves is much, much larger. One of the chief aims of this book is to change teacher behaviors. If you want to take charge of your classroom, you'll need to examine how you do things and find better methods for managing behavior.

Teacher moves that help you take charge are found in the third through fifth sections of the book (anticipate, reinforce, and grow). Behaviors are represented only by the tip of the iceberg, however. While your behaviors are visible to you, your students, and your administrators, they are driven by elements below the surface. Influencing your behaviors are your beliefs.

Too many classroom management programs fail not because they have faulty ideas but because they only scratch the surface. Driving your behaviors are your beliefs, the part of the iceberg directly below the surface. Before learning how to streamline and align your teacher behaviors, the second section of the book (heart) speaks to what you believe about students, their value, and the true purpose of teaching. If you want your behaviors to permanently change, you must strike below the surface to your beliefs.

And yet changing beliefs isn't as easy as it may seem. You hold some truths about yourself, about your students, and about education in general that are deeply rooted in your psyche. Many educators can trace the seed of these ideas all the way back to their own experiences in school. Beliefs can change but will not become new mindsets unless the deepest part of your being is affected.

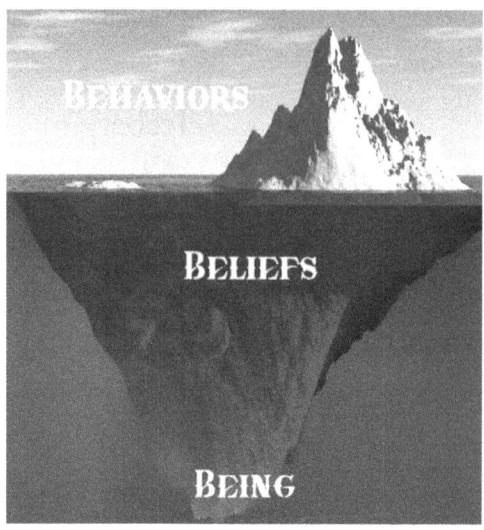

At the bottom of the iceberg, in the depths of the ocean that reach so far down that the light barely penetrates, is your way of being. Who you are. How you define yourself. The first part of this book (confidence) starts at ground zero, asking you to examine who you see in the mirror. You can't take charge of your classroom until you take charge of yourself.

Thus the first five sections of the book proceed sequentially up the iceberg. From the bottom, you examine your way of being and learn to gain the confidence needed to take charge. Next, you evaluate and modify your beliefs to align with the heart of teaching. Once you crack the surface, your teacher behaviors change through anticipation, reinforcement, and growth.

And there's an elephant on top of the iceberg.

Elephant and rider

Adapting your teacher behaviors to take charge is all about change management. And change is hard.

INTRODUCTION

I first read about the elephant when I ran across *Switch* (Heath & Heath, 2010), a fantastic read for anyone wanting to guide change in a new way. The metaphor they use to discuss strategies for effective change management is that of a rider and an elephant. So, when you think about the iceberg, once you get above the surface, if you zoom in you'll see an elephant and rider on top.

If you are riding an elephant and want to get it to move to a certain location, there are three elements or angles you can use to achieve your desired result. One method is to shape the path. Tweak the environment so that the path of least resistance is in fact the path toward your destination. In the Take CHARGE model, this relates to the third section (anticipate). You can help set your students up for success when you eliminate obstacles to good behavior.

In addition to shaping the path, you can also motivate the elephant. The elephant itself represents your emotions and is by far the biggest driver in change management. This element is represented by the fourth section (reinforce) and looks at how to use the power of your attention to mold behaviors without relying on negative emotions such as fear or shame. Emotions drive behavior, so leaning on negative emotions will never lead to positive behaviors.

Finally, there is a rider on top of the elephant. He might not be in full control but the rider can direct the elephant toward a desired direction. For our purposes, the rider represents our rational minds and is examined in the fifth section of the book (grow). As educators, we should teach much more than content. In addition to instructing students in reading and math, we can also teach them emotional literacy and empathy, grit and curiosity. Teaching and practicing these positive habits will pay large dividends.

As I previously disclosed, I never met a metaphor I didn't like. When thinking about how to best package the Take CHARGE model to make it more easily understandable, I kept running into a problem. I first thought of the iceberg model and thought to myself, *Sure, why not?*

After reading *Switch*, I immediately latched onto the elephant and the rider metaphor and, with a little bit of finessing, found a way to integrate the two by putting the elephant on top of the iceberg.

But both metaphors exclude what might be the most important part of the entire model – engage. The sad truth is, you can set up your procedures, maintain positivity, build strong relationships, teach about having a growth mindset, and focus on desired behaviors all day long. If

INTRODUCTION

you give your students worksheets or low-level tasks, they will misbehave.

While some of you prefer to think that your students' behavioral problems all stem from poor parenting skills or other factors outside your control, oftentimes they are simply bored. Bored students misbehave. Engaged students are too interested to act out.

Thus, the final section of the book (engage) closes out the Take CHARGE model with key principles for student engagement that draw from some of my previous books.

And yet engagement doesn't quite work with the elephant or iceberg metaphor.

Anyone that knows me knows that I am a huge sports fan. Living in the Dallas/Fort Worth metroplex since 2000, I have enjoyed the ups and downs of our local sports teams for several decades.

And if you think of Dallas sports, you can't avoid thinking of the #1 franchise (in terms of net worth) in the entire world.

How 'bout them Cowboys!

Football

Thus a third metaphor that uses football terminology encapsulates everything you will find in this book. If the iceberg with the elephant on top doesn't quite work for you, this metaphor captures the entire Take CHARGE model.

Anyone that watches a lot of football knows that games are won, lost, and played in three phases. Ask any football aficionado what wins championships and they will most likely answer *defense*. While the defensive side of football can score points, its primary purpose is to keep the other team from scoring. In your battle to take charge of your classroom, your best defense is found in the first two sections of the book (confidence and heart). When you come into the classroom with strength and purpose, focusing on relationships, you'll have won before any students ever darken your classroom door.

Others subscribe to the notion that the best defense is a good offense. It's the offensive side of the ball that is tasked with scoring points, so when combating poor classroom behavior you have two offensive skills to deploy that are found in the third and fourth sections (anticipate and reinforce). Building in procedures, increasing productivity, and reinforcing desired actions and attitudes with the power of your attention can score you more than enough points in your classroom management struggle

---

You can't take charge of the classroom until you take charge of yourself.

While casual football fans might only be able to name the first two phases, defense and offense, hard core fans know that there is a third phase that can completely flip the field. Special teams, which consist of kickoffs, punts, and field goals, can take a simple punt or kickoff from five yards deep in the endzone and run it all the way back for a touchdown. In the span of thirty seconds, special teams can make or break your chances of winning.

For our purposes, the final two sections of the book (grow and engage) represent special teams. If you were to stop reading the book after the first two phases, defense and offense as represented by confidence, heart, anticipate, and grow, you could become a competent teacher. You could successfully learn to manage your classroom and eliminate poor behavior.

INTRODUCTION

	Iceberg	Elephant and rider	Football
Confidence	Being		Defense
Heart	Beliefs		
Anticipate	Behaviors	Clear the path	Offense
Reinforce		Motivate the elephant	
Grow		Direct the rider	Special teams
Engage			

Table 1: Metaphors Comparison

But if you want to move from surviving to thriving, from managing to empowering, you'll need to engage special teams. The final two sections speak directly to student achievement while simultaneously working to minimize negative behavior.

Because that's the true secret of this book. It isn't you that's supposed to take charge.

It's your students.

If you are looking for hope in the midst of the COVID-19 pandemic, if you are thinking of quitting the profession, or if you are simply frustrated and losing the joy of teaching, it's time to take charge.

Keep reading to find out how.

Confidence

Heart

Anticipate

Reinforce

Grow

Engage

1 – 1 Introduction (Confidence)

Behaviors flow from beliefs and beliefs flow from your being.

If you want to take charge of your classroom, you'll have to keep two fundamental truths in mind.

First, you can only control yourself, and even that is hard. You cannot make others (i.e., your students) change.

Second, lasting improvement comes only when you've drilled down to the core. Surface level hacks might work for a season but cannot stand the test of time.

Thus, the first step in taking charge of your classroom is confidence.

Your confidence.

How you show up to the classroom, your energy, your mojo, sets the tone for everything else.

Everything.

You are the deciding factor in your classroom. You are the difference between success and failure, growth and stagnation. If you can improve yourself, your students and your classroom environment will be unable to resist the pull of your power.

Working on your confidence first, before we look at procedures, strategies, and classroom management tips, honors the fact that everything flows from your being.

Who are you? Why are you a teacher? What are you hoping to accomplish this year? What are you willing to do for your students?

Answers to questions like these speak to your identity as an educator. Prior to examining your beliefs, which shape the very behaviors you want to improve, the first step is to come into the classroom with confidence.

When crisis situations erupt, like a natural disaster or any other scene of mass confusion, some people rise to the occasion and lead. It's not always those with the titles and positions. It's not always those with the most charisma or magnetism, though these people tend to initially stand out in stressful situations. More than anything, when you're on the 18th floor of a building that's collapsing, you want to follow someone that has a plan.

It's the person who is cool, calm, and collected that ends up as the leader. The one who knows how to keep everyone together, to gather ideas from the group and put forth a viable escape plan while allowing everyone to feel heard, is the one who has the followers. Ultimately, these leaders serve others, rather than dominating them, and their impact is drawn from their followers.

Confidence increases your performance during stressful situations. You can more easily influence others through a commanding presence and positive attitude. Additionally, confidence grants you freedom. You gain energy and motivation while losing anxiety. You feel like you can handle anything that comes your way.

You might not ever find yourself trapped in a crumbling building, thrust together with a group of strangers and forced to get everyone to safety, find a love interest, close three separate subplots, and battle your own inner turmoil while exorcising the demons of your own conflicted past. Your task is much harder.

You are a teacher.

Your students are coming to you fragile and needy. Some have little to no faith in their ability to succeed. A few might have serious trauma they are dealing with while others are suffering from systemic racism. They might be several grade levels behind academically, have few positive role models, and only attend school because of compulsory attendance laws. You are their leader, whether you wanted to be or not, and you must be confident.

Confidence is not cockiness. It's not dominance nor is it bluster. *Fake it 'til you make it* works less often than you think. You need to enter the classroom each morning sure of your role, your place in the learning environment, and with a plan to help every child succeed. You also must be confident in your ability to adjust on the fly, to keep things rolling when your finely crafted lesson plans derail at 8:08 a.m.

Confidence is not cockiness.

When you grow in confidence, you nurture strength in the core of your being. That confidence will serve as the foundation for the second part of taking charge, heart. Yet it's not as simple as repeating positive statements to yourself or being blindly optimistic. When you try to manufacture confidence, the only person you fool is yourself. Everyone else, your students especially, can read you like a week-old newspaper.

In the classroom, confidence comes from connecting with three powerful aspects. The first is purpose. What drives you to show up early each day and stay late into the evening? Your purpose is your power source, refilling you when your reserves are running low. Purpose pushes you through obstacles when all you want to do is turn around and run from them.

Purpose is power and when you claim it, you claim confidence.

The second aspect is positivity. We spend a large majority of our lives presuming the intent of others. We see their actions, hear their words, and ascribe intentions to them. Someone says something kind to us, and we apply an intention of graciousness (*She's really kind. She's such a nice person.*) or malice (*What does she want? She's just saying that to get on my good side.*) without ever truly knowing the actual intention of the other person. We think we do, but in fact we are just continually projecting our own doubts and fears onto others and interpreting their actions through our unseen filters.

What happens if we presume positive intent? When we give people, especially our students, the benefit of the doubt, our confidence in our own ability grows. Instead of constantly being under assault because of the malicious actions of others, we can stay curious and open to new possibilities. Positivity keeps learning paths and solutions accessible while negativity shuts them down.

The third aspect is protection. So many times we plan diligently, making sure everything is ready for a lesson, and then watch it land with a thud as students remain unengaged or fail to show mastery on the assessment. While the problem might be with the planning, the activities, or the rigor of the tasks, sometimes the issue lies with the students. They don't feel safe.

Confidence

A learning brain is a safe brain. When students feel protected, socially and emotionally, then and only then are they ready to learn. Taking on the mantle of *chief protector* gives you the confidence to know that you are giving your students' brains the one thing they must have before learning becomes possible – safety.

Confidence is not drawn simply from positive self-talk but by aligning your being with these three aspects. That confidence will power your journey toward taking charge of the classroom.

The two most important days in life are the day you are born and the day you discover the reason why.

- Mark Twain

1 – 2 Purpose (Confidence)

So, you're a teacher.

Why?

Ages ago some people viewed education as an easy career to fall back on. With three months off each summer, how hard could teaching really be?

I'm not sure if that fantasy ever truly existed. If it did, it doesn't any longer.

Teaching is hard. It keeps you up at night, takes you away from your own family and your own household duties. It asks too much of you, and when you've given everything, it still asks for more.

Oftentimes teaching is thankless. You're yelled at by parents, demeaned by administrators, and made to feel inept by students. I'm not quite sure if there's another profession in existence that makes so many of its members rethink their life choices on a weekly basis.

Before we dive deep into taking charge of your classroom, into getting a handle on classroom management and reducing off-task behavior, we have to talk about you.

The first part of taking charge of the classroom is confidence, both yours and your students'. It all starts with you, however, and the first step in growing your confidence is tapping into your purpose.

Accidental teacher

If, when I was a boy, you would have asked me what I wanted to be when I grew up, I wouldn't have a firm answer until high school. I was too busy playing baseball, riding my bike around town, and generally having fun with my friends to worry about the future. As the son of a minister, and an identical twin to boot, both my brother and I decided that we would follow our father and join the ministry after college.

With that major decision made, our college plans lined up nicely. We went to a private Baptist college in California, both with full scholarships, and each graduated in three years with double majors (being a twin can be incredibly annoying when everything you do is identical). With a bachelor's degree in religion and history, my brother's life and mine broke into distinctly different directions post-graduation.

You see, after my freshman year in college, I met the love of my life, Heather, when she was a summer missionary to California in 1997. We dated for a year, were engaged in 1998, and got married a few months after I graduated in 1999. While I was starting my new marriage adventure, my brother became a missionary to Botswana for two years.

Still operating under the guidance of my decision to become a minister, my wife and I lived on the college campus for a year after my graduation while I worked in the campus ministries department. Though I already knew that ministry underpaid, I struggled again with that stark reality as a new husband. To supplement my eager income, I also started to serve as a substitute teacher for the local school district on Fridays.

I don't remember much of my few stints as a substitute teacher, but my overarching reaction was one of relief that teaching was not in my future. It was absolutely crazy! Sometimes the students were fine, and then sometimes it seemed as if they were possessed! No matter what I did, it seemed to be wrong. I felt as if I had been dealt a losing hand and that all the students could see my cards.

Fast forward to May 2000. Heather and I decided to move back to her hometown of Fort Worth, TX to be near her family. There is also a nice seminary in the city and I was going to start my graduate work there in the fall. But to pay for my education, and for the family that Heather and I wanted to start, I needed a real job that paid real money. A friend at church told me that, since I had a bachelor's degree, I could get an alternative certification and become an elementary school teacher. While it wasn't a dream scenario, especially with my brother gallivanting around South Africa as a missionary, it would pay the bills.

How hard could teaching be?

Taught by a ten-year-old

I began my modest education career as a 4th grade teacher in Fort Worth, TX. I had sixteen students and nary a clue about what to do with them. Luckily, the friend from church who talked me into teaching was also a 4th grade teacher at the same school. By sheer dumb luck, and the grace of God, I somehow survived the year. During that eventful trial run, I celebrated the birth of my first son and continued to volunteer at my local church while taking a few seminary classes at night.

Desperate to cling onto the thin hope that I knew what I was doing, I coasted through teaching, treating it like a standard 8:00 – 3:00 gig, and poured my all into ministry. I studied and got good grades in all my seminary classes. I fervently did all I could at the church, both on Sundays and Wednesday nights. And even though I was quite dense, I couldn't help but notice a trend starting to emerge.

Everything I did at the church wilted and died. The harder I tried, the less I seemed to connect to the youth I worked with, to the point that they mostly stopped showing up. By no great effort on my part, on the other hand, I happened to do quite well at teaching. My school students were pretty well-behaved, they seemed to be learning, and they did alright on the state test at the end of the year. I felt as if I was in an episode of *The Twilight Zone* where everything I wanted to accomplish at church was funneled into the wrong outcome (school).

All of that came to a crashing halt sometime at the end of my first year. As students are wont to do, one of mine wrote me a little note and put it on my desk. She wrote just two sentences, but they made me rethink everything.

Dear Mr. Daffern, I'm so glad you became a teacher instead of a preacher. I'll never forget you.

What was painfully obvious to my students, but hidden by my refusal to accept reality, was that I was their teacher. While they knew that I wanted to be a preacher, and that I was attending seminary classes at night, they didn't care. The simple reality was that I was a stable factor in their lives. I was there, day in and day out, and we had fun together. Sure, sometimes we learned as well, but that wasn't my driving force.

I found that little kids were very funny! Watching them understand my jokes, try out puns, and learn to appreciate sarcasm was intensely interesting. While I'll never be a people watcher, like my wife Heather, who could sit on a bench at Walmart for four hours and be entertained by simply watching people walk by, I did enjoy interacting with the students. I liked them, and they seemed to like me.

That note from one of my students, however, made me rethink everything. What if I actually tried to be a good teacher? What if I did those teacher-y things like lesson plan on the weekends or spend time trying to make fun activities? How good could I actually be?

It took a ten-year-old to teach me that what I did mattered. Once the scales fell from my eyes, I looked around me with a fresh perspective. Here was a group of students that would probably never darken the door of a church. For many, I was the first male teacher they had ever had. For those without a positive male role model in their lives, that was powerful. I had the opportunity to redefine how children saw themselves and how they related to the world.

I literally held their future in my hands and I nearly missed it. Does teaching matter? Does it touch the human soul as much as pastors and ministers do?

You better believe it.

The reality

And so here I am, more than 20 years later, still in education and loving every minute of it. My brother is still in the ministry and I couldn't be happier for him. He found his thing and I found mine.

What's your thing?

Here's the ugly truth. Everything sucks most of the time.

Everyone loves being a teacher at the start of the year when the desks are lined up nicely and floors still have wax on them. Teacher appreciation week is pretty enjoyable as well, but sometimes that's all you have.

In between comes the parents who drop their kid off on the first day of school and say, as they are leaving, "He's bipolar and ADHD. Good luck."

Happened to me once.

There are the principals who are either way out of their league, were bred in laboratories designed to rob them of all people skills, or possibly both. Nothing can suck the joy out of teaching quicker than administrators who don't understand how to get the best out of their teachers.

And we haven't even discussed the rude, uncontrollable children who are assigned to your roster by some demented twist of fate. Your job is to teach them and possibly get them to score well on a standardized test at the end of the year. If you can't, your job might be on the line. Never mind the fact that they live below the poverty line, move several times a year because their family can't afford the rent, stay up until midnight each night playing Fortnite, and never have money for field trips but have a better phone than you and an inexhaustible supply of Takis and Funyuns.

Fuel

Once the veneer gets scratched off what you thought teaching would be, you're left with a hot mess of unfunded mandates, district initiatives that seemingly change weekly, pressure beyond belief to help kids pass a test you don't even believe in, and ungrateful students with disinterested parents.

Are you okay with that?

While teaching in itself is difficult, that's only one of the job titles you unofficially hold. You are also a surrogate parent, counselor, social worker, behavioral therapist, curriculum developer, test proctor, crisis interventionist, and party planner.

To bring this opening conversation back around full circle, one of the most challenging things about teaching is behavior management. If students would just do what they're told, everything would be easier, right? And if I suddenly became the heir to Jeff Bezos, the founder of Amazon.com, things would also be easier, but that's not going to happen either, is it?

The struggle is real. Teaching is incredibly difficult and taxing to your physical, emotional, and spiritual reserves. It also can give your life meaning and purpose.

You're reading this book right now because you'd like to know more about how to take charge of your classroom, how to get your little imps to behave. We're going to dive deep, pulling from neuroscience, social-emotional learning, behavioral therapy, traditional classroom management resources, and even parenting books. What I'm probing for in this initial section is your resolve.

There are no quick fixes. There are no panaceas. Learning how to take charge in your classroom ironically means that you give most of the control to your students.

Go figure.

What's your fuel? What's your purpose? If things get tough, what do you do?

If you could say without a shadow of a doubt, if you knew that you knew that you knew, that teaching is what you were supposed to do, it would be a source of great strength. The first step in taking charge is confidence. The first step in confidence is purpose. When you can walk into your room each day with the assurance that you're where you're supposed to be, that you are doing what you were made to do, that knowledge would give you an underlying sense of swagger that would propel you through even the most difficult times.

Are you willing to struggle through all the idiocy that comes from central office (or the front office) for the sake of your students?

What are you willing to sacrifice to give your students a fighting chance? Your time? Your money? Your emotional reserves?

What injustices gnaw at you? What do you see in your students or in your community that drives you to show up each morning at 7:00 am, rain or shine?

Teaching is not for the faint of heart. It isn't fun most of the time.

But it matters. More than you will ever know.

To make the changes necessary to take charge of your classroom and to take charge of each moment with your students, you're going to need to unlearn. A lot.

You will be asked to try things that make you uncomfortable and that you doubt will work.

These things will work but they're hard. There are no silver bullets in education, but if you have a solid purpose, if you know why you are a teacher, then let that be the fuel to guide you through this journey.

Because without fuel you'll never reach the end.

CONFIDENCE

What can you do tomorrow?

Claim your purpose. Write a short statement that describes why you are a teacher and what you hope to accomplish. Think about your motivation for continuing even when things get tough.

Ground yourself. Every morning before school, look into your mirror and tell yourself why you are a teacher. Repeat it again and again until it becomes a mantra.

What does this look like in the classroom?

Classroom tasks are **designed with purpose** to support student learning by:

- Reflecting students' cultures and interests;
- Stretching students to reach increasing rigorous goals; and
- Aligning with curriculum standards and assessment tools.

How can you reflect on your learning?

Why are you a teacher?

_____

_____

What is the fuel that keeps you going when teaching becomes difficult?

_____

_____

Student purpose

Here's a crazy thought.

What if kids don't know why they're in school?

You could probably assume that they knew at one point. Either their parents or their kindergarten teacher told them at one time or another that school was where you learned new things. Assuming that the students found that to be a motivating factor, that should have been enough to get them through a few years at least.

But if you have ever taught older students, you know that they sometimes have learned different reasons for going to school.

School is where you're made fun of for being wrong or different.

School is where you feel anxious every time you have to go to lunch in the cafeteria and find a spot to sit.

School is where disinterested adults make you do tons of worksheet packets.

School is where you are forced to go, day in and day out, whether you want to or not.

Before moving on to other aspects of confidence, I'd like to take a moment and try to redeem one of the foundational truths of education that gets lost far too often.

School is where students are loved, supported, and stretched to learn and do things they couldn't do on their own.

If that truth isn't obvious to your students every single day, then that's going to be one of your first steps in taking charge of the classroom.

Make the purpose for coming to school explicit and obvious.

Control is an illusion

When a well-minded adult says to a teacher, "You just need to get those kids to behave," I want to laugh. Might as well ask for a balanced federal budget or peace and harmony between Democrats and Republicans.

This unfortunate reality was made clear to me several years ago. Serving as an instructional coach, one of my many roles was to serve as the go-to guy for any troubled classrooms. Viewed as a jack-of-all-trades, I was sent to assist teachers that might need help due to a variety of reasons.

Sometimes the class was staffed by a long-term substitute and I needed to help get the curriculum and instruction back on pace. At other times, there were certain behavioral situations that I helped teachers troubleshoot. Add to that data disaggregation, small groups tips, and a host of other educational tools, and my job was never dull.

And until I went into Mr. Goshen's class, I thought I had a pretty decent handle on classroom management.

His students taught me otherwise.

Teaching is not for the faint of heart.

Most classes have one or two (or three or four) unruly students. Those are the ones that teachers would do well to befriend and make their special helpers. What I had never experienced before Mr. Goshen's class was the inverse of that principle.

There were about three or four docile students and the rest were off the chain. I actually don't even know if there ever was a chain for some of these students.

I'm always open to learning new things. That being said, Mr. Goshen's students taught me a few things that I didn't really want to know.

My sense of control over a classroom was an illusion.

They outnumbered me. Significantly. One, or even two, adults can not sufficiently put out fires if the entire room is a raging inferno. Floating on a lake of gasoline. And every student has a flamethrower.

I needed to know a lot more about human behavior if I wanted to help Mr. Goshen because my skill set at the time was completely inadequate.

Before you get all judgmental, here are a few facts. Mr. Goshen did not yell at his students. He was positive, supportive, and the students liked him. The problem was not a flaw in his personality, his interactions, or his attentiveness. His students enjoyed seeing him and, after a day of tearing up his classroom, most would give him a hug or fist bump, anxious to see him the next day.

When a class loses its way

Reflecting back on my short and ineffective time with Mr. Goshen's class, which is serving as a significant part of my motivation for writing this book, I now have a clearer picture of what went wrong. All of my little tips and tricks were useless. My eagle-eyed teacher looks, repeated directives, positive options, and everything else I tried were completely futile.

I was standing in front of a category five hurricane trying to keep myself dry with a dollar store Paw Patrol umbrella that was torn and broken.

If I could talk to myself back then, I would give myself some advice that I'd like to share with you.

School is a place of discovery. School is for trying, failing, and getting back up and trying again.

School is for students to learn not only content but how to manage themselves and learn how to learn.

While it was obvious that I knew these things, and Mr. Goshen did as well, the students had forgotten that purpose. To them, school was a place in which they were either predator or prey. School was a place of failure, because that is how they viewed themselves. They were several years behind in reading and math. Many of them were illiterate.

Before they worked on procedures, class commitments, or any kind of behavioral management system, Mr. Goshen's class needed to retrieve its true purpose.

A powerful ritual

Instead of assuming that students know why they were there, Mr. Goshen's class would have benefited from a daily chant or ritual that set the tone for the class. I should have recommended a call-and-response similar to this:

Teacher: Why are we here?
Students: To learn as much as we can.
Teacher: How do we best learn?
Students: By helping each other succeed.
Teacher: Who is responsible for learning?
Students: I am – we are!

Before you write this type of mantra off as silly or gimmicky, consider a few things.

Behavioral science has vetted and validated several foundational truths that we would be wise to abide by (Willans & Williams, 2018). The first fundamental axiom is the need for a common purpose. For a group to be functional, members must unify to accomplish an agreed upon objective. In this context, everyone can excel when a class of students unifies as a group of learners.

Imagine whitewater rafting with your students down a churning river.

You're coming up to a set of rapids, classified as moderately difficult (class 3). You should be able to make it through but you'll need a few students to help row at key points. As you grab your oar and look back to give directions to your students, you see chaos. Three children are fighting over one of the oars, a fourth has thrown his oar into the river, and the last two are no longer in the raft. Instead, they jumped out 30 seconds ago without life vests.

Without everyone on the raft rowing in the same direction, with the same purpose, your raft is at the mercy of the rapids. That is not a pleasant feeling, either for recreational rafters or teachers in the classroom.

Now don't misunderstand me. Even if you could convince your students to participate in a morning chant, your classroom wouldn't change on its own. The chant, or mantra, is representative of some deeper truths that will be explored throughout the remainder of this book. The purpose of the chant is to bring into the open what is sometimes forgotten.

School is for learning.

Learning is only possible when students feel safe, both emotionally and psychologically.

For that safety to exist, it requires cooperation, empathy, leadership, and agency.

Why are we here?

The opening refrain from the mantra asks students a simple question: Why are we here?

While this might be common sense, one thing I've learned throughout my years in education is that common sense is not all that common. Sometimes you have to call out what's hidden and assumed because, until you can agree on the definition of key terms, oftentimes people can use the same words but mean entirely different things.

Some students don't know why they're in school. Some go because their parents make them. Others attend because of a sense of obligation, as their parents have preached the benefits of getting an education for years. Still others attend to get good grades, focused on larger goals like graduation, college, or careers. A sizable portion of students attend school because that's where their friends are and they're social creatures.

So, one wonders, how can teachers steer students toward a beneficial goal orientation, such as learning for learning's sake?

First and foremost, make it explicit. Make it evident and repeat it daily.

Teacher: Why are we here?

Students: To learn as much as we can.

Notice the response is not, "To get good grades," or, "To pass the high-stakes test," or even, "Because we are legally required due to compulsory attendance laws."

I would actually be quite frightened if students answered with the third response.

Second, back up the mantra with actions. Students are going to have a hard time focusing on learning if the tasks they are assigned lack meaning. Fill-in-the-blank worksheets, repetitive tasks, and low-level questions that require simplistic answers don't fool students. They communicate that learning is not a process of discovery but instead a required action that results in a grade and/or time being filled.

How do we best learn?

If teachers seek a true partnership in learning, the roles of both teacher and students need to be clear (Birnie, 2017). While learning as much as they can is a great start for students' purpose at school, it's only the beginning.

Learning is communal. It is a process that grows not just between a teacher and a student but within a larger community context. What was missing from Mr. Goshen's classroom was a sense of unity. The students were not there to help each other or even be friends with each other. Like first-class passengers scrambling for limited lifeboats on the Titanic, his students were concerned only with meeting their own needs.

Relatedness is our psychological need to be a part of something bigger than ourselves, to be connected to others. It's why we live in communities, why family bonds are so powerful, and why inclusion in a group, whether it be a gaming club, a church, or other social group is so important. Teachers have the ability to tap into that need if they are aware of its value and how to access it.

Teacher: How do we best learn?

Students: By helping each other succeed.

Schools and learning do not need to be a zero-sum game. In a zero-sum situation, all outcomes must add up to zero. So, if I'm winning, someone else must be losing. Everyone can't get a trophy, so my success comes at your expense. While sports is an area that definitely qualifies as zero-sum, school and learning doesn't have to.

Just because one student succeeds doesn't mean another has to fail. Everyone can learn. Everyone can win. This win-win mentality provides a communal aspect to the learning atmosphere that teachers hope to build and maintain in their classrooms.

But that's only the beginning.

Who is responsible for learning?

Students helping each other is typical when teachers place an emphasis on everyone working together (Willans & Williams, 2018). Once students accept that they have a responsibility to everyone else, they learn how to help each other. This shared responsibility, not only for their own learning and behavior but for others' as well, is the final piece of the relatedness puzzle that, I now know, was missing from Mr. Goshen's classroom.

Those students were disconnected from each other and either did not care about or got sadistic pleasure from watching others fail. This toxic environment, which I could sense but couldn't clearly enunciate, destroyed any chance of building momentum toward productive learning. In a true community, the members are responsible for each other.

Learning is only possible when students feel safe, both emotionally and psychologically.

Teacher: Who is responsible for learning?
Students: I am – we are!

The response to this basic question has two parts. First, students own their own learning. Students, as humans, seek control. They need to feel a sense of direction, of power, of order in their lives. In the chaotic world that they live in, oftentimes the only sense of order they can create is through misbehavior.

They have learned, through trial and error, that certain actions, like dropping the F-bomb, will always result in predictable responses, such as being sent to the principal's office. While we might see the consequence as not being beneficial, for students with little to no order, that sense of predictability is extremely valuable. If they want attention, all they have to do is punch the student next to them. They'll get attention, albeit negative, in a predictable manner.

Showing students how to learn, how to grow, and how to work constructively with peers is very empowering. They can make wise choices that impact their future. They are not at the mercy of the vicissitudes of fate.

Additionally, students respond to the last question with a second answer – "We are!" This brings things back around to their communal purpose, to learn as much as they can. They only succeed if everyone succeeds. While there are individual awards in team sports, most players would give up all individual accolades if they could win the championship with their team. Once students view their classmates that way, once they begin to see how they are responsible for their friends, that it's not a zero-sum game, learning becomes empowering.

They are not alone. They have a strong, beneficial purpose for going to school every day. They have a team of friends that has their back.

That's what Mr. Goshen's class was missing, what I unfortunately could not vocalize in time to help him.

So if I were to stop by your classroom in the near future, or, heaven forbid, your evaluator does, and either of us were to drop down next to one of your students to ask, "Why are you here?", how would they answer?

What can you do tomorrow?

Cast your vision. Create a class purpose statement with your students and practice reciting it daily. If it has multiple layers, build it slowly with your students so they understand and believe in every component. Share your purpose. Make sure every student can explain why they're there and what their purpose is.

What does this look like in the classroom?

Classroom tasks contain **clear learning objectives** that build student success by:
- Outlining what students are learning;
- Describing how students will know that they've met the objective; and
- Making connections to students' lives and the real world.

How can you reflect on your learning?

Why do your students come to school?

_____

_____

How does creating in a classroom community impact behavior and learning?

_____

_____

Immediate impact: Go to 6 – 4 Making meaning (Engage) – pg. 459

Keep your face to the sunshine and you cannot see a shadow.

- Helen Keller

1 – 3 Positivity (Confidence)

How does one take charge of the classroom?

I work with a lot of teachers in my current capacity at a large urban district in north Texas. I see great schools and struggling schools, strong teachers and weak ones. Educational leadership is powerful but not the deciding factor. Curriculum programs affect learning but not student behavior directly. What's the x factor?

I have good news and bad news.

There's only one factor that decides, in one fell swoop, the level of productivity, instructional focus, and management in a classroom.

It's not the principal.

It's not the students themselves.

It's not their zip code, socio-economic status, parental involvement, race, or even the culture of the neighborhood.

It's the teacher.

So, great news! You have the power to change your classroom, to take charge of learning and make your instructional program run like a well-oiled machine!

So, bad news! You can't blame it on your school atmosphere, your lack of administrative support, the 83 district initiatives that start up each August and fizzle out by February, or anything that relates to the students. It's simply not their fault.

Are you ready for that type of responsibility?

Clear is kind

Brené Brown, noted researcher and author, states a painfully simplistic but powerful maxim for communication specifically and living life in general (Brown, 2018).

Clear is kind. Unclear is unkind.

I'm not going to sugarcoat it. For a strong majority of educators that pick up a book on classroom management, reading is largely an exercise in skimming until they find the silver bullet. Looking for that quick fix, that panacea, they flit along the surface, searching for that one tweak that will finally get their kids to behave.

I have news for you. Your students aren't the problem.

If they aren't the problem, then there's only one person left in your classroom to take responsibility for your current situation. That's both the good news and the bad news.

Just for the sake of argument, let's say the students were the problem. What would happen if you could lay blame for your classroom discipline woes squarely at the feet of the miscreants currently on your roster?

Absolutely nothing! For one thing, you can't get rid of them. You don't make the roster and there's nowhere else for them to go. More importantly, however, you can't change anyone but yourself. Let's pretend there is a magic formula hidden somewhere in this book. It would only work if you applied it to yourself.

That's the frustrating myth about classroom management that we need to dispel here and now. You can't control children. You can't make them behave. That's not what this book is about.

It's about changing you. When you've accepted that, feel free to continue.

Clear is kind.

A living example

I didn't always know this. As a teacher, I used to believe, like most of my fellow educators, that classroom atmosphere largely depended on factors outside of my control. I did my best but, sometimes, I was dealt a bad hand. A few years ago I was faced with a situation that made me rethink all of that.

This particular school was not a strong school. The atmosphere that permeated the hallways was one of resignation and blame. *Those kids* were not going to be successful for a whole host of reasons, many revolving around culture, race, and parental support (or lack thereof). As classroom after classroom struggled, some teachers became comfortable in their ineffectiveness. They were doing all that they thought they could. It just wasn't their fault.

And then I walked into one of the kindergarten classrooms. The students looked like all the other ones. The parents of these students were no more capable in providing a stable environment at home, nor were they further away from the poverty that affected the area. Several times difficult students were moved from other kindergarten classrooms into this one throughout the year. Those students, almost like magic, started doing well almost immediately.

It wasn't easy. The teacher had to grind out every single day with her students, fighting against the tsunami of disadvantage that her students brought in with them from home. The difference was not her curriculum, her pedagogy, or her instructional materials.

It was her.

Clear is kind. Unclear is unkind.

This teacher made a conscious choice every day to believe the best in her students. She saw them as able, as capable, as worthy. When the whole school started to crumble around her, and it did, her room was one of the only bastions of hope around. Her positivity translated into love for her students. When they struggled behaviorally or academically, she assisted them with strength and goodwill. She viewed their misbehavior as out of character, not a definition of who they were. Many of the other teachers held the opposite view and their students' struggles only went to prove that they were somehow deficient and incapable.

It was largely due to this wonderful teacher, who I was supposed to coach ironically enough, that I started to wonder about the power of one person. If she could do it in the face of adversity and toxicity, why not others? How could teachers learn to take charge of their classrooms and set their students up for success rather than feeling as if they were subject to powers outside their control?

It all starts with positivity.

Scenarios

A classroom's climate is its background noise. It's the energy, mostly unseen, that fills in every space and shapes how you and your students interact with each other. For example, a student might bump into another student while walking up the aisle toward your desk. In a positive climate, the student that was bumped would most likely think that it was an accident. The errant student would apologize quickly, set anything right that was knocked askew, and the matter would be over. If you even noticed it, you might thank the offending student for apologizing and ask the student that was bumped if he or she was okay.

Imagine the same situation in a negative climate. The student who was bumped jumps to the worst possible conclusion and believes the bump was either an intentional act, a precursor to more intimidation to come, or both. That student immediately retaliates, shoving back and yelling something sharp and profanity-laced. The initial student, regardless of the purposeful or accidental nature of the bump, is now on the defensive. Not willing to lose face, this student responds in kind and a simple situation becomes a rapidly deteriorating dumpster fire.

You, as the ever-vigilant teacher, are on the lookout for your little hoodlums to show their true colors. Whichever action you happen to see first, either the bump or the reaction, raises alarm bells in your mind. Not wanting your authority to be diminished in any way, you jump in feet first, yelling at the students, shaming them for such an insensitive act and demanding that everyone take their seats immediately. Throwing gasoline onto the fire, one or both of the students involved resent the injustice of your quick judgment and decide that backing down is not an option.

It largely depends on the climate of the classroom. This emotional dark matter that fills every crack and cranny of your room is influenced over time by one small act after another. It doesn't get created in a day or a week but, over time, permeates the space between the four walls of your room.

Ultimately, it's your choice as to what the climate looks and feels like.

Your strength

You are outnumbered. Sometimes your students surpass your physical presence by 25 or even 30 to 1. But what students have in sheer force, you more than make up for in presence. You are the teacher. You are the adult. Students naturally look for order, for predictability. If your classroom is one that provides for those psychological guardrails within a positive framework, then they will be far less likely to challenge you.

Mind you, I didn't say that they will never challenge you. They will. It's in their nature and it's actually a good sign. We don't want children to grow up weak-willed and subservient. Passive students become adults led around by the nose by those with the loudest voice. Instead, we want students who know where the boundaries are and can operate within them with agency and autonomy. Sometimes simply telling students what those behavioral boundaries are is enough. More often, though, students have to experience those limits personally.

It all starts with positivity.

This is where your positivity sets the atmosphere for your classroom. How you react to misbehavior, to challenges, and to rudeness goes a long way toward shaping the feeling of your classroom. If you are a dog owner, you know that as you go for a long walk, you'll need to bring a plastic bag or two to courteously clean up your dog's messes. You'll also walk in starts and stops as your dog sniffs. Every. Single. Bush. And. Tree.

That's simply in your dog's nature. To not urinate on and sniff every piece of flora would actually be quite strange. It's the same with children. They are going to push your buttons. They'll forget their homework, call out in class, bump into neighbors, and snatch pencils and other shiny objects from others. That's what they do. Rather than letting those instances in which children do what children do unnerve you, approach them with positivity.

Every bad thing that happens in your classroom is not an attack on your authority. Even though it might seem like it at times, your students are not actively plotting to overthrow your regime and institute anarchy within your domain. They're simply being kids. When they mess up, they are showing you that they need help managing their emotions, their tongues, or their bodies. They need someone to show them, with love and positivity, a better way.

By maintaining a positive outlook on everything that happens, by not taking things personally but observing them from a detached perspective, you get to choose your response and its flavor. Your positive responses will begin to overpower any negativity that your students bring in with them. That's your strength as a teacher. Do you want a more positive, trusting atmosphere?

It all starts with you.

Positivity

We cannot teach peace or happiness (Srinivasan, 2014). There isn't a curriculum guide or scope and sequence for making our students show higher proficiency on a positivity scale. Instead, we must be positive, be peaceful, and be happy. If we begin to change ourselves, then our reactions, which tend to happen automatically, become more positive and loving. We transmit our own state of being to our students not through a six-week program but through how we show up each and every day.

Medicus cura te ipsum – physician, heal thyself.

So, here's the good news about taking the giant leap toward taking charge of your classroom. It's not going to take anything beyond your knowledge or skill level. You don't have to stop teaching something important to carve out 15 minutes a day for instructing students on positivity. Though there are some interpersonal skills and intellectual behaviors discussed in other sections that can be taught explicitly, a positive climate comes not from direct instruction.

Positivity comes not from what you teach but how you teach it. The love and joy behind your teaching is perhaps the strongest impression you will leave with your students. Underneath every word you speak, every expression that crosses your face, is another message. That message, the message behind your words, is what your students truly hear in their hearts.

While you might think that your students are listening to your wonderful explanation about the standard algorithm for multiplying numbers, they aren't. You can imagine that they are enthralled with your literary analysis, but that's much more important to you than it is to them. Your students are listening for other messages, such as, "My teacher likes me," or, "My teacher believes in me," or, "My teacher thinks I'm capable and intelligent." It's the tone behind your voice outlining your daily interactions that contributes to the positivity or negativity of your classroom culture.

Growing positivity

Intentionally cultivating an attitude of thankfulness and gratitude can be kick started by instituting some tried and true habits (Sage, 2017). These ideas work both for teachers trying to improve their own positivity quotient but also as classroom activities to begin empowering students to choose their outlook.

First, gratitude, or the attitude of being thankful, is something that can be grown by focused attention. Each day, teachers can take out a journal or spiral notebook and, before the students show up, jot down a few things they are thankful for. What is going right? What is helpful in their lives? What are things they take for granted that, if absent, would make their worlds darker?

As teachers, we have a lot to be thankful for. Not even counting our personal blessings, we are gifted with the responsibility to shape the future of students. We can be thankful that we are employed and essential. Writing this sentence in the midst of the COVID-19 lockdown of 2020, parents across the world are now very aware, if they weren't already, of how hard teaching is and how lucky they are to have us.

Positivity comes not from what you teach but how you teach it.

We can be thankful that we have students who show up every day. We can bless the parents that feed and clothe our students, the administrators that do so much behind the scenes to keep things going, and the support staff, like cafeteria servers and janitors, that all pitch in to make learning possible. There is a lot of goodness that happens every day in a school. It's always been there, it's just up to you to notice it. Consistently writing down a few things you're grateful for can produce a marvelous change in your attitude in just a short time.

Also, once a day doesn't have to be the only time that you take a moment to be thankful. Many teachers utilize alarms on their smartphones to remind them about various daily occurrences, such as when to take attendance or when to pick up their students from lunch. In the same way, teachers can set a simple chime to go off every hour or two. When they hear the chime, they can simply take a moment wherever they are, pause, take a deep breath, and silently name one thing they are thankful for at that moment. This would be a great opportunity to teach this simple habit to students as well. The more they reflect on what they are thankful for, the more that the atmosphere of your classroom will slowly fill with positivity.

Finally, teaching yourself to pause in stressful moments can be a lifesaver in regards to your outlook. Sometimes we say and do things reflexively that have a strong negative impact on our classroom. If we can train ourselves to stay in the moment when our emotions begin to rise, we can stop and consider before acting. Something as simple as saying to ourselves, "1-2-3, is it good for me?" allows us a moment to consider our response and decide whether it's helpful or hurtful. If we can catch some of our words before they make a situation worse, we can inject positivity rather than negativity into the situation.

What you focus on becomes your reality.

Choose wisely.

What can you do tomorrow?

Practice. Take time each day to practice gratitude and thankfulness. **Write it down.** If it would help, start a journal that you can use to gather your thoughts. Set aside a designated time each day to not only jot down what you're thankful for but to review previous entries and keep thankfulness always before you.

What does this look like in the classroom?

Students and teacher build and sustain a **supportive environment** through:

- Positive expectations for students;
- Demonstrations and/or time set aside for gratitude and thankfulness; and
- Instruction delivered in a warm tone of voice.

How can you reflect on your learning?

How is the fact that you are the deciding factor in your classroom both good news and bad news?

_____

_____

How does your positivity or negativity affect student behavior?

_____

_____

Intent

Why won't kids simply behave?

Wouldn't it be easier if they just acted obediently and stopped getting into trouble?

What's wrong with parents these days? Why won't they discipline their children?

If that was my child, he would act like that only once and then I'd put a stop to it. Don't parents know the power of a good butt-whooping?

Questions like these roll through the minds of teachers frequently, more often when they step out of the classroom momentarily to speak with a colleague only to step back in and find the room has turned into a mosh pit at a heavy metal concert.

As valid as some of these questions might be, as squarely as some of these judgments might land on the lack of parenting ability possessed by the families at our schools, they are ultimately useless. Focusing on deficits, missing traits, and behavioral gaps ultimately perpetuates a negative climate, something we must move away from in order to take charge of the classroom.

No one is perfect. Everyone is doing the best they can with the best they have. Parents aren't keeping their most promising children at home and sending the dysfunctional ones to school. Students aren't saving their best behavior for home and running amok at school for sheer variety. What you see is what you get.

It's easy to stay positive and non-judgmental when things are going right. But sometimes a student mouths off to you and finishes with, "And my momma said you can't do nuthin' to me cuz you ain't the principal!" Those are the situations in which, as a teacher, it would be helpful to have already done some work on assigning intent to students' actions.

Here's the thing with intentions. The only intentions you can ever really know are your own, and even those are often hidden from you. So many adults believe that, unlike other mere mortals, they possess the magic ability to truly gauge the intentions behind students' actions. Teachers are quick to lay malice and subversion at the feet of students because they know, beyond a shadow of a doubt, that the student is inherently wicked and thus his actions must come from a place of evil intentions.

Everyone is doing the best they can with the best they have.

The only person that truly knows another's intentions is God. And you're not Him.

So often, things happen in the classroom that aren't explicitly good or bad. They are somewhere in between, in that area of gray that is a lot larger than we'd ever like to admit. When deciding on whether the action is or is not worthy of punishment, then, most of us go for the intentions. Why did the child do that? What was he trying to accomplish? Is this the first step toward rebellion or simply a mistake?

When these conclusions are drawn from flimsy or non-existent data, we sit in judgment over the student, declaring our interpretation of the action as the correct version and decreeing punishment for not only what happened but also for what the child intended to happen. We assume to know the intentions behind the action and, more often than not, include those as a large part of our decision-making process.

But we can never know the true intentions of children. When hard pressed, it's hard to even put our own aims into words. To believe that we are so thoroughly aware and perceptive that we can peer behind every action and accurately discern the objectives of others is at best problematic and at worst delusional. We simply can't.

Yet intentions matter. Why not assume the best?

Positive intent

Holding positive intent for our most difficult and challenging children is essential (Bailey, 2015). More than likely, these children will have defined themselves, either partially or completely, as *bad* or *unworthy*. These judgments begin to seep into their self-conceptions and children perpetuate them by living them out at school.

If students only see themselves as bad, as unintelligent, as incapable of anything that resembles quality work or behavior, their energy is going to be largely spent on defending themselves psychologically and meeting their needs in various ways. There won't be anything left for trying to rise above the labels placed on them by adults.

Positive intent is a choice that teachers ought to make. There are many other things that teachers must decide every day, such as what tasks to assign, how to group students, and what instructional practices to employ. Why not choose, at the beginning of each day, to assume positive intentions for your students, especially the difficult ones?

Positive intent defines the core of the student as good enough. The child's behavior, not the child, is what needs to change.

Positive intent keeps us, the teacher, in the higher centers of our brain where solutions and change are possible and accessible. In this frame of mind, we can wisely discern which executive, academic, or behavioral skills the child is missing and begin the teaching process.

Positive intent defines the child as one who makes mistakes and is willing to learn in the eyes of classmates and teachers.

These intentions are largely hidden from both students and teachers. When in doubt, why not reach for positive intentions as an explanation? The alternative is not very palatable.

Negative Intent

What happens when we believe the worst about children? How does our judgment affect their attitudes, actions, and self-beliefs?

Negative intent defines the core of the child and his or her behaviors as bad.

Negative intent throws us, the teacher, into the lower centers of our brains where blame and punishment are the only options. Solutions and positive change are not available here.

Negative intent defines the child as bad in the eyes of classmates and fellow teachers.

Surprising as it is, in that it produces a result that all teachers would admit undesirable, negative intent encourages children to be more oppositional. There is nothing quite as motivating as feeling slighted or perceiving yourself to be a victim of injustice and using that as fuel to rage against the machine.

Negative intent also subconsciously labels and defines children as bad, mean, selfish, or inconsiderate. Children usually accept these labels over time and become aggressive, withdrawn, and/or exhibit bullying behaviors.

Emotional contagion

So what? You become all happy and sappy, holding positive intentions for your students, but how will that affect them? What good does it do, you ask, if you drink the happiness Kool-Aid all day but your students continue to be ornery and argumentative?

I'm glad you asked.

There is an important connection between neuroscience and how we teach and interact with students. Emotions are contagious. If one student in the room gets hijacked by his amygdala and goes into a rage, others will also become infected with anxiety, resistance, or disengagement (Hammond, 2014).

The opposite is also true, however. If one person in a room is happy, laughing, and smiling, others will also likely become infected with this attitude. A large part of this is due to mirror neurons that reside in each of our brains. These "smart cells" help us understand others' actions, intentions, and feelings by firing when we see someone else experiencing an emotion, such as happiness, fear, anger, or sadness. Mirror neurons serve as a basis for empathy because they allow us to share the emotions of others vicariously.

Mirror neurons are why I want to scream, "Freedom!" at the top of my lungs with Mel Gibson's William Wallace in *Braveheart*. They are why I turn away when I see too much blood and gristle and why my wife knows not to go into too much detail as she excitedly describes someone's injury and the operation used to repair it. We all, deep inside our minds, can feel the feelings of others simply by watching, hearing, or even reading about the experiences of others.

We are wired to empathize, so use that to your advantage.

Everything we do, as educators, is a teachable moment. Positivity does not mean sunshine and daffodils 24/7. As I stated earlier in the book, everything sucks most of the time. When we choose positivity, we choose to embrace the suck and let it grow us rather than define us. Even when our students see us consciously work through difficult emotions like hurt, frustration, and being overwhelmed, they are learning through that example (Shapiro & White, 2014).

Positivity is a choice we make every day, much like the choice you made this morning to put on a dress or slacks, jeans or shorts. As a teacher, you can choose to put on positivity, to clothe yourself in it every morning. As you put on these rose-colored glasses, you are making an intentional decision to see others with positive intent. You are choosing to take the trials of the day as they come and respond with love and acceptance rather than by taking every fluctuation as a personal assault on your authority.

The child's behavior, not the child, is what needs to change.

And the students are watching.

As they see how you handle the stresses of the day, with a large part of these stresses coming from misbehavior and plans gone awry, they are learning how to handle these situations. When they see you calmly talk to one of their peers about his behavior and you lovingly expect the best from him, they are internalizing these interactions through their mirror neurons. When they see you viewing troubled students with positive intent, they are more likely to do the same. This, then, affects their own interactions with those students. You are unintentionally teaching your students how to interact with each other simply by how you interact with them yourself.

Do you want them to view each other with love and acceptance or with suspicion and fear?

Collect data

A classroom environment that is focused on positivity, hope, optimism, strengths, the ability for growth, and the like, can be beneficial for not just students but you as well. This takes practice, and one of the first steps is to gain an accurate assessment of where you and your classroom currently stand on the positivity continuum (Sage, 2017).

Remember, what you pay attention to shows up more and more in your life. It might take some mental aerobics to begin focusing on what is right rather than what is wrong and believing that all students, even the misbehaving ones, are capable of growing and learning. The first step to take, therefore, is to collect data. One area of study should be the ratio of positive to negative/neutral statements that you make in a typical class period.

One option for collecting these data would be to invite someone you trust, a colleague or coworker, to come and observe your classroom. While you would know the purpose of the visit and would probably act a little unnaturally with someone watching your every move, most people revert back to form after just a few minutes of observation. The observer, sitting unobtrusively in the back of the room somewhere, could take simple notes on statements and create a tally chart, scripting the exact wording if time and circumstances allow.

For those of you that don't have the luxury of inviting someone to come in and observe your classroom, or if your students would act so differently in the presence of another adult that the data would be skewed, a digital option remains. Place a tablet or even your smartphone in an indiscreet place, perhaps on top of a filing cabinet, and hit record. Though the sound quality might not be ideal, this serves as a simple solution to the problems that arise from an in-person observation.

While there is no set standard for the ideal ratio between positive and neutral/negative interactions, the former should largely outweigh the latter. If the ratio drops below 5:1 (positive:neutral/negative), then the classroom could most likely be described as one with a cold or even negative atmosphere.

Practice

Presuming positive intent is a significant change for many educators. Like any new skill, it will take time, persistence, and grace. You will mess up and you will lose your cool. Perfection is not realistic so go ahead and forget about that.

Take a moment to think about your most troubled student. It can be a current student or one that is seared into your memory because of negative interactions. Think about some of that student's most heinous actions and narrate them using positive intent. What was the child thinking or doing that caused the behavior? Here's an example.

Daniel is in one of his moods. He runs in from the hallway, shoves past two students also walking in, and jumps onto the bean bag in the library center. The book balancing on the edge of the bean bag flies across the room, smacking Desiree in the face and causing her to instantly tear up. Drew, sitting next to Desiree, thinks that the whole thing is hilarious and laughs harder once he sees that Desiree is crying!

It would be easy to assign negative intent to Daniel. But perhaps he was just excited. Coming in from recess, he typically has a hard time settling down to silent reading time. He's still full of energy and he usually roams throughout the room for several minutes before finding a seat.

Today, his group was going to be able to read in the library center. Maybe he wanted to claim the bean bag for himself. While his actions still need to be addressed, they can be discussed from a different frame of mind when viewed through positive intent.

Emotions are contagious.

In the scenario above, Daniel would have probably been willing to practice walking into the classroom and even apologizing to Desiree if the teacher recognized his eagerness and gave him an opportunity to try again. If fussed at, however, he would have gotten defensive and a negative spiral would have begun.

CONFIDENCE

What can you do tomorrow?

Reflect. Recollect a recent experience and revisit it through a positive lens. How would that assumption have changed your interactions? Could the subsequent power struggle have been minimized or even avoided if you had approached it differently?

Try it again. Replay the situation in your mind while presuming positive intent and note how the outcome might have changed.

What does this look like in the classroom?

Students and teacher maintain **positive communication**, as evidenced by:

- Presuming positive intent regarding student misbehavior;
- Students being open to discussing misbehavior and rectifying it as needed; and
- Students seeking support and guidance from the teacher.

How can you reflect on your learning?

How does presuming positive intent improve your environment?

_____

_____

What's the best way for you to collect data on the ratio of positive to negative comments you make to your students?

_____

_____

Immediate impact: Go to 6 – 3 Memory (Engage) – pg. 439

The ache for home lives in all of us. The safe place where we can go as we are and not be questioned.

- Maya Angelou

1 – 4 Protection (Confidence)

Confidence is an essential component of taking charge of your classroom.

While the first two aspects of confidence, purpose and positivity, are characteristics that teachers direct and guide with student involvement, the third aspect is one that only you can provide for them.

If you want to get a handle on student misbehavior, to help students successfully inhibit their unproductive urges, you must provide protection. Without a felt sense of safety in your classroom, nothing positive is going to happen.

Brain needs

Safety is as essential to learning as oxygen to a flame. Neurobiologically speaking, students can't learn if they don't feel safe, known, and cared for within their schools (Minahan, 2019). This is a strong statement. We're not talking about choosing not to learn, or students willfully ignoring instructions or goofing off. In our brains, certain conditions must be met before the parts of our consciousness responsible for learning can be accessed.

In the presence of aversive stimuli, the hippocampus and amygdala, responsible for memory and emotion respectively, remain on high alert for continuing distress. These brain systems are designed to keep us safe when danger is sensed (Willans & Williams, 2018).

For example, if you are walking down a wooded path and you hear a growl and a blood-curdling, high-pitched scream about 50 yards behind you, what you don't want to do at that moment is analyze. If you continue strolling down the path, quietly musing to yourself, "Hmm, that's strange, I wonder who that person is and why she's screaming?", you could be putting yourself in danger. Your natural instinct is going to be to turn around, look for the source of the sound, and make a split-second decision as to what to do.

Safety is as essential to learning as oxygen to a flame.

The stress of the moment is pumping cortisol and adrenaline through your body as your senses seem to be on overload, taking in more information than you can cognitively process. The cortisol is increasing sugars to your bloodstream and curbing functions that are non-essential, such as idle thoughts about the rare flower you just saw before you heard the scream. Adrenaline is also elevating your heart rate, your blood pressure, and your energy. With increased perception, you can instantly act in a way that will keep you safe, whether that be fight, flight, or freeze.

What you can't do, unfortunately, is use logic, think abstractly, or do anything that doesn't immediately assist you. Trying to match the growl to a specific species (e.g., "Was that a mountain lion? Cougar? No, too throaty. Something deeper…maybe a bear. Are bears native to this area? If so, I wonder if it's a brown bear. I read somewhere that those are pretty large….") would not happen because it's non-essential.

Trying to look and identify the woman by her size and outfit would also be non-essential (e.g., "That looks like my aunt Sara. What's she doing here? She lives down in Houston and I know she would have called me first. She's not much of a walker, maybe it's not her. Sure looks like her, though…"). Your first and best instinct would be to evaluate the danger and figure out how to stay away from it. If you took your Superman vitamins that morning, maybe you rush in to help the stranger. Either way, you're reacting on instinct because your brain is designed to do just that when danger is sensed. Analysis and reasoning can come later. First, make sure you're not eaten.

So, here's the really scary question.

What if every time a student walks into your classroom he feels like there's a wild animal in there?

What if his stress levels are so high that he's continually in a fight, flight, or freeze frame of mind?

First and foremost, learning isn't going to happen. That's completely out of the picture. You'll also probably see some erratic behavior. A classmate might do something or say something innocuous and the child suddenly snaps, losing it for no apparent reason.

That's a reaction due to stress and anxiety. If schools are to provide an appropriate learning environment for children, they must strive to keep anxiety to a minimum.

Lack of protection

So, unless you are harboring any wild animals in your classroom, you can probably knock that off your list. But what else causes students to live in chronic stress, a term used to describe the emotional pressure suffered for prolonged periods of time in which people feel unsafe and/or powerless?

Lots of things.

Some factors are out of your control. Poverty, domestic violence, drug and alcohol abuse, neglect, homelessness, hunger, mental illness, and discrimination simply start the list. The chains of stress that children bring in with them every day, if somehow made visible, would stagger us. That's one of the reasons why teachers are mandated reporters for suspected child abuse and neglect. It's that important and we are in a position to learn things that other adults can't.

Now consider that one student you've had, either in the past or currently, that drives you bonkers. The one that you pray falls ill (though not dangerously ill, obviously) so that he's out of your class for two weeks. What are your interactions like with him? How does he perceive your feelings toward him?

If he feels that you don't like him, disapprove of him, or sit in judgment on his every action, then you're creating an anxiety-filled environment for him. That's pumping him full of cortisol and adrenaline, two hormones that are useful for getting away from brown bears but not helpful for learning. That's why positivity is so vital. Keeping positive intent in mind for those students can do much to reduce their stress and anxiety.

Priming

One final word on the power of our brains, both for helping us to not be eaten and potentially keeping us from learning. Think back to the previous example of the bear in the woods. If, for some strange reason, you decided to walk down the same trail a week later, you'd be on the lookout for danger. As you passed by the portion of the trail that was so dangerous last time, your brain would automatically start pumping stress hormones through your body, getting you ready for an impending attack.

This automatic reaction is called priming (Siegel & Bryson, 2012). Implicit memories cause us to form expectations about how the world works based on previous experiences. The last time you walked down that path, something horrible happened. Thus, walking down the same path would cause those memories to resurface and the same reaction to occur again. This isn't done consciously but subconsciously, as a defense mechanism, to keep you safe. It would probably take many more trips down the same path with no incidents for those alarm bells to stop ringing every time you walked it.

Priming keeps us safe and out of danger because it frees us to be able to react quickly and automates our responses in moments of danger without having to actively or intentionally recall our responses in similar situations. These repeated experiences, or even a single experience in some cases of trauma, help us predict what will happen next. We don't have time to go through the start-up process of getting ready for danger every time we walk down that path. Priming automates that for us.

This wonderful survival feature, however, can work against students that habitually face stress and anxiety from school. When the relationship with the teacher is cold and/or their peers are critical or even hyper-competitive, that influences their expectations for the classroom. With enough repeated experiences of stress and anxiety, priming can trigger that child's defense mechanisms every time he walks into the classroom. This means that even on days in which nothing overtly hostile might happen, the student's ability to learn might be severely compromised because of his anxiety.

Thus, classrooms must offer protection to students. If we, as teachers, want to prepare students to participate in learning as healthy individuals, to communicate with us and their peers in open and trusting ways, we need to nurture within them a receptive state instead of a closed, reactive one. If a student's entire focus is on self-defense, the wonders of our lesson delivery and the excitement of the activities will do no good. Instead, the child's whole focus will be on staying safe.

So if this resonates with you, if you can envision a particular student when thinking about this defensive state, what's the solution? How do you shoo away the brown bear so that the student's cognitive processing doesn't go on hiatus every time he enters your classroom?

Trust.

Protection

Trust deactivates the amygdala.

For students to inhibit negative behaviors, one necessary environmental factor is a sense of trust that the teacher will protect the student from emotional injury and psychological pain (Willans & Williams, 2018). Walking down a lonely path, fearful of bears jumping out of the woods, would make anyone anxious. If, however, you were driving a tank down the path, then any bears that stumbled into your way would be annoying but not dangerous.

More than being a friend or a buddy, teachers first and foremost must be protectors. We do not know all of the unseen bonds of stress that children bring with them every day nor can we eliminate all of them. What we can do, though, is make our classrooms a fortress of protection. Students can be primed not for fear but for relief, safety, and openness if they know that they will be protected from shame when they cross your threshold.

Protection is not control. It is not dominance. If teachers try to eliminate threats by exerting ultimate authority over students, theoretically keeping the fragile ones safe from the hooligans, compassion is thrown out the window. Effective relationships, between the teacher and students and between the students themselves, thrive on trust. They wither in the face of power imbalances.

When students trust their teachers, they feel free to take off the armor they carry around to protect them from wounds. Protection offers them the possibility of being seen, being known, warts and all, and still being accepted. When trusting relationships put this option on the table, students are now, finally, in a position to learn.

Because learning can actually be quite dangerous.

Zone of proximal development

For those of you not familiar with the common educational term *zone of proximal development* (Vygotsky, 1978), it refers to the difference between what a learner can do without help and what he or she can achieve with guidance from a skilled partner, usually a teacher.

In other words, it's the sweet spot of teaching.

Some tasks are too easy. Students can do them on their own and, already having mastery, are not really adding anything to what they already know.

Other tasks are simply too hard or complex. Even with adult guidance, it simply is beyond their ability to process. Teaching calculus to a first grader would be an extreme but fitting example.

In between, though, is where learning happens. Not so hard that the learner can't get there even with significant support. Not so easy that the brain can coast through the task on autopilot.

The zone of proximal development (ZPD) is an area of stretching, risk, and the possibility of failure. Students won't go there without trust and a sense of protection.

Students naturally care about their identity and how they are perceived by others. Wrapped up in that identity is a host of factors, such as physical appearance, social standing, and skills. In the school setting, another factor rears its ugly head – academic reputation.

If you put 25 random students into a room, within an hour they would have a pretty good sense of who the smart kids are and who are the dummies. It's a type of sixth sense that students develop, the ability to quickly and accurately identify their place in the academic pecking order. In classroom atmospheres that do not provide a feeling of protection, students are loath to enter the ZPD.

Trust deactivates the amygdala.

It's simply too risky. Failure is a possible outcome, and with that failure all the shame and verbal abuse that accompanies being wrong in an unsupportive environment. Resistance to stretching the limits of understanding decreases the learning of new knowledge and skills, thus making academic achievement stagnant or declining.

Maximum learning happens in the ZPD. That's a scary place for many students because it's high risk/high reward. That level of danger might be too much for them unless they feel safe. While emotional protection is necessary for quality relationships and social-emotional well-being, it also plays into academics, the underlying reason for education. Without trust and safety, learning simply isn't possible.

Many students are burdened with anxiety and stress from their homes. Their lives outside of school may be filled with trauma, uncertainty, and fear.

But your classroom can be an island of hope in a sea of chaos.

You have the ability to set a positive tone and steer your class toward a learning orientation, favoring community over competition, growth over grades. When students feel supported by their teacher and their classmates, they can take their armor off, even if it's only temporarily. If you, as a teacher, can create and sustain a safe environment for students, if you can banish the bears lurking in the woods, then students will feel safe enough to percolate in the ZPD, opening themselves to learning and to being seen.

This is the true outcome of confidence. It is when students can cast off their anxiety and stress that they are ready to begin learning.

What can you do tomorrow?

Visualize. Take a mental field trip into your classroom through the eyes of one of your students with behavior challenges. Are there dangers on the path? What trauma does he bring in with him? What's his morning like before he shows up?

Be proactive. As you consider a typical day from his point of view, think about how you might reduce his anxiety and banish the dangers.

What does this look like in the classroom?

The teacher provides **emotional and psychological protection** by:
- Anticipating potential problems and planning for them accordingly;
- Providing comfort and assistance to students; and
- Showing appropriate affection toward students.

How can you reflect on your learning?

Think about one of your more behaviorally challenged students. How safe does s/he feel in your classroom?

_____

_____

Why are emotional, physical, and psychological safety important for learning?

_____

_____

Trust

Do you trust yourself?

The answer is not as obvious as it may seem.

For students to feel safe and to have the confidence needed to successfully learn new things, they have to feel protected. The atmosphere that the teacher creates can do much to build this trust, both as a result of the teacher's sense of purpose and spirit of positivity.

Yet it's hard to encourage students to trust you when you don't even trust yourself.

The first wave of trust is actually self-trust (Covey & Merrill, 2008). It's the confidence that we have in ourselves, in our ability to set and achieve goals, and to keep our commitments. The ability to walk the talk inspires trust from others. This credibility, stemming from high character and high competence, translates into influence.

Key to all this, however, is our trust in ourselves. When we repeatedly fail to make and keep commitments to ourselves, it hacks away at our self-confidence. We lose the ability to inspire trust in our students because, deep down, we don't truly believe in ourselves. This rot at the core of our character oozes out and destroys security in the classroom.

When you make a commitment to yourself, how often do you come through?

If, at the core of our being, we know that we are fundamentally unreliable, that our talk never quite aligns to our walk, then trust will be hard to come by in the classroom. A lack of self-trust translates into poor trust in external relationships.

At first glance, most of us would state that we trust ourselves. But before blindly moving on, let's explore that for a moment. What seems like a solid history of faithful execution might instead be a backdrop littered with broken promises.

When you start that new fad diet, how long does it normally last before you're off it? That commitment to wake up early a few days a week to work out, how's that going for you? Or even your promises to either drastically reduce or even eliminate your social media consumption? Do you get at least one week into your self-imposed exile before you simply have to know what people are saying and doing online? Or can you make it two weeks?

These questions aren't asked in judgment but in an effort to clear the air. Students need us, more than we can possibly ever know, to be dependable, trustworthy, and protectors. If we don't trust ourselves, even if that suspicion is at a subconscious level, then we won't be able to provide them with all the protection they need.

And here's another dangerous line of thinking that people will sometimes use as a defense.

As long as I don't break commitments to others, they think, then it's okay not to keep commitments to myself.

That is simply untrue.

Our ability to trust and be trusted stems from our own sense of dependability. By not believing in ourselves to come through when we make internal promises, we erode the potential for others to trust in us. When we don't, deep down, believe that we'll make good on our commitments, we don't offer that option to others. We hold it back, not wanting to be shown as faithless in their eyes.

So, how can we reverse the trend and start to trust ourselves?

By making and keeping small commitments.

Small commitments

Your trust in yourself, if not at 100%, most likely eroded one small bit at a time. And that's exactly how you repair it.

Start small. Instead of committing to wake up early four days this week to work out, commit to one day. Wake up tomorrow morning and work out or go to the gym. Keep your focus on the commitment right in front of you rather than making it an all-or-nothing proposal.

If you follow through and work out tomorrow morning, then you've gained trust in yourself. If you didn't, take a moment to reflect. What kept you from meeting your commitment? Did you stay up too late the night before? Do you need to limit your screen time while in bed so that you can go to sleep faster? Or maybe mornings simply aren't your thing. Would it be better to try to exercise after work?

Our ability to trust and be trusted stems from our own sense of dependability.

Just because you don't keep your commitment doesn't mean all is lost. Reflect, refine, and try again. Go for short goals, baby steps, before pushing for the stretch goals.

In the classroom, these small commitments will look different.

Commit to coming into the classroom tomorrow with a positive attitude. Forget what happened today or yesterday and start fresh tomorrow.

Commit to greeting some students at the door as they walk in. You don't have to spend 18 minutes performing a personalized hand-shake or fist-bump ritual with every student. Instead, try to tell five students, "Good morning," as you greet them by name.

Commit to giving your most difficult student the benefit of the doubt. Before blowing up at him, think about what might have caused his behavior. Chase the why.

Once you start seeing yourself keep these small commitments, you'll change how you view yourself. You'll begin to see yourself as someone that can make and keep promises. With confidence in yourself, you can begin to build the foundation of trust with your students.

Trusting yourself

If you were to ask my wife, she would tell you that I don't struggle with trusting myself. In fact, she believes, I'm way too cocky most of the time.

She's right, of course.

But this confidence in myself slowly built over time. One example is my authorship.

In 2016, I had an idea. It was really more of an itch, but something that had been nagging me for a while.

What motivates students to learn?

I had to find what research said on the topic because, after a few quick Google searches, I realized that the majority of what was available online consisted of sundry bags of tricks peddled by charismatic educators. Nine times out of ten, those results couldn't be replicated without also conducting a teacher personality transplant.

Fast forward to March 2017, and my first book came out. Titled *Solving Student Engagement*, it answered (for me at least) the riddle of what makes learners tick. Consisting of over 250 pages and over 60,000 words, it explored the five facets of student motivation – competence, relationships, autonomy, value, and emotions. I was an author!

February 2018 saw my second book come out titled *Don't Quit Your Day Job*. It looked at the same research as the first book but repackaged it into a 30-day guidebook that teachers could use to learn more about student motivation. While my first book was like drinking from a fire hydrant, this was more of a water fountain.

I was an author twice over but I was beginning to lose faith a bit. My second book didn't push new boundaries or take a large amount of work to write. I had already done the heavy lifting by diving into 30 years of social cognitive research for *Solving Student Engagement*. I began to wonder if I could start the arduous process all over again.

Finally I decided to take the plunge and start a new project.

Worksheets

So many teachers used worksheets in the school I served at the time that students and parents were starting to quickly tire of education. The quantity of work became more important than the quality or rigor of instructional design. Teachers gleefully spent hours each Thursday and Friday putting together worksheet packets for the following week.

Yet one cannot simply say, "Worksheets are weak and bland. Do something more exciting!" Even if teachers agreed with the preceding statement, it simply tells them what to stop using, not what to start doing. If I was going to help, I needed to come up with usable worksheet alternatives that teachers could easily implement.

After playing around with the seed of an idea, I finally had it! I was going to call my new book *Worksheets Don't Work* and use the word *worksheets* as an acrostic to list ten different worksheet alternatives.

It sounded so easy.

I dove back into the research and started exploring the first worksheet alternative, word work. There is a surprising amount of strong educational research on vocabulary instruction and oral language development. As I kept traveling further and further down the rabbit hole, I slowly began to realize that I had a problem. I had too much research on vocabulary development. It wasn't simply a chapter in my nascent book. It was a book in itself.

I shifted gears and wrote a smaller book, *Wrestling with Words*, which came out in August 2018. I was very pleased with it because it details the five parts of a powerful vocabulary program, something all educators could benefit from.

But it was a distraction.

Worksheets Don't Work still hung over me. I jumped back into it but then lost steam. If you've ever written anything before, you know that you must harness your creative energy when it's flowing. Take a day off work, pump yourself with energy drinks, and bang it out when you're in the right headspace for it. Because for most of the time, writing is tedious. It's a slog.

Ultimately I quit. My initial idea was still valid but the scope was far too large. The way I had envisioned it, each of the ten worksheet alternatives would have five separate examples. Thus, my book would have 50 worksheet alternatives for teachers to use. Great idea in theory but difficult to execute. Each alternative was roughly 2,000 words.

Not doing the math ahead of time, I slowly began to realize that the finished product, if I continued at my projected pace, would be about 100,000 words. That would be almost twice as large as my first and largest book, which in itself was about the length of a doctoral dissertation.

I gave it my best shot but then just quit. I couldn't last any longer. I had about half of the book written (though not proofread or edited) and I was done. I felt like a sponge left outside on a Texas summer day.

My confidence started wavering and I thought my authoring days were over. They'd be a nice footnote in my unwritten biography, but nothing more. It was just too big.

Fast forward again to March 2020. *Worksheets Don't Work*, consisting of 360 pages and over 100,000 words, was finally published. After stopping cold for over a year, I began to reflect on my lack of confidence in writing. My difficulty lay in my perspective. I had the finished product in mind and that was too overwhelming. Instead, I changed my perspective and looked closely at what the finished product would consist of.

Each subsection, or worksheet alternative, was about 2,000 words. That wasn't too bad! That was about the length of a long blog post and I had been blogging for years. And, to make things better, I only needed 50 alternatives to finish the book and I already had 27 of them done! Suddenly, the perspective changed and I saw small steps. Instead of being daunted by the enormity of the task, I took it one chunk at a time. I kept hacking away, knowing it would end eventually, and lo and behold, it did.

Baby steps

Don't be overwhelmed by the enormity of the behavioral problems in your classroom. Keeping your eyes on the big picture might paralyze you into inaction. Instead, begin by taking baby steps toward improving your classroom environment. To begin with, utilize the action steps I provide throughout the book to incrementally build a safe and supportive culture.

Whichever goals you set, focus on the first step rather than the end result in the distant horizon. As long as your initial target is worthy and your plan of execution is aligned, you can keep your focus on the next action rather than on the distance still ahead of you. Each step you take builds your confidence in yourself. You begin to see yourself as reliable and trustworthy, able to make and keep promises.

Your students will see it too and also see you as someone that can be trusted. This is the foundation for a feeling of protection.

Secure attachment

Meeting the needs of students reduces their misbehavior (Shapiro & White, 2014). All behavior is communication, in one form or another. Many students, by their acts of anarchy, are shouting at the top of their lungs, metaphorically speaking, that they need something. They might not know what it is, and you probably don't either, but they definitely need something. They'll keep acting out until their needs are met.

In the presence of trust, however, having unmet needs becomes less scary. When students are in a protective environment, they know deep down that they will be taken care of. Young infants have one form of communication to share their needs and they use it expertly. Mothers can often distinguish the needs of their babies simply by the types of cries they use. There are different wails for hunger, sleepiness, and even needing their diaper changed.

In the same way, children have a sure-fire way to communicate their needs, and that's through behavior. Obviously, it would be better for everyone involved if they used words, either spoken or written, but sometimes children aren't even consciously aware of their needs. Their random acts of violence and destruction might be their only viable form of communication.

To continue the young infant metaphor, how parents react to their children's cries goes a long way in shaping their personality and resilience. If parents respond warmly and soothingly to their crying babies, working through the various options until they figure out how to soothe them, the children will grow up with what psychologists call a secure attachment (Siegel & Bryson, 2021). This wordless communication between parents and their children ensures that the children feel calm enough to ride out the various peaks and valleys of their nervous system and natural development. Secure attachment helps children's brains to organize properly, providing a sense of safety, self-awareness, trust, and empathy.

Meeting the needs of students reduces their misbehavior.

Except in rare circumstances, teachers rarely teach their own children. They don't have any direct impact on the security or insecurity of their students' attachments. However, teachers can serve as secondary attachment figures. Educators, along with other important adult role models, such as caregivers, therapists, clergy, and others, can fill in the role possibly left vacant by distant or disconnected parents.

That means you.

You have the ability to set each of your students up for a future building on optimism and a healthy self-awareness. You can repair damage made as a result of adverse childhood experiences. You hold the key to your students' futures.

It's a big responsibility, but like the adage says, the best way to eat an elephant is one bite at a time. Take small steps to develop trust in yourself and trust in your classroom.

Commit to yourself that you'll greet at least five students at the door for three straight days.

Commit to yourself that you'll say one nice thing to your most troublesome student every day or even every hour for a week.

Take small bites out of the elephant and pretty soon it won't seem so large – though I can't say anything about the taste.

What can you do tomorrow?

Start small. Find an area in which you've struggled in the past to keep commitments. Scale down next steps until they are bite-sized and take them one piece at a time.

Be accountable. To make it more actionable, communicate these steps to someone else who can serve as an accountability partner. Be sure to give yourself grace when the inevitable happens and you miss a commitment.

What does this look like in the classroom?

The teacher provides **secure attachment** for students by:
- Being emotionally available for them;
- Attuning to their emotional states; and
- Building trust through fulfilling commitments.

How can you reflect on your learning?

When you make a commitment to yourself, how often do you come through?

_____

_____

What is one action step you can take to provide protection and secure attachment for your students?

_____

_____

Immediate impact: Go to 6 – 2 Motivation (Engage) – pg. 419

1 – 5 Conclusion (Confidence)

Your behaviors, which we'll get to soon, play a big impact on classroom management and student achievement. Those behaviors, however, flow from your beliefs. What you envision the true heart of teaching to be will ultimately direct your behaviors as they permeate everything you do. That's what we'll look at in the next section.

Before we do that, however, we need to build confidence. Confidence comes from our core being, who we are deep down where the sun don't shine. Our being dictates our beliefs and our beliefs dictate our behaviors.

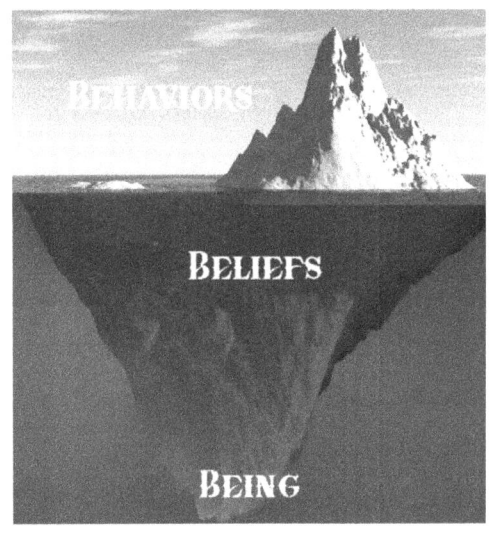

Want to learn some techniques for improving classroom management?

Those are teacher behaviors and they come after beliefs which are built upon your being. That's why we start with confidence.

Think of your confidence as the cornerstone on which taking charge of your classroom will be built. There will be good days and bad days. Some strategies will work and others might cause a meltdown. The key is not to read from a script but to maintain flexibility and think on your feet. If you can do that, and pair it with some grit, you can overcome any type of misbehavior.

Those abilities are grounded in confidence.

Confidence first emerges from finding your purpose. Brené Brown (2018) reminds us that everything sucks most of the time. Teaching definitely can fall into that description and so purpose is what will push you through the tough times. You don't teach for the money or the status. It isn't for notoriety or the laid-back working environment. You teach because you want to change the world. You teach because every time you touch a life, you touch eternity. That's powerful stuff, enough to give you confidence in the face of anything.

You teach because you want to change the world.

You also can build your own efficacy by choosing positivity. Most everything has a degree of ambiguity. We don't know why things happen or what the intentions are behind the words and actions of others. Our brains don't like mysteries so we are constantly filling in the gaps with stories we create.

If our stories are negative, if we believe the worst about others, then that will put us in a defensive frame of mind. We'll always be waiting for the other shoe to drop, searching for a cloud on a sunny day. We will begin to close ourselves off to solutions and growth as we hunker down to try and survive the coming storm.

Positivity changes all that. It fills in missing pieces of information with data that uplifts and energizes. It finds the best in people and, when in doubt, presumes positive intent. This foundational attitude, flowing from our being, affects everything and everyone. It can make us more confident because we don't feel under attack or insecure. Instead, it provides us with a beneficial narrative structure to make sense of our world.

Finally, protection is often overlooked when thinking about classroom needs. Without a felt sense of safety, students don't have the mental capacity to grow academically.

To learn new things, students must feel secure enough to try something that is beyond their current ability. Without safety, it's much easier to not try at all, even if that means taking a bad grade. Learning is scary, when you get right down to it, and requires emotional protection.

Trust, however, is built over time and cannot be given by others if it's not first given to yourself. Some teachers, deep down, feel they are unreliable due to a string of broken promises to themselves. A lack of self-confidence erodes their ability to be trusted by others, a wound at the core of their character.

Instead of bluster, you can build trust in yourself by making and keeping small commitments. Create a track record of success, even if it's on a small scale, and let that propel you to larger and larger gains.

When you gain confidence in yourself and your abilities, you take the first step in taking charge of your classroom. It's not a Boy Scout badge you can earn or something that is granted after six clock hours of continuing professional education credit. Confidence comes when you have a healthy view of your professional calling, your interactions and daily events, and your primary duties in the classroom.

Though your home life might be stable, your family safe and secure, and your outlook rosy, your students oftentimes aren't as fortunate. They're the ones trapped on the 18th floor of a collapsing building. They're looking around for an adult to lead them to safety. If they don't have faith in you, they'll have to look after themselves, and children are not equipped or designed to be completely self-reliant. They're wondering if you, the one with the title and college degree, can actually get them to the ground floor safely.

Learning is scary, when you get right down to it, and requires emotional protection.

When students sense your confidence, when they feel that you not only have a plan but can adapt it on the fly, and when they see that you aren't phased by interruptions or changes, they'll begin to relax. They still might be anxious, and their home life might not be any better, but they'll know that at least there's one adult in their world that knows what's going on and how to navigate the obstacles that threaten to overwhelm them.

With confidence in you, they'll begin to open up to your instruction. They can take feedback and reprimands knowing that you have their interests at heart and have a clear idea of what's going on. Even though it might be overwhelming to them, they won't worry about it too much if you have everything under control.

It's your confidence that opens up the door to learning.

CONFIDENCE

HEART

ANTICIPATE

REINFORCE

GROW

ENGAGE

2 – 1 Introduction (Heart)

What is teaching?

Is it a collection of information, skills, and ideas that we attempt to transfer to students by any means possible?

Is teaching only a means to an end, that final goal post being competent performance on a standardized assessment?

Or perhaps, if you're more jaded, is education simply a tool of an intrusive government to push its agenda and shape the ignorant masses?

Before moving on too far, it might be good to define teaching, both what it is and how it's accomplished.

Easier said than done.

What makes these inquiries so interesting is that the answer to the first question, *What is teaching?*, should be obvious. When asking a football player about his sport, it's easy to identify the objective (score more points than the opponent) and how it's accomplished (offense, defense, and special teams).

In fact, most professions, organizations, and even recreational groups can give you a quick and easy approximation of both their purpose and the methodology used to achieve it.

Before you get too excited that I might reveal some never-seen-before purpose of education, I believe most of us can agree on the aim of teaching. Education, as defined by many a district mission statement, aims to provide students with the knowledge and skills to succeed in a global workplace. Sometimes schools will include a goal of success in college, career, military, and/or community leadership.

No matter what the phraseology looks like, most schools take the long-term view of education. They seek to prepare their students for entry into the world as adults prepared to contribute to society, participate in democracy, care for themselves and others, and generally make the world a better place. That's not the issue here.

The question is, How?

How do we best teach? What conditions are necessary for learning to have any chance at success? This is the sticking point, the question that many teachers would have to take a moment to think about before responding. If you were to ask teachers about the best way to teach, the responses you get would be as vast as the Milky Way.

Some would point you to specific instructional methodologies, named after famous educators in the past and sworn to with dogged determination. Others would reply using a catchphrase such as *research-based* or *best practices* but, when pressed, couldn't go into much more detail than that. A significant portion, however, would simply shrug their shoulders in acquiescence. Their job is to teach and it's the students' job to learn, they might say. They don't get too worked up about it.

If you want to take charge of your classroom, the first section of the book focused on the confidence you bring. This speaks to your being, who you are, and it affects everything you believe, say, and do. Without confidence, you've lost before you've even started.

In subsequent sections, we'll discuss behaviors that set your students up for success (anticipate, reinforce, and grow) and close the book out with key engagement truths. Yet between your being and your behaviors lies your beliefs.

What do you believe about teaching?

Assuming we can agree on a general purpose of education, that being to prepare students for future success in the world at large, we still must decide on the best way to accomplish that goal.

How do we best teach? What's the most effective methodology? Which pedagogical practices rise above the rest? It's safe to assume that if you increase your teaching practices, you'll also reduce misbehavior at the same time. Students that enjoy learning, and are successful at it, are much less likely to exhibit maladaptive behavior.

Teaching and learning boil down to one factor – relationships.

The heart of teaching, your beliefs about the best strategy for instructing students, revolves around the truth that we are social creatures. We seek and crave connection with others because that need is biologically hard-wired into all of us.

Do you want to become a better teacher? Build better relationships.

Want your students to stop acting out? Build better relationships.

Interested in boosting student achievement on high-stakes testing? Build better relationships.

Relationships act as the mediator for instructional practices. All your fancy teaching tips and tricks get filtered through the relationships you've built with your students. Those relationships enhance or diminish the content you're trying to teach and the pedagogy you use to share your message.

While relationships form the first part of the heart of teaching, two other related aspects deserve our attention. The respect you have for your students, and the beliefs you hold about their abilities, inadvertently filter into all your instructional choices. While most teachers would adamantly claim that they love and respect their students and the communities they serve, digging a little deeper might prove otherwise.

Relationships act as the mediator for instructional practices.

Many teachers who serve in underprivileged schools, teaching students in communities that are historically under resourced, do so with a savior mentality. They come, with honorable intentions, to save their students from the degradation of urban blight and broken homes. Holding these deficit mental models, often tied to racial inequities and/or systemic white supremacy, show a lack of respect for students and the strengths they bring with them. Ultimately, it stymies relationships between teachers and students and erodes your ability to teach and your students' ability to learn.

Finally, the heart of teaching also includes release. The better you get at teaching, the more successful your students are, and the closer your relationships grow, the less control you have.

Now there's a scary thought.

Maintaining power and control is a sure way to guarantee that you'll never take charge of classroom management. Instead, you'll spend the rest of your career chasing after students and putting out fires.

Heart

A sure way to improve classroom behavior is to give students autonomy and responsibility. Hold them as capable partners in learning rather than deficient laborers that need to be managed. All humans, in addition to craving relationships, desperately seek autonomy. We all want to feel like we have a say in our daily lives.

If you are an American football fan, you know that there are three major parts to any team and winning organizations focus on all three. The first two parts of the Take CHARGE model, confidence and heart, are like a football team's defense. While defenders guard their own end zone and try to keep the other team from scoring, confidence and heart are geared toward guarding yourself. If you get yourself right, if your being and beliefs flow together in harmony, nothing will be able to stop you.

When you explore and ingest the heart of teaching, that learning is a function of relationships, respect, and release, you're ready to take the next step toward taking charge of your classroom.

I define connection as the energy that exists between people when they feel seen, heard, and valued; when they can give and receive without judgment; and when they derive sustenance and strength from the relationship.

- Brené Brown

2 – 2 Relationships (Heart)

The year was 2000 and I was extremely bored. Fresh out of college and an alternative teaching certification program, someone thought it was a good idea to give me sole responsibility for 16 nine- and ten-year-olds for seven hours a day. Don't get me wrong, I had a lot of fun with my students. One of the worst parts of my teaching day, though, was recess.

The kids played and had fun for 15 or 20 minutes each day. All I had to look forward to was standing around with a bunch of really old teachers underneath an oak tree (they must have been in their 30s at least). Their favorite pastime was complaining about the principal, the parents, and their students. As a 22-year-old rookie teacher, this was the equivalent to being sentenced to solitary confinement.

The reason I mentioned the fact that I was alternatively certified is because I had no formal education training in college. I didn't know that there were actual teaching strategies. I thought the textbook was the curriculum. If the kids were having fun, I figured, they were probably learning (I wasn't too far off there). I knew absolutely nothing about student motivation or classroom management. I did, though, stumble into an effective practice proven to improve both.

One day, I started playing soccer with my students during recess.

It turned out to be an eye opener for me even though it took me a decade and a half to figure out why. Remember that my motivation for doing this was very selfish – standing around and adult-ing for 20 minutes every day was torture for a 22-year-old first-year teacher. I didn't know that I was fulfilling the psychological need for relationships by playing soccer with my students. I just wanted to play (though my wife didn't want me to after I ruined a second pair of khaki pants with grass stains).

Because I played soccer with my students at recess, my students became putty in my hands in class. I was a young Anglo-Californian teaching in a predominantly Hispanic school in Texas. I didn't have the first clue about my students' worlds and, honestly, I didn't even know that I should try to understand their backgrounds. Inadvertently, though, I had brought myself into their world by playing soccer. I had opened a connection with them and, for some of them, that was all they needed.

They might not have cared about the subjects I taught but they started to work hard for me. I developed a close relationship with them by letting them destroy me on a soccer field for 20 minutes a day. They saw me reach out to them and they reciprocated.

Neurology

Funny thing, the brain. Ignoring what neuroscience tells us about the brain and how it intersects with teaching and learning is foolishness. If we know how our brains function, we can better plan our teaching and interaction strategies to leverage our physiological realities.

And we know.

Heart

Children's neurology is affected by the relationships they form with their teacher and other students (Bailey, 2015). Personal connections create the brain circuits responsible for such basic things as the formation of meaning. Relationships also affect the regulation of bodily states, the modulation of emotion, the ability to focus and sustain attention, the organization of memories, and the capacity for interpersonal communication.

Basically, relationships affect everything.

Positive, nurturing relationships, whether they be between students and parents or students and teachers, lay the groundwork and mental infrastructure for all learning activities. Without these support systems in place, trying to teach is as difficult as trying to run up a greased metal ramp in your socks.

Why is that?

Our brains have a hierarchy of needs that must be met for us to be open and receptive to new learning. First, we must feel safe. If there is an imminent threat to our safety, whether physical or psychological, our mental energy will be spent on finding safety rather than diving into the complexities of adding fractions with unlike denominators. Students don't have time to learn when they are full of stress or fear.

More than that, though, is our need for connection. Once safety has been established, we must feel loved and connected to enter into a beneficial learning state. For our brains to develop fully, for us to enter into the sweet spot that lies between security and challenge, we must feel cared for. From this strong student-teacher partnership flows optimal brain development, academic success, emotional well-being, and the willingness to cooperate.

So why are relationships so important? Because nurturing, attuned alignment with others builds neural connections within the brain that literally wire it for willingness and impulse control.

Do you want your students to stop fighting every time you ask them to do something? Focus on deeper relationships.

Do you want your students to resist the urge to lash out at their peers when angry? Focus on deeper relationships.

Our brains are wired to connect, attune, resonate, and learn with each other. Only when children feel safe and loved can they begin to develop skills like setting and achieving goals, regulating themselves, and getting along with others. When children have positive interactions, their neural pathways are being strengthened for future success.

Unfortunately, many teachers operate out of a fear-based approach. They seek to control their students through punishment and rewards, doling out the former while withholding the latter when students have the audacity to be human and err. This approach eliminates a large portion of social problem-solving that is inherent in warm classrooms. In consequence, the prefrontal lobe development of students in these cold, hard classrooms is suppressed because they are focused more on not angering the teacher than working through everyday problems with their friends.

Relationships literally shape the function and structure of our brains.

Oxytocin

Oxytocin is your friend.

This chemical is related to many learning-friendly actions or emotions, such as bonding, generosity, empathy, and trust (Bailey, 2015). As oxytocin rises, so do these desirable abilities. Healthy relationships are just one of many ways to release this wonderful hormone into your brain from your pituitary gland.

When oxytocin is released it calms the amygdala, the brain's watchdog that is always on the alert for danger.

Imagine walking by a deserted lot between buildings and hearing a snarl. You turn your head sharply and you see a blur of motion as a 50 pound pit bull races toward you. At that moment your amygdala flares into action, giving you instant access to energy and clarity as you seek safety.

What you don't have time to think about are the intricacies of urban decay and the plight of inner cities as they fight to hold back the tide of crime and suburban flight. No, the logical centers of your brain are on a short hiatus as your amygdala tries to keep you from being eaten.

Relationships literally shape the function and structure of our brains.

Now imagine that the dog is on a heavy chain leash. While still disturbing, the threat from the dog would greatly diminish as long as the leash holds. Better yet, there's now a twelve-foot high chain link fence between you and the leashed dog.

These barriers to danger, the leash and the fence, act as oxytocin does. They calm the amygdala (the pit bull), keeping your heart rate normal as you saunter past the deserted lot.

Our polyvagal nervous system, sometimes known as the *social engagement system*, uses oxytocin and other hormones to keep us connected to others when in their presence (Hammond, 2014). Social activities such as laughing, talking, and even hugging release this all-important bonding hormone. When we feel safe in the presence of another, our breath comes more easily, our heartbeat is regulated, we don't sweat nervously, our thinking is clear, and we feel open, expansive, and in sync. Oxytocin is the brain's signal to the amygdala to stand down.

Yet how does all of this affect learning?

It's imperative for teachers to understand how to build positive social relationships that signal to the brain, specifically the amygdala, a sense of emotional, psychological, and social safety so that learning is possible. When the brain doesn't feel safe, suddenly the chain link fence and the leash vanish, leaving survival as the only remaining thought.

The brain is always seeking to minimize social threats and maximize opportunities to connect with others. It can't do that, however, if it perceives others or the environment to be threatening to its social or psychological well-being. Positive relationships keep our safety-threat detection system in check. The oxytocin that positive relationships trigger helps the amygdala stay calm so the prefrontal cortex can focus on higher order thinking and learning, such as adding fractions with unlike denominators.

Relationships should not be viewed as merely emotional. Instead, they also have a physiological component. They exist at the intersection of both mind and body. It's only when our neuroreceptive mechanisms confirm that our surroundings are physically, socially, and intellectually safe that we can enter into a state of relaxed alertness, primed for new information and experiences.

Relationships are the precursor to learning.

Connected or disconnected

Our brains, then, are hardwired for connection. Hormones flood our system when we form or perpetuate meaningful connections with others. In addition to oxytocin, our brains have mirror neurons that fire when we see or hear something happening. We can vicariously experience the emotions of others through these mirror neurons and those experiences help bind us together.

Mirror neurons are why I tear up when Jennifer Lawrence's Katniss Everdeen volunteers as a tribute for her sister Primrose in *The Hunger Games* movie. From the bland color palette used to visually display the horrors of a dystopian future to the shaky cam that captures the scene, that moment in cinematic history has always moved me emotionally. When Katniss runs out and screams that she volunteers as tribute, her voice breaking, and she hugs her sister who is now safe, I'm done for. I weep like a baby because my mirror neurons are firing madly, connecting me to that moment and those visceral emotions.

Relationships are the precursor to learning.

In the absence of authentic connection, we suffer. Everything in us, from our hormones to our genetic makeup, support interdependence over independence. It's the level of children's connectedness that governs their behavior.

Mirror neurons help transmit your warm, receptive state to your students. When you feel open, calm, and ready to engage in learning, your students feel the same. You are not a thermometer in your room, merely reflecting the ambient temperature but unable to change it. You are a thermostat, directly influencing the emotional states of your students through authentic relationships and the power of mirror neurons and empathy.

When children feel connected to their school family, when they feel a sense of acceptance and identity with their teacher and peers, the conflicts that arise naturally as a part of the day become opportunities to learn missing social and emotional skills (Bailey, 2015).

Connectedness turns punishment into discipline.

Disconnected students, however, are disruptive. Sometimes a teacher might, after seeing that her students are not following the routines, decide that her students need more modeling, more specific visuals, or more practice. Every time students fail to meet the teacher's expectations, it should not be viewed as the gateway to Armageddon. Sometimes there's a lack of clarity or familiarity with the routine or expectation that gets in the way.

If after reteaching or additional modeling, however, a student or two continue to ignore the rules or the expectations, there's usually something deeper at play. Oftentimes, the relationship between the teacher and student is strained or non-existent. Disconnection causes misbehavior.

No reward or punishment system can make a child behave appropriately. Even when teachers swear by the effectiveness of their sticker charts or behavior folder systems, they are being tricked by fool's gold. Compliance based on fear is not the same as good behavior. Instead, connection activities should be built into every lesson every day. When students begin to build relationships with each other and the teacher, it strengthens the wiring in their brains essential for problem-solving and positive social interactions.

Trying to make a disconnected child behave is like trying to drive a car across the country without gas. Or tires. Or even a steering wheel.

When teachers ask students to follow class rules or abide by certain procedures, they are, in essence, asking them to submit their wills. The teacher's routines are in effect saying, "I know what's best for you. Just do as I say and everything will run smoothly." Whether or not children choose to submit themselves to the care of their teacher depends on a wide range of factors, one of the most important being the health of the relationship between the student and the teacher.

One final word on connection. Teachers of older students will often hear three words as a retort when they ask disruptive students to follow the rules or expectations. "I don't care."

Connectedness turns punishment into discipline.

Those words can take a relatively minor situation and blow it way out of proportion. If the teacher isn't careful, she can take this as a personal attack on her authority, typically because the phrase is uttered with a high degree of scorn and contempt. Yet, if we can stop a moment and view the message behind the words, we'll see something else entirely.

When a student says, "I don't care," he often really means, "I don't feel cared for."

Let that sink in for a moment. Students want to please teachers they feel connected with. They don't want to antagonize their friends or classmates when in a warm, reciprocal relationship with them. Misbehavior, then, can sometimes be boiled down to a lack of connection. Successful behavior management is not about complex systems, procedures drilled into children's muscle memory, and blind obedience. It's about successfully connecting with students.

Connection fosters cooperation. Disconnection fosters disruption.

What can you do tomorrow?

Observe. Choose one of your troubled students to shadow for a week. Get to know him, learn his likes and dislikes, and even eat lunch with him.

Forge connections. Find ways to spend time with him outside of instruction and see how your relationship changes. Imagine a typical day through his eyes to gain a clearer picture of his world.

What does this look like in the classroom?

The teacher develops and maintains **positive relationships** that are reflected in:

- Social conversations between teacher and students;
- Interactions with students that are relaxed and open; and
- Frequent laughter and nurturing facial expressions.

How can you reflect on your learning?

What impact does oxytocin have on learning?

_____

_____

What's the relationship between teacher-student connections and behavior?

_____

_____

Heart

Belonging

Humans are hard-wired for connection.

Much like oral language abilities, humans are born with the genetic makeup needed to connect with others and live in a community. And yet so many of our students are missing that in their daily lives.

Imagine trying to hold a track meet if every competitor had nagging or suppurating leg wounds.

How effective would basketball practice be if every player was handcuffed?

In both instances, parts that are essential to the execution of the sport are removed from play. In both instances, the only result would be frustration and failure.

Can you honestly say, then, that every one of your students comes in with his or her relational needs met? That none of your students suffer from a sense of being alone, of not having anyone to support them or watch their backs? Many of our students suffer not from ADD but BDD – belonging deficit disorder.

And you hold the cure.

There are many ways to develop a sense of belonging in the classroom. One of the most effective is the one that has the widest effect.

Help students help others.

Encouraging children to help their classmates creates a communal sense of belonging. The intrinsic desire to be of service can be nurtured and send attention-seeking behaviors into remission. Built on a foundational belief of connectedness, fostering an environment of aid and assistance creates a compassionate culture that focuses on unity and togetherness.

There is value in emphasizing the triumphs of the whole class over individual wins (Willans & Williams, 2018). Students who are committed to the success of the class are less likely to disrupt others. As the pronoun shifts from *me* to *we*, behavior problems surface less and less. Students who lash out are likely to do so toward strangers or those they are disconnected with. They have difficulty, however, maintaining their negative behaviors toward those close to them. Those actions become self-inflicted wounds.

Teachers who want to take charge of their classroom do well when emphasizing pride in class achievements over individual ones. In hyper-competitive classrooms, students begin to scheme and sabotage in an effort to move forward. When strong communities are built and maintained, however, success becomes dependent on everyone, not just the few at the top.

Help students help others.

As a disruptive student, I'm less likely to lash out when my success is tied to yours. If I want to win, then you must as well. Rather than trampling you on my way toward the finish line, I must stop and help you up. For me to reach the ultimate level of achievement, I must work together with you and accept responsibility not only for myself but for you as well.

For classrooms to be effective learning centers, students must develop constructive relationships with each other. This is especially important in the upper grades where many students are beginning to restrict their friendships. Unification of a class is even more important as peer mores push students to identify themselves with one group over another. Togetherness is integral to success. What some students might not understand from the teacher's lesson, they might understand if a friend explains it to them.

But how can teachers build this sense of community?

Rituals

Relationships develop organically, as people spend extended amounts of time in close proximity to one another. Just because it happens naturally, however, doesn't mean you can't help speed up the process.

Connection rituals, or repeated activities or traditions that are designed to encourage camaraderie, are essential to any and every classroom. Connection fosters willingness and willingness is a wonderful thing (Bailey, 2015).

Willingness means being prepared and ready to meet behavioral and academic expectations.

Willingness means being open to correction if needed.

Willingness means working for, rather than against, the good of the class.

Authentic rituals are true rituals jointly created by the teacher and students. Though you, as the instructor, might bring the ritual to the students, planned for a particular part of the day, the execution of the ritual itself is wildly variable. True rituals are interactive, and by very nature, anything involving students has a tendency to get off track.

Students will sometimes become shy all of the sudden when it's their turn to speak. They might break down into uncontrollable giggles when a classmate says something funny. When preparing for rituals, keep in mind that it's supposed to be fun and connecting, not prep for a college entrance exam. Students should feel comfortable enough to make it their own.

So why are rituals so important? Remember that students enter the classroom each day with two questions that, once answered in the affirmative, signal their willingness and ability to learn.

Am I safe?

Am I loved?

The first question deals with physical, emotional, and psychological safety that comes from positive and protective classroom cultures. It's the second question that becomes answered partly through rituals. Remember that our social brains are wired for connection. We need community as much as we need food, water, and air. It's the daily rituals of a classroom that make us feel like we belong. Like we're on the inside rather than the outside.

Togetherness is integral to success.

There are many rituals that teachers use all across the world to form deeper relationships and networks of inclusion. Here are a few starter ideas to get the ball rolling.

Welcome students at the door each morning with a handshake and a warm greeting. Your face might be the first one they've seen all morning that wasn't angry.

Form students in a circle and have one stand up and state one thing he or she likes. For example, a student might stand in the middle and say, "I like baseball." If another student also likes baseball, he or she stands up (just one student at a time) and says, "Just like me!" while linking arms with the first student. The new student then starts again with something new he or she likes. Another student that likes the same thing stands up, links arms, and says, "Just like me!" until all students have joined.

Jokes are some of the easiest ways to break the ice and foster social conversations in the classroom. Bring one or two jokes or puns to share each morning before starting instruction. As students come to anticipate this, they can volunteer to bring an appropriate joke to share the next morning.

Give students five minutes at the beginning of class to partner up to walk around the playground or through the hallways to discuss an academic topic, such as something they learned yesterday. This simple walk-and-talk ritual gets their blood flowing, fosters connections, and integrates academics all at the same time.

Emotional literacy is an important part of social-emotional learning. To build this, students can play a quick emotions guessing game in the morning. Have them partner up and each pair has one partner facing the screen while the other has his or her back to the screen. Show a word on the screen, such as *sad* or *anxious*, and the partner facing the screen tries to display that emotion using only their face while their partner guesses. Not only will the students enjoy playing this simple game, it opens the door to much broader discussions about emotional literacy (discussed again in section five – grow).

Noncontingent reinforcement

One of the messages our troubled students receive from teachers year after year is actually quite sad. From the responses they get from the adults in their lives, these students have internalized a message of conditional affection.

I will be nice to you when you behave. If you want my affection, I need you to stop acting out. My love and care for you is only evident when you're on your best behavior.

This message that is internalized by many troubled students is one that is built up over time. As their behavior gets worse and worse, the affection they receive from adults dwindles. Unable to manage their emotions, adults withhold from them the one thing they need to regulate their bodies, brains, and feelings. Instead of conditional affection, teachers would do well to send a different message.

I am with you. I've got your back. Even when you're at your worst and I don't like the way you're acting, I love you, and I'm here.

Now that's a powerful message.

Remember that students have a built-in need to be connected with others. Every student wants to be accepted by the other students and by the teacher. When their actions disrupt that, their connection begins to weaken. While in some students this weakening causes the aberrant behavior to decrease or even stop, in some the opposite occurs. Unable to deal with the emotional rejection their behavior engenders, they push others away even further with negatively escalating actions.

How can we send a message of unconditional affection to our most troubled students?

Simply put, noncontingent reinforcement (NCR). In the context of school classrooms it means giving the troubled student positive attention or positive interactions throughout the day regardless of his or her behavior (Minahan & Rappaport, 2012). This reduces the child's need to act poorly to receive attention.

Think of NCR as planned random acts of kindness.

NCR has many things working in its favor. First, implementing it is rather simple. Set a time interval and, at each interval, give the student brief positive attention. Smile at him, walk by and compliment his work, or simply make eye contact and wink. Using a timer, chime, or some other time-keeping device, it does not take much effort to plan or implement.

Second, the intervals can increase as the behavior improves. Though a dense schedule might be necessary at first, the length of the interval can increase over time. Start strong and slowly wean the child off NCR as needed.

Finally, NCR works. It's been shown to be an effective treatment for destructive behavior maintained by social attention (Hagopian, Fisher, & Legacy, 1994). If one of your students is driving you nuts with attention-seeking behavior, NCR is a proven technique that psychologists and behavior therapists use.

For students whose negative behavior is driven by a need for attention and connection, they don't have the rational ability to understand that their actions are undermining the very thing they need.

NCR delivers a message of acceptance and kind regard. Through planned random acts of kindness, students slowly begin to have their relational needs met. As their sense of connectedness and belonging grows, their aberrant behavior begins to decline. Rather than waiting for the student to do something correct in order to show affection, a wait that is usually very long indeed, purposefully schedule NCR. Show the student that you love him in spite of his actions.

Vulnerability

Other than NCR, one of the greatest weapons you have in the fight to form connectedness lies within you. There are five actions or factors that generate trust: selective vulnerability, familiarity, similarity of interests, concern, and competence (Hammond, 2014). While the other factors may seem like common knowledge to educators, it's the first one that at first seems dissonant.

Selective vulnerability means to share your story. Come out from behind yourself and enter fully into the classroom. Become a human being with follies and dreams rather than a cardboard cut-out purchased in bulk at a wholesale distributor.

There's only one you. That's who the students want to know. Your biggest ticket to building relationships and taking charge of your classroom is your vulnerability.

Yet vulnerability is both powerful and dangerous (Brafman & Brafman, 2010).

> *Vulnerability and self-disclosure accelerate our ability to connect with those around us. It helps the other person trust you precisely because you are putting yourself at emotional, psychological, or physical risk. Other people respond by being more open and vulnerable themselves. The fact that you are letting down your guard helps to lay the groundwork for a faster, closer, personal connection.*

There is power in vulnerability because our willingness to put ourselves at risk deepens the quality of our relationships and makes us more likely to connect with others.

I told you it wouldn't be easy.

Connection fosters cooperation. Connection comes from many factors, but one that's entirely within your control is vulnerability. Take your armor off and bring your hobbies, your dreams, and your mistakes into the

HEART

classroom. While you might not want to detail the intricacies of your recent divorce to your eight-year-olds, all students love to hear stories of the trouble their teachers got into while at school. If you collect llamas, decorate your room with domesticated South American camelids. Your classroom should be filled with you as well as with contributions from students.

Come out from behind yourself and enter fully into the classroom.

Vulnerability is dangerous. It carries risk. Your students might not find your jokes funny or might laugh if you bring in your guitar to sing for your students. In any relationship, whether it be between teachers and students or between newlyweds, intimacy always carries the danger of rejection. The only way to ensure that you will never suffer emotional damage is to tear that part out of you and lock it away, refusing to connect with anyone.

Students need to belong to a school family, but so do teachers. Both groups need each other emotionally and socially to fulfill their built-in need for human connection. The ticket to that train is bought with vulnerability.

Are you ready to climb aboard?

What can you do tomorrow?

Plan random acts of kindness. Think about how you can integrate noncontingent reinforcement into your daily interactions with a student. Choose a student with whom you have few positive interactions and decide on an initial interval, from five to ten minutes. **Stay consistent.** When your notification or reminder dings, have a short positive interaction with the student (e.g., smile, gentle touch, kind word). Note how the relationship improves.

What does this look like in the classroom?

The teacher develops and maintains **connection rituals**, which can include:

- Greeting students at the door with a smile and handshake;
- Classroom rituals (e.g., walk-and-talks); and
- Using humor (sharing jokes, puns, or comics) with students.

How can you reflect on your learning?

Which connection rituals have you found to be successful?

_____

_____

How can you use noncontingent reinforcement to increase positive relationships in your classroom?

_____

_____

Immediate impact: Go to 3 – 2 Procedures (Anticipate) – pg. 187

If we lose love and self-respect for each other, this is how we finally die.

- Maya Angelou

2 – 3 Respect (Heart)

All Aretha Franklin asked for was a little.

For students to thrive, and for your classroom to become a haven of learning, your students will need much more than that.

Respect.

While most teachers would argue that they do respect their students, that they believe the best about them and hold them to high expectations, sometimes the lack of respect shows up not so much in blatant disregard but a lack of faith in students' ability to behave and succeed.

If you treat your students like animals, you can't complain about being a zookeeper.

I remember having this truth slammed in my face over a decade and a half ago. I was a fourth grade teacher, still less than five years into my new career, and had attended a professional development training in my district. I can't even remember the content or even where the training was held. What I do remember was the conversation two of my tablemates were having.

Sitting with other fourth grade teachers from across the district, I quickly realized that I had been pretty isolated to begin my teaching career. While I had one or two disciplinary issues in my room, my woes were apparently nothing compared to these teachers'. Partner teachers that taught across the hall from each other, these educators delighted in regaling me with the antics of their students.

What began as harmless fun with a few amusing kid stories quickly devolved into a gripe session about the human condition. These teachers did not think very highly of their students and the steps they took to keep their students under control grew progressively more extreme as the stories continued.

If you treat your students like animals, you can't complain about being a zookeeper.

They took the personal pencil sharpeners away from students because a few had left piles of pencil shavings in their desks before switching classes. Then they took the pencils away from students because they drew on their desks constantly. Students were only given pencils when asked to write something and then had to immediately give them back. Finally, the students still managed to leave messes in the desks. Thus, all the desks had been turned around so that the openings faced away from the students.

While the teachers thought these stories amusing, hoping to garner pity from me, I was shocked. I literally had nothing to say because I couldn't believe what I was hearing. As the discussion wound to a close for the day, they were trying to figure out if they could take the chairs away from the students as well because they kept leaning back in them.

That experience professionally scarred me for quite a while. Those two teachers had stopped viewing their students as capable learners, or even as human beings deserving of respect. They had started to treat their students as animals and were shocked when the students behaved in a similar manner.

Percentile scores

Mr. McPherson finally had something to look forward to as an educator. Even though he'd been teaching at the high school for seven years, he was still the newest teacher in the mathematics department. This meant that he usually got stuck teaching the remedial courses. His days were filled with ninth and tenth graders attempting to make it past Algebra 1. Though he did the best he could, his results were less than stellar. His students came to him defeated and usually left in the same frame of mind.

This year was going to be different, though. He looked at his roster for first period Algebra 1 and liked what he saw. The class was filled with freshmen and each student name had a number beside it, ranging from 72 to 94. He couldn't believe it! 94! He had never taught a student who scored in the 94th percentile on last year's end of course exam. It looked like the school's move toward utilizing data for instruction finally resulted in him getting the pre-AP class he always wanted.

He looked at his lesson plans that he had been using year after year and knew they wouldn't suffice. These students performed in the top 20% on their math exam last year and they did not need remediation. No, what they needed was to be pushed. Instead of dawdling with basic properties of operations, he wanted to start the year out with a bold project-based learning task.

"Students, my name is Mr. McPherson. I'm so excited to be your teacher this year," he began on the first day of school. "I've been working with teachers in other disciplines and we've come up with something we think you'll enjoy." The students rolled their eyes but were definitely interested. "This project will start today and take the entire first month of school to complete. In connection with your science, English, and social studies classes, you will be working together to stop a serial killer.

"You and a group of three other students will work as crime scene investigators to not only identify the murderer but also define the motive and how the killings took place. Clues will be scattered all throughout your classes and since I'm your first period teacher, I'll be serving as your base of operations. When you come across something you need help with, your job will be to go to the appropriate teacher and get the assistance you need. For instance, today we've received a coded message from the killer in the form of linear functions. If you can solve the equations, you'll crack his coded message and begin to unravel his devious plot," Mr. McPherson concluded.

A hand slowly shot up. "Uh, teacher, this all sounds hard. We've never done anything like this before. Are you sure this is what we're supposed to be doing?" a student timidly asked.

"Of course I do, young lady. The school included your scores on last year's exams and I couldn't be happier. You are all very capable and I know you can do it. Let's get started!" Mr. McPherson replied.

The students looked at each other wordlessly and shuffled forward to receive the coded message. That first day didn't go so well and Mr. McPherson had to do a lot of reteaching on linear functions. He figured they had just forgotten a lot over the summer and didn't let up on them.

HEART

He constantly pushed them and challenged the class to extend their thinking because he knew that they had the ability to do great things.

At the end of the month, his students had solved the mystery of the serial killer. Working together as a group, with teachers in various classes, and even before and after school, the momentum slowly built until the class seemed like a juggernaut. They entered school each day ready to tackle the next task, confident in their ability to work through any problems and find success. Mr. McPherson was especially pleased with their performance and was planning the next set of lessons when he was called into the principal's office.

"Mr. McPherson," Ms. Miller began. "I understand that your first period class took a different approach to Algebra 1 this month. I was a little worried until I saw the results from our common assessment. Your students outperformed every other Algebra 1 class in the school, even the pre-AP courses. How did you do it?"

"Ms. Miller," Mr. McPherson replied, "Thank you very much. The students you gave me deserve all the credit. If they hadn't been so bright, none of this would have been possible. I am a little confused, though. You said my class outperformed the pre-AP courses. My first period is a pre-AP Algebra 1 class."

"No, it isn't. That's why your success is so amazing. What did..."

"I'm sorry to interrupt, Principal Miller, but I'm now very confused." Mr. McPherson brought out his roster. "Look at this roster. These students are mathematically gifted. See Michele here? She scored in the 94th percentile on her test last year."

As Ms. Miller examined the roster, she nodded and looked up. "I'm the one who needs to apologize. I guess I wasn't very clear about these numbers on the first period roster. You have the same type of students you always have, Mr. McPherson. Your first period class is a remedial Algebra 1 class, just like normal."

She looked up and flashed him an embarrassed smile.

"These are their locker numbers off to the side."

Ability to behave

Students will rise or fall to the level of your expectations. Called the Pygmalion effect (positive) and the Golem effect (negative) in psychology, student behaviors and achievement are heavily influenced by the attitudes and expectations of the teacher.

Do you want your students to act better? Do you want them to regulate themselves and their emotions? Believe they can and you'll go a long way toward making your dream a reality.

Student will rise or fall to the level of your expectations.

Many schools and districts include phraseology about high expectations for all students in their mission statements. Too often, however, those lofty goals don't extend past academics. While teachers routinely hold their students to rigorous learning expectations, they sometimes simultaneously hold a belief that erodes trust in the students' abilities to act appropriately.

See the problem?

Some teachers would counter that with a vociferous defense of their classroom rules and regulations. "I have tons of expectations," they would argue as they point to their list of rules. "I have seven rules and most students can't even keep three of them!" they might say, triumphing in their moral superiority.

While the above platitudes about believing in all students' ability to behave might be generally true, you might not think they apply to you and your unique situation. I don't know *your* students and the challenges they present to *you*.

Let me share a little secret with you. Rules don't teach expected behaviors. Instead, rules simply hold us accountable to those behaviors.

Imagine a first grade teacher going to her principal three weeks into the school year. Frustrated with her students, she's taken as much as she could but then loses it after another failed day. Desperate to the point of quitting, she texts her boss and asks to meet with her after school.

Barging into the office without preamble, she launches into her diatribe. "I just don't believe these students! I've had problems before, but never to this degree. Usually I'm a pretty confident person but these kids are making me rethink my life choices. My sister-in-law is in real estate and she's been trying to get me to start selling houses for years. If things don't shape up by Thanksgiving, I might just take her up on it."

Realizing that this was quickly turning serious, the principal holds up her hands. "Whoa, slow down a bit. What exactly is the problem? Maybe I can help."

"Problem? I'll tell you what the problem is! They can't read!! Not a single one of them knows how to read and it makes my job almost impossible. I've never seen a group of students so low that not one of them can recognize more than his or her first name. It's simply unbelievable," the teacher rails in desperation.

Expectations

As ridiculous as that scenario sounds, it's not too far from what happens in classrooms across the country. The irony, of course, lies in the fact that most first graders don't know how to read nor should they be expected to. If kindergarten teachers can drill into their students the ability to recognize all 26 letters, both upper and lower case, their related sounds, and a smattering of sight words, then they've done their job. A first grade teacher complaining about her students coming in without appropriate reading abilities is as ridiculous as obedience school employees complaining that the dogs they get are so wild.

That's their job!

First grade teachers have many duties but first and foremost their job is to teach students how to read.

Rules don't teach expected behaviors.

You get paid to teach history or mathematics, physics or elementary social studies. Whatever your content area expertise is, there's a hidden curriculum you are also responsible for. Your job is to teach your students not only how to read, write, compute, or analyze socio-political theories, you have also been hired to teach them how to act.

The expectations you hold for your students will tell much about the results you'll achieve. If you expect them to act like hoodlums, then don't be surprised by the anarchy you engender. If you expect them to demonstrate decorum and civility, that's a wonderful start.

But what if they can't?

Heart

It's a good thing they have a teacher!

Many educators fail to take charge of the classroom because of a huge assumption. They presume that their students know how to behave and are simply choosing not to. While that might be the case in rare situations, for the most part students are behaving the best they know how. If their best isn't good enough, then it's up to you to show them how to improve.

When a child doesn't know how to read, you don't suspend her but teach her to decode.

When a child doesn't know his multiplication facts, you don't assign him detention but work with him until he develops automaticity.

When a child doesn't know how to behave, what do you do?

What expectations do you hold? Do you respect him enough to teach him a better way?

What can you do tomorrow?

Evaluate your rigor. Take an inventory of the tasks, grouping strategies, and learning activities that you employed over the last few weeks. Are they the highest-level, most rigorous ones you could have used or did you water them down because you didn't think your students could handle more?

Expect more. In the same way, how do your students rise to the level of your behavioral expectations? If they act like animals, is that because you expect them to do so?

What does this look like in the classroom?

Students are held to **high expectations**, as evidenced by:
- Being assigned rigorous tasks that do not water down the curriculum;
- Receiving thoughtful instruction on how to act; and
- Being spoken to with dignity and respect.

How can you reflect on your learning?

How high are the behavioral expectations you have for your students?

_____

_____

Whose responsibility is it to teach children how to act and behave?

_____

_____

Honoring culture

Some people claim they are culturally color blind, that they don't see race but instead view all people equally.

How unfortunate.

My orientation on race and culture will always be shaped by my upbringing but is not restricted to it. Typing this in the midst of the 2020 COVID-19 pandemic, an event that is beginning to feel as earth changing as the Great Depression was for our grandparents, racial tensions have boiled to the surface.

The national exposure of the Black Lives Matter movement, coming shortly after the #MeToo movement, has thrown open the doors on some bitter truths that American society has ignored and downplayed for far too long.

There are groups of people, whether they identify by race, culture, sexual orientation, or gender, that are minimized, slighted, assaulted, and handcuffed by poverty, violence, and institutional discrimination. To blindly claim that everyone is equal is optimistically naive at best and a tool to perpetuate evil at worst.

Claiming that race is irrelevant is like believing that gravity is just a human construct. Try jumping off a tall building and see whether or not gravity truly exists. Both race and gravity are alive and well and to ignore either is dangerous.

A solid approach to this sensitive topic, especially if you hail from a privileged upbringing, is not to avoid it but cherish it. The culture that students bring through the door with them shapes who they are and how they think and learn. Being blind to students' background, whether it be racial, cultural, linguistic, or religious, is harmful.

Imagine that you have a new student entering your classroom six weeks into the school year. Coming in alone and with no supplies except for an broken pencil, she sits in the back of the room quietly. Refusing to engage in the lessons, it takes you a week to get even a simple response from her. After six weeks of little to no results, you ask for the educational diagnostician to test her for a suspected learning disability.

After contacting the special education department, you find out that there has been a major oversight. Your new student is not only in the system already, she is supposed to receive at least 60 minutes a day of intense reading support for dyslexia. Her reading difficulties cause her to withdraw and, much to your horror, you realize that your new student has lost six weeks of instruction because you didn't know her background or the individualized education plan developed to support her.

To blindly claim that everyone is equal is optimistically naive at best and a tool to perpetuate evil at worst.

As detrimental as that scenario is, some of your students face something similar year after year when their teachers and schools are not sensitive to the power of their cultural, linguistic, and religious diversity. Students might come to you with poverty and violence peppering their background, but they also come with the strength of their heritage. Honoring that is a solid first step in building respectful relationships with them.

There are many ways for teachers to integrate inclusive practices into their pedagogy (Hammond, 2014). A solid first step is to think about deep culture and to consider its group orientation toward collectivism or individualism. In America, the dominant culture is individualistic, with an emphasis on direct communication styles and internal guidance. Students growing up in this type of culture, myself included, define themselves more on internal factors rather than external or community influences.

Collectivist cultures, which are prevalent in many African-American, Latino, Pacific Islander, Native American, and Asian communities, are quite different. Rather than independence, these cultures tend to put greater value on interdependence. Students growing up in a collectivist culture place a large degree of importance on cooperative learning and relationships. Maintaining social harmony, getting along with others, and communicating indirectly are hallmarks of these influences.

So how does this affect you? Disrespect toward culture shows up in many different areas in the classroom, whether intentional or accidental. Placing your desks in rows and discouraging group work and discussion ignores the learning strengths and communication styles of certain cultures. Demanding that a child look you in the eye while disciplining him might disregard the cultural norms instilled in him by his parents. Cultivating a competitive classroom environment that pits students against each other completely ignores how many students from collectivist cultures are raised to value group accomplishments.

Teaching with cultural sensitivity

One method teachers can use to tap into the cultural strengths of their students is the use of auditory connective anchors. In cultures that have a strong oral tradition, the use of alliteration is extremely powerful. Word play, such as alliteration, tongue twisters, and even puns can tap into the brain's memory systems that process oral language (Hammond, 2014).

Additionally, movement and emotion play a large part in making meaning for students. When these elements are woven into instruction, they leverage the cultural identity of those with a strong oral tradition and tap into it for increased engagement and memory retention. Sing, dance, rap, move, and do everything you can to cast a broad pedagogical net. Even though you might prefer quiet lectures in straight rows, there's a good chance many of your students don't.

Culture is more than simply a child's background or values. Culture guides how students process information at the most basic level. When trying to teach a newcomer to the country, pantomiming and gesticulating will only provide so much information. The best option, if available, is always to speak the child's first language and use that as a bridge to your content and the English language. For many students, learning in school is like trying to pick up a second language. If they come from a different background, the way their brain processes information might not be aligned with the way you present it.

Common cultural learning aids include music, call and response, and other attention-grabbing strategies. These devices signal to the brain that something important is about to happen and they should pay attention. When these preferred neural pathways are utilized, learning happens much quicker because active brain networks already exist that utilize these strategies.

Attention drives learning. All children (and adults as well) have a reticular activating system (RAS) as a part of their neural network. This RAS is the attention center of the brain, a network of neurons that mediate behavior and attention, among other things. Everyone's RAS is tuned to novelty, relevance, and emotion. Those elements send strong signals to the rest of the brain to pay attention because something interesting is happening or about to happen. Cultures based on oral tradition rely heavily on the RAS to activate learning. They use music, call and response, and other attention grabbers to let everyone know that what follows is valuable.

So what does all this mean?

Look at the children in your classroom. If they all look exactly like you, attend the same type of church you do, and speak the same primary language as you, then your teaching is probably on point. If that were the case, however, you probably wouldn't be reading this book.

For many students, learning in school is like trying to pick up a second language.

There's a good chance that some, or even most, of your students come from different cultures. Their heritage and value systems might not be individualistic but collectivist. That means that group work, team building, and community are going to be far more important than individual competence and competition. Additionally, some of your students might identify with cultures based on a strong oral tradition. This means that, to respect the worth that each child brings with him or her every day, your teaching should reflect those values. Song, dance, rhythm, and other oral strategies are invaluable techniques to tap into a child's cultural identity for learning.

Rather than guessing at a student's heritage and how to fully leverage it, you can jump start the process by asking students to bring in a cultural artifact. During a morning circle, a few students each day can bring something from home that represents their culture, language, religion, or anything else important to them. As the child places it in the middle of the circle, his or her classmates can ask questions about it and its significance. Through this questioning, you learn more about your students and the class as a whole adds to its cultural pool of knowledge.

Free will

There's a secret buried deep within the core of taking charge of your classroom. It doesn't happen when you impose your will on your students. It's not a result of training your students to obey your every command like army recruits in boot camp.

Taking charge, at its deepest level, is about honoring the free will of your students. It's about not trying to take from them something that cannot be removed, their ability to choose and direct their own lives. When you, as the teacher, attempt to supersede that basic human reality, you artificially remove a child's role in the process and place the entire burden of maintaining classroom order on your shoulders.

It's exhausting. And it doesn't work.

Recognizing that our students have free will seems obvious but can be hard for some teachers of younger students. Even though you might be old enough to be their parent or even grandparent, giving students the respect to honor the choices they make each day is key to classroom management. The power that students need to make the right decisions about how they interact with you and their peers comes from choices, not from force.

For students to be motivated to work toward the common good, and to have the ability to regulate their emotions and behavior, the choices they make must be self-driven, motivated from within, and lacking in coercion

HEART

(Bailey, 2015). When students make a choice based on their needs, their values, even their aspirations, the reward center of their brains are activated, releasing feel-good chemicals like dopamine. Choices made from internal desires enhance self-regulation.

Once students accept that they are constantly making choices, they can take charge of their actions and lives. They realize that their power lies within them and cannot be taken from them. When you try to control or manipulate their students, you falsely send a signal of powerlessness to your students. Your message of *you can't control yourself so I need to help you* runs contrary to their own internal sense of free will. Often the result of these manipulations is the exact opposite of what's intended.

Choices made from internal desires enhance self-regulation.

When students lash out behaviorally, oftentimes their actions signal a need for control. They are attempting to fix the boundaries of their identity so they know where they end and others begin. Teachers who recognize the free will of their students, who honor them and respect them enough to appreciate their individuality, give their students the very strength they need to self-regulate.

And that's the secret of taking charge. When you first read the title of this book, you probably thought it would give you tips and tricks to control your classroom. Someone does need to take charge of the classroom, but it isn't you.

It's your students.

Respect and responsibility

Ultimately, it's your students that are responsible for their behavior. You can certainly attempt to threaten them and manipulate them into submission, but that's a recipe for frustration and disappointment.

When we try to make others, children in this case, do things according to our timeline and agenda, we prepare ourselves to rely on force. The strong-arm tactics we are driven to employ teach children that using power to influence others is a valid and acceptable strategy. Our use of brute force to make children behave strips them of their willpower and self-worth, either rendering them flaccid or rebellious.

There is a better way.

As strange as it may seem, children learn to better internalize our values and directions if given a chance to reflect on the feelings, choices, and outcomes that are a result of their actions. When teachers assign punishment and blame, they don't begin the reflective learning process; they stop it.

When someone is drowning, they have only one thing on their mind. They don't care about how they got into the situation, whether or not they had waited 30 minutes after eating before swimming, or what they'll be cooking for dinner that evening. Instead, taking just one more breath is the only thing on their mind. Air is key to life and if we go without it for more than a few moments, we die. Our bodies are designed to respond instinctively to our need to keep breathing.

Psychologically, you can say the same thing about autonomy.

Human nature also demands freedom, the ability to choose and be in control of our lives. When that choice is stripped from us, like a drowning man, all we can think of is taking the next breath and making our own choices. Teachers who attempt to exert their will over students and rule through sheer force of determination often find that they can turn a serene class of rule-followers into a mob of anarchists in just a few days.

Respecting our students means more than simply honoring their culture, their linguistic heritage, and their individuality. Respecting students, even the smallest and youngest of them, begins with recognizing that they are responsible for their choices. They make decisions every day about what they will say or do and your task as the teacher is not to control them but to guide and empower them.

The secret lies in that shifting of responsibility. Once students feel a sense of agency, they can stop flailing about in the water, take a few deep breaths, and begin to learn.

What can you do tomorrow?

Think about strengths. List the cultural value that each child brings to the classroom with them. Think about their primary language, religion, family, traditions, and recreational activities.

Celebrate. Plan a few ways to integrate cultural strengths, such as diversifying your classroom library or having students bring cultural artifacts.

What does this look like in the classroom?

Students' **cultural and linguistic heritage** is valued, as evidenced by:

- Diverse environmental print and a classroom library collection that reflects the student population;
- Engagement strategies that maximize cultural strengths (e.g., movement, call-and-response); and
- Artifacts from students' culture on display.

How can you reflect on your learning?

How do you honor your students' cultural and linguistic heritage?

_____

_____

Why is respecting students' free will so important to classroom management?

_____

_____

Immediate impact: Go to 3 – 3 Productivity (Anticipate) – pg. 209

If your actions inspire others to dream more, learn more, do more and become more, you are a leader.

- John Quincy Adams

2 – 4 Release (Heart)

Agency.

The term might conjure up thoughts of spies or even advertising, but in the world of social science, agency means something entirely different. It's defined as the capacity of individuals, students in our case, to act independently and to make their own free choices. In other words, it's exactly what is needed for you (and your students) to take charge of the classroom.

Agency, in practical terms, means that students have control over themselves and their actions. They feel empowered to make choices, regulate their emotions, set goals, and pick themselves up after failures. Rather than viewing agency as a large, nebulous trait that students are either born with or lack, it can be cultivated by breaking it down into component parts. When viewed separately, agency can be subdivided into three time-bound elements and one overarching attitude.

When students have agency, they have the ability to look ahead and aim, setting goals that are both self-driven and beneficial. They can peek around the corner, decide on something they'd like to have or accomplish, and then plan efficacious steps to make that dream a reality. Secondly, students have agency when they can act in the moment. Not paralyzed by fear, timidity, or even confusion, students with agency can not only aim and set advantageous goals, they can take any necessary actions to bring the plans to fruition. Simply put, they know what to do.

Third, students with agency can look back at past actions and analyze, reflecting on their progress toward their goal and how to adapt their current strategy for achieving it. Rather than blindly flailing around in the dark, these students can make mid-course adjustments to meet the demands of new situations. Finally, students with agency have an overall attitude of alliance. Operating from a safe space of secure attachment, they have a felt sense of safety, knowing that someone, typically a caregiver or teacher, has their back. More than simple support, an attitude of alliance empowers students to spread their wings and fly because they know that someone is in the trenches with them, supporting them. They aren't working alone but on a team striving for mutually beneficial goals.

Aim

For students to feel a sense of efficacy, they must experience control over their lives. Even if only temporary or minimal, this sense of being able to set and meet goals is crucial for agency. This, then, shows the folly of many traditional approaches to classroom management. In those systems, the classroom culture is built around control. The teacher's job is to manipulate, coerce, plead, and cajole students into following classroom and school expectations.

Yet no matter how often teachers succeed in their daily whack-a-mole game, desperately trying to head off potential disasters before they come to fruition, that task never ceases. In their attempts to keep the classroom safe through sheer force of will, they undermine the very element needed for long-term success. Positive and supportive classroom environments can never be built through coercion, threats, and control. Instead, they are built through self-regulation.

Take the example of two different money managers. The first worked hard every day, hustling to and fro trying to grow his clients' portfolios. From seven in the morning to seven at night, he's day trading on the floor of the New York Stock Exchange. Through effort, determination, and endurance, he successfully ekes out a living for himself and dividends for his clients. Yet however successful he may feel, he's only one bear market away from losing everything.

For students to feel a sense of efficacy, they must experience control over their lives.

A partner in the same financial firm takes a different approach. Rather than frantic, fevered activity, he wisely invests in a broad spectrum of mutual funds, bonds, and other securities. Though his potential return might not be as great, his risk is far less and the energy needed to keep up with his accounts is close to zero. He spends his days playing golf and getting high-priced haircuts, letting his money work for him rather than the other way around.

Building students' ability to make and set goals for themselves, to aim toward a brighter future, is much like the experience of the second money manager. No matter how much energy the first manager put into his portfolios, it was solely supported by his own effort. He had to order the trades, work the phones, and put in hours of work to make ends meet. Teachers who likewise attempt to maintain classroom discipline through control often find themselves in the same situation. Exhausted, worn down, and on the losing end of the numbers game, they spend so much energy trying to quell riots that they have little room for improving their teaching craft.

To keep the classroom safe and build positive relationships with students, the key is not control but empowerment. When the students feel a sense of agency, when they are shown how they can aim for certain targets and meet those goals through effort, reflection, and determination, they see themselves as able. That sense of self-efficacy translates into self-discipline and, like the second money manager, the students start to govern their own behavior.

Intrinsic motivation

The most beneficial motivation for students to develop in life, whether it relates to personal or professional goals, is intrinsic motivation. When students are pushed to succeed and achieve because of internal reasons, they become unstoppable forces that are resilient in the face of alterations and disruptions. Extrinsically, or externally, motivated students, on the other hand, mainly work for some type of reward or achievement. These students always need a carrot in front of them to lead them on and even then their motivation begins to wane if they aren't too interested in the particular vegetable being waggled before their eyes.

Either of these types of motivation are reinforced daily through teacher interactions and elements of control. For teachers that attempt to dominate their classrooms through rigid adherence to guidelines and the threat of punishment for disobedience, they are instilling in their students an external sense of motivation. They teach their students that obeying the rules is right because someone other than them (i.e., the teacher) is watching, judging, and delivering justice.

As long as teachers and parents are fine with having to always motivate their students to act through punishments and rewards, this approach is fine. But if and when teachers and parents want their students to take initiative, bear responsibility, and make decisions on their own, they might find that those traits were driven out of them a long time ago. Teaching students to self-regulate and giving them the space to do so, no matter how messy it might be in the short term, is the only viable long-term solution.

To keep the classroom safe and build positive relationships with students, the key is not control but empowerment.

One key to developing this sense of internal motivation is for teachers to slow down and dig into emotions when students misbehave. For example, if a student pulls another student's hair, our instinct might be, upon seeing this infraction, to immediately snap out summary judgment.

"Dave, pulling hair is not okay. You've just lost five minutes off your recess."

While to the teacher this might be acceptable and even align with the posted rules and consequences, this rapidity eliminates the one thing that will help Dave regulate his behavior in the future – his feelings. How children feel about the results of their actions is what will become the driving force for learning better ways to handle the situation next time (Bailey, 2015).

Instead of rapid fire condemnation, walk over and talk with Dave. Ask him how it might feel to have his hair pulled. Ask the little girl in front of Dave to share how she feels having her hair pulled. His thoughtless action caused harm to another human and, unless Dave has serious psychological issues, that's not going to sit right with him. He's most likely friends with the girl and thought, in his own illogical way, that it would be funny to pull her hair. Letting him stew in the hurt that he caused momentarily, letting him feel the consequences of his actions, is what he will remember. The next time he's tempted to pull her hair, he'll remember how he felt and that will give him pause.

If we want students to set goals, whether they be academic targets or behavioral checkpoints, they have to first feel a sense of control over their lives. They can't aim toward a better future when they feel powerless to affect it. By taking a step back and giving students opportunities to make their own choices, teachers give them the space needed to grow and mature.

Like the second money manager found a way to make his money work for him, empowering students to self-regulate helps your students begin to monitor themselves. This becomes vital as we look at the larger picture of teaching and learning. The ability to self-regulate gives students the key to unlocking their learning potential. When they can process their emotions and transform their inner states for optimal learning, they have agency. They can set goals, aim for learning targets, and make adjustments.

Act

How much control do students really have over their lives? At what point do students begin to make choices for themselves? That's another misconception about classroom management and control. Teachers mistakenly believe that they are the ones making the choices and that if they keep tight enough control, they can keep students from making poor choices.

And if you super glue wings on pigs, maybe you can teach them to fly.

I learned this the hard way through an encounter I had years ago with a student when I was an administrator. During my time as a principal, I instituted stricter rules about missing work for students. Those that chose not to turn anything in eventually made their way to my office. I spoke with them, disciplined them, and tried to set them straight. Like the claims on a can of Lysol, it worked for 99.9% of my students. Jenny was the one that got away.

I tried everything with her. I ranged from hard-nose disciplinarian to friendly counselor. No matter what I tried, she had no interest in doing her work. Punishments, threats, parent conferences – all useless. She beat out the clock, made it to May, and somehow managed to be promoted to the next grade. She didn't come back the following year and I've never seen her since.

In all my years of education, both as a teacher and as an administrator, I've never been so stumped. I could understand outright defiance, anger issues, or even mental health concerns. Jenny, on the other hand, was politely non-compliant. The more frustrated I got, the calmer she became. I never reached her. I never found a way to motivate her to learn.

Years after my experience with Jenny, I still couldn't completely move on. Something nagged at me, making me think that I was missing something. I felt like I was looking at education with blinders on. While I could see what was in front of me, there were things in the periphery that I couldn't quite make out. From an adult perspective, everything should have worked for Jenny. The instruction, systems, and support were all there. Jenny appeared to have no interest in learning.

Ultimately, my frustration came from my inability to make her do her work. That was a time in my career in which my understanding of student motivation was nascent or non-existent. I was the adult (the principal, for crying out loud!) and my instructions should have been followed and that's all there was to it.

Once we accept, however, that students are constantly making choices, we begin the process of empowering them. They can take charge of their actions, their emotions, and their futures when they realize that true power lies within them, not us. Our attempts to control and manipulate them are ultimately futile, as Jenny taught me, and short circuits the very qualities we want to instill in them.

As educators, one of our many jobs is to teach students about life in addition to the content specific to our grade level and subject area. In life, no one can make you do anything. Laws and regulations are there to strongly encourage and/or threaten you, but ultimately you are in charge of yourself. If we want students to begin to take responsibility for their actions, our language and disciplinary style should mirror this reality.

Autonomy

One of the deepest psychological needs humans have is the need for autonomy. There is a universal reaction to bondage, whether it be physical, emotional, religious, or some other type of subjugation. Humanity as a whole instinctively fights to be free. This trait is something we are born with, not one that is cultural or geographic. It's in our DNA.

All humans, including our students, pursue their psychological needs throughout their daily lives. In addition to autonomy, humans seek socialization, avoiding psychological pain, and intellectual stimulation. When these needs are largely satisfied, students are better able to delay gratification of their needs and to inhibit responses that are contrary to classroom rules (Willans & Williams, 2018).

In other words, a key element to classroom management is largely counterintuitive. Instead of trying to control students, emphasize their freedom. Use language that highlights their choices and how the decisions they make affect themselves and others. When students come to grips with the fact that, as a part of the human race, they have a need for and the ability to exercise autonomy, that recognition empowers them. They begin to feel themselves efficacious and experience a sense of agency.

One of the deepest psychological needs humans have is the need for autonomy.

And once they feel in control of their lives, they're much more likely to comply. They take less umbrage from rules and regulations when they know they have the ability to obey or disobey them (with consequences, of course). Instead of trying to keep students under your thumb, celebrate their power to choose. By doing so, you help satisfy their need for autonomy and, strangely enough, empower them to follow your behavioral expectations.

Reflecting back, that's what Jenny was trying to teach me. Every adult in her life, including me, was trying to control her. Even at a young age, she was flexing her autonomy, desperately shouting that she needed to be in control of some part of her life. When her whole life was falling apart (her parents were going through a nasty divorce at the time), she was controlling the one thing she could – her work at school. The more we tried to coerce her, the further she slipped from us.

What can you do tomorrow?

Set goals. Goal setting is a key part of agency. Think of something you'd like to do differently in the classroom, whether it be academic or related to classroom management, and write it down in a journal.

Share them. Share a goal you have for yourself with your students, modeling for them how to set and reach learning goals. Encourage those that are interested to begin setting their own learning goals to begin to build their own confidence.

What does this look like in the classroom?

Classroom tasks **empower** students by:
- Embedding authentic choices within them;
- Providing clear instructions and expectations; and
- Aligning with learning goals and curriculum standards.

How can you reflect on your learning?

How does feeling controlled affect students' desire and ability to set goals?

_____

_____

How can teachers support student autonomy?

_____

_____

An outdated model

Parents universally want their children to be successful.

If asked what some of their hopes and dreams are for their offspring, you would inevitably hear the same refrain over and over.

I want my children to be strong and independent.

I want my children to have options and opportunities.

I want my children to be successful and lead fulfilling lives.

As teachers, we serve as surrogate parents for so many of our students. This happens not because their actual parents are deficient in any way but simply as a result of our close proximity to them. Spending hours upon hours with students day in and day out naturally develops an affinity between us. As stand-in parents, teachers should also want the best for their students.

They should want their students to be strong and independent.

They should want their students to graduate with many career choices and opportunities.

They should want their students to be academically successful and lead fulfilling lives.

None of this happens, however, when we operate out of a traditional discipline mindset. Instead of trying to get children to behave, we need to instead focus our attention on helping them be successful.

Over a century ago, public education closely resembled a factory, the model of productivity in an industrialized world. The factory's goal is to make as many standardized widgets, or products, as efficiently as possible. Factories use quality control standards to keep the end results of their labor as near to perfection as possible. Factory managers rely on external motivators such as removing or punishing workers who do not meet the daily quota. Inversely, workers who meet or exceed the daily quota might be rewarded for their dedication.

Widgets that do not conform to factory standards are rejected in order to keep the high level of quality output. Overall, the feeling in some factories is one of apathy, boredom, or fear of not meeting the daily quota. That, in addition to the possibility of not earning possible bonuses, keeps the motivation on the external rather than the internal.

Does any of that sound familiar?

While the rapid industrialization of America after the Civil War led to a more uniform educational environment of students, as public education broadened and largely left behind the one-room schoolhouse model, it wasn't until the standards-based education movement of the 1980s that education became fully industrialized. Students, as widgets, were moved along a curriculum pace in lock step, batched together by birth year, and progressed from one grade level to the next along a conveyor belt of textbooks and examinations.

While this reform movement did much to improve education, it brought with it the factory model of discipline. If students were widgets and the curriculum the production line, then the job of the teacher was to manage the students in their studies. Using punishment and reward, two tools well-known to many factory floor managers, students were disciplined and rewarded based on their conformity to behavioral and academic standards.

There is nothing as dehumanizing and antithetical to agency than being managed like an inanimate object. Any system, whether it be classroom management or school governance, that relies on controlling others through punishment and reward by its very nature limits the social interactions needed to strengthen the development of problem solving skills.

The answer, then, is not to limit choices but to expand them.

Choices

Offering students choices fosters the general well-being of children (Bailey, 2015). Choices increase prosocial behavior and responsibility while improving academic achievement. It also raises teacher morale, enhances all classroom relationships, and advances self-regulation and intrinsic motivation.

Who wouldn't want all that?

With choices, however, comes the very real possibility that students will make the wrong ones. Thus, in order to spare them (and us) the discomfort of those wrong choices, many teachers fall to the other extreme and limit student options. Through power and control, they seek to run a tight ship and limit any and all behavioral fluctuations.

There is nothing as dehumanizing and antithetical to agency than being managed like an inanimate object.

Yet remember that no one can make you do anything. You, of your own free will, are reading this page. Even if you claim to be heavily-influenced by some other motivation, such as this chapter was assigned to you, you still choose whether or not to comply. The same reality exists for students. No matter how closely you hold classroom expectations in your fist, how vigilantly you seek and destroy behavioral loopholes, students still ultimately choose whether or not to comply.

Yet this battle for control is not one worth fighting. When people, students included, make internally-motivated choices, helpful chemicals are released in the brain that support everything you want as a teacher. Students making choices have a more optimistic attitude, better decision making, more focused attention, and increased compliance.

Rather than hiding the fact that students ultimately make the choice whether or not to obey, celebrate it! Give back to them the power that was rightfully theirs to begin with. Highlight to them that they choose to make poor decisions or helpful ones. While it might seem risky to bring this out into the open, to deny it would be futile, like trying to hide the moon on a cloudless night.

Reflection questions

One of the many dangers of attempting to control children's behavior is the limited scope of the approach. For those teachers that would argue with the previous section, citing personal experience of maintaining control through force, I would counter that any compliance through this method is temporary. Behavior can be coerced for a single instance or even continue for a few minutes, true. However, a child coerced into a response cannot and will not maintain that behavior long-term, especially if the coercion lightens up.

Coercion is a short-term solution to a long-term problem.

When compliant behavior is forced onto students, it deprives them of another factor of agency, that of analysis. A key part of empowering students is providing them with opportunities and structures to look back on their decisions and think about whether or not they made the best ones. And it's difficult to analyze past decisions to shape future ones if those opportunities to make decisions are never given.

In reality, students are making decisions all day long. Teachers can build up the agency of their students by facilitating their analysis of the decisions they make. Instead of blowing past the consequence of their actions, teachers can help by slowing down and asking students a few questions.

What were you trying to accomplish? Sometimes students aren't too sure about the reasoning behind their actions. Instead, they act instinctively. Asking this question can help slow the tempo and give students an opportunity to process their motivations or goals.

Did you get what you wanted? Instead of placing a value judgment on whether or not what students wanted was worthy, instead ask them to reflect on the efficacy of their action. If they realize that their actions are sometimes counterproductive, it will help them stop and think in the future.

Was there a better way to do that? Reflecting on the intended outcome and the strategy used to accomplish the goal is integral to developing agency. Maybe students achieved their purpose but took some collateral damage, such as hurting their friend's feelings. This question helps students begin to think of win-win strategies that limit negative consequences.

Alliance

For true agency to develop in students, they need to move beyond developing the skills of aiming, acting, and analyzing. The final level is gained when students operate with an attitude of alliance. Knowing that someone is not only watching their back but actively engaging in combat with them gives students the sense of security needed to take on any and every challenge (Hammond, 2014).

While most teachers would say they are definitely not their students' enemies, not nearly enough take it to the other extreme of alliance. To continue the metaphor, many teachers form a non-aggression pact with their students. The difference between the two can be quite staggering.

Non-aggression pacts are neutral at their core. The two sides agree to neither harm nor help each other. Both sides commit to staying out of any conflicts involving the other, using distance to keep their spheres of influence separate. Unfortunately, teachers who fail to become emotionally invested in their students often find themselves in a non-aggression pact with them. While they don't actively work against them, they also don't go out of their way to help them out. Instead, they focus on their content and getting through the curriculum.

This mentality is sometimes evident by the answer to a simple question often posed by one teacher to another. "What do you teach?"

Coercion is a short-term solution to a long-term problem.

The expected response is usually a grade level or content area. Educators answer this query with something like, "I'm a second grade teacher," or "I teach chemistry." What if, however, our answers were a little more personal?

"I teach students."

When teachers form an emotional alliance with their students, they move far beyond an attitude of, "I won't bother you if you won't bother me." An alliance is a sympathetic connection with a student that results in the warm, friendly feeling of being in sync. It's more than simply being nice to students. An alliance is a relationship of mutual support in which partners walk through a situation or period of life together.

Allies defend each other and fight for each other. Allies take on the burdens of their friends and carry them as their own. Allies are willing to lay down their lives for each other.

For some students, having an alliance with their teacher is nice but not a necessity. Some students grow up in stable homes with two parents, adequate food, and little to no domestic violence, emotional abuse, or other adverse childhood experiences. When students come to school with a secure attachment to one or both of their parents, they are psychologically grounded and ready to explore the outside world with a knowledge that if something bad happens, they won't be alone, that their parents will always love and comfort them.

But how many of your students can say that?

Calming the amygdala

Obviously, many students can't claim the benefits of the domestic serenity described above. Instead, their lives are filled with chaos, violence, and abuse. As they come into your classroom, psychologically shell-shocked from the trauma that is their daily lives, you asking them to let their guard down to learn long division or the periodic table of elements is almost laughable. They are in a battle every day and they're losing. Why would they worry about a silly assignment when they aren't even sure that they'll be safe that night or have anything to eat?

Most learning activities ask students to take a leap of faith. They put students in a deficit position because they expose their lack of knowledge.

While this isn't problematic for emotionally healthy students, those with psychological baggage balk when put into this situation. They lash out at any sense of weakness and jump into attack mode or simply retreat. This type of behavior is all too prevalent with students who don't feel safe.

The alliance, however, works to calm the brain's fight or flight response. When the student feels safe with the teacher, when they feel as if someone has their back and will walk through the struggle with them, their violent or withdrawal reactions are curbed. Becoming vulnerable does not seem so frightening when you're not all alone. When it's you against the world, however, defensive behaviors and shutting down are typical responses to feelings of jeopardy.

While you can't fix their home lives, you can be an ally for students by your actions. Realize, however, that this means more than simply being there for students. Offering your presence is step one but these at-risk students need something more. They need an ally to fight for them, to initiate actions that will assist them. Instead of passively waiting for students to come to you, advocate for them. When they can't clearly communicate their needs, take time to dig a little deeper.

Maybe they need meal assistance and you can introduce them to a community liaison. Maybe they lack health insurance and would benefit from a visit to a neighborhood clinic. Many schools even bring dentists into the school to provide low-cost or free examinations for students. Non-aggression participants leave each other alone. Allies actively support each other, fighting side-by-side against a common enemy.

Which arrangement do your students need?

What can you do tomorrow?

Practice reflection. Choose a few of the reflection questions mentioned above and use them after a behavioral incident. Instead of interrogating the student while her emotions are still high, wait until things have settled down.

Listen deeply. Accept all answers, simply trying to provoke reflection in her, rather than using the questions to lead her to a particular answer or shame her for her actions.

What does this look like in the classroom?

Classroom tasks develop **student agency** by:
- Allowing freedom in how students complete them;
- Providing students opportunities to analyze and correct mistakes; and
- Including supports to meet the needs of diverse learners.

How can you reflect on your learning?

How do you encourage your students to reflect on their actions?

_____

_____

Is your approach to teaching more like an alliance or a non-aggression pact?

_____

_____

Immediate impact: Go to 3 – 4 Planning (Anticipate) – pg. 229

2 – 5 Conclusion (Heart)

The heart of teaching is relationships.

It's through your connection with your students that learning occurs. Your relationship with them, and their relationships with each other, form a large part of the culture and climate of your classroom. It's the dark matter that fills in all the cracks, that remains present but unnoticed, affecting everything that happens.

Ignoring relationships, which form the context of teaching, and just paying attention to the content and instructional strategies is just downright ludicrous. Imagine a golfer out on 7th hole of his local course, not sure of what to do. He doesn't have a caddie to ask for advice, so he calls his buddy up in in the next state who advises him to hit the ball in the hole.

The advice the friend gave is ridiculous and ultimately useless. It doesn't take into account the context of the lie. Is the golfer teeing off or in the fairway? If so, a driver might be appropriate, assuming he's still several hundred yards from the green. Is he in the rough or maybe even a bunker? Then definitely an iron is better, maybe even a wedge.

What about the wind? Where is the hole on the green and how does it slope? Does the ball have to carry over water?

You get the point.

Trying to give golf advice from a distance with no appreciation of the current conditions of the course and the lie is silly. In the same way, however, too many teachers and schools implement one initiative after another, plug in several remediation programs in quick succession, and employ a host of other frenetic actions in an attempt to boost student achievement.

While the intent is honorable, most fail to launch because they don't pay attention to the climate and culture of the classroom. Armed with a sand wedge, they're swinging at everything they can find, whether they're already on the green or teeing off from 450 yards away. Context matters.

The heart of teaching is relationships.

Relationships, then, are the conduit through which learning occurs. Without nurturing supportive and beneficial relationships, learning will be hard to come by. Time and energy invested into developing close relationships in the classroom pay dividends down the road. They not only greatly reduce off-task behavior, they also enhance achievement. Ignoring relationships in a classroom is as useful as ignoring a shark while swimming with it in a pool.

Genuine relationships are deeper than niceties and platitudes. Students need more than a beginning-of-the-year scavenger hunt to learn about their classmates. As the professional educator in the classroom, you can set the tone for strong relationships by respecting your students. Respect their abilities, their potential, and their heritage.

When teachers hold a deficit view of their students, they are doomed before they even begin. This type of thinking is readily observable in actions, comments, and assignments given to students. If you've ever spoken with a colleague and a statement begins with, "These kids," followed by a generalization, you know you've run into a lack of respect.

These kids can't handle difficult work.

These students only understand threats and punishments.

The students from this neighborhood either end up in a gang or in jail.

Students rise to the level of your expectations. When you think little of them, you shouldn't be surprised when they prove you right. Instead of seeing what they can't do, dream big for them. Hold them to high standards and provide the scaffolding needed to reach those expectations.

Another factor in respecting students is to honor their culture, heritage, religion, and host of other strengths they bring with them into the classroom. Too many middle-class educators come to urban schools with a noble but errant goal of saving the poor ghetto kids from misery. This type of thinking not only holds a deficit view but perpetuates the systemic racism that is deeply rooted in many educational systems.

Even the term *achievement gap*, one I've used for over 20 years in education to denote the very real difference in performance between white students and minority students, is in itself implicitly racist. It doesn't respect black and brown students because it assigns them a status as lesser than their white peers and doesn't hold out hope for change. Switching the terminology to *opportunity gap* shows more respect and builds deeper relationships. It doesn't dismiss the gap but attributes it to a lack of opportunity and something that can be and will be overcome.

Relationships are further strengthened in the classroom when teachers release control. When they honor students as sentient beings, capable of ordering themselves and making wise choices, they pour worth and value into their souls. Control is in itself an illusion, since we can't ever truly make anyone do anything, and holding onto it as a form of classroom management is counterproductive.

Instead, releasing control means empowering students and building their agency. It means giving them the opportunity and skills needed to make goals, act on them, and reflect on progress. It means that things will get a little messy because students don't always make the best choices.

But they're their choices. And we can't take them away.

Students who feel in control of their learning and their actions increase in their ability to regulate their behavior. If we, as educators, try to keep a firm grip on every single child throughout the day, we strip away their autonomy and will. We are the only ones producing effort to maintain equilibrium in the classroom and it's exhausting. And impossible.

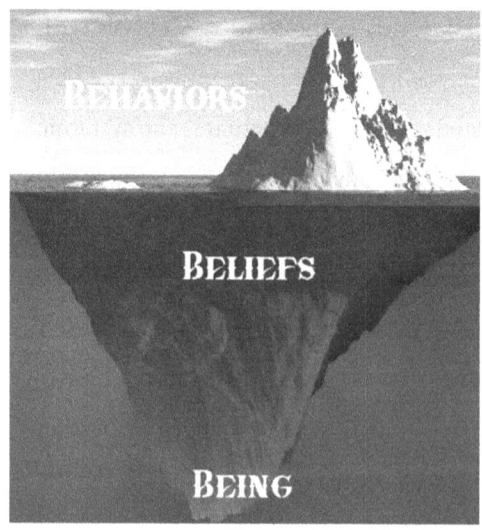

The more we try to control students, the more they fight us. It's simply human nature.

We cannot build strong relationships with students if we don't believe in their potential, if we don't value their culture and the strengths they bring with them into the classroom. If we do those things, however, we'll clear the

Heart

path for true engagement and powerful learning.

Confidence as a teacher, which speaks to the core of your being, comes from purpose, positivity, and protection.

The heart of teaching, which flows from your beliefs, centers around relationships, respect, and release.

With those two under your belt, you're now ready to adapt your behaviors to take charge of the classroom.

CONFIDENCE

HEART

ANTICIPATE

REINFORCE

GROW

ENGAGE

3 – 1 Introduction (Anticipate)

In the book *Switch* (Heath & Heath, 2010), the authors use a powerful metaphor to explain how to produce change when change is hard. To effectively manage change, they argue, there are three different aspects of the situation that must be addressed and managed.

The image they use is a rider on an elephant. Imagine yourself atop an Asian elephant with more than four tons of muscle, sinew, fat, and will underneath you. You might, as the human on top, think you're driving the elephant. You might hold reins or an elephant goad. You might even consider yourself a mahout, or a professional elephant rider and trainer. In all actuality, though, the elephant is the one in charge.

Let's assume that the desired change is represented by getting to a certain destination. If you want the elephant to take you to a specific location a kilometer away, three elements must work together to make it happen. First, you as the rider or driver must know where you're going. The elephant probably doesn't know, so you'll need to be the one with the goal in mind. You, as the rider, represent the rational side of your mind.

You can use logic, reasoning, and willpower to attempt to move the elephant in the right direction.

The elephant represents your emotions. While sometimes placid and pliable, at other times your emotions erupt and take you to places you never even intended to go. To make the change, to arrive at your destination, you must motivate the elephant to keep going in the right direction. Without your emotions, or in this case the elephant, as a willing partner, you'll never get anywhere.

Finally, you can make things easier for the elephant by shaping the path. Why walk through a thickly wooded forest when a smooth trail is available 100 yards to the west? You're much more likely to reach your destination when you attend to the context and adapt the environment to make the journey as easy as possible.

The next three parts of the Take CHARGE model (anticipate, reinforce, and grow) roughly parallel these three aspects of change management. To direct the rider, and help students cognitively attend to their behavior and learn to better manage themselves, you'll have to help them grow their interpersonal, intrapersonal, and intellectual skills.

When you reinforce positive behavior through the power of your attention by focusing on desired actions and attitudes, you motivate the

Anticipate

elephant. The weight of differential social attention, and the emotions it generates, is enough to keep any elephant (or student) headed in the right direction.

Finally, the topic we'll look at in this section of the book is anticipation. By doubling down on procedures, productivity, and planning, you can clear the path and make change management both natural and desired.

While the first two portions of this book, confidence and heart, are sequential and build upon each other, the next three all work simultaneously. Though presented in a sequential order simply because one of them must come first, any of these topics can be tackled next after confidence and heart. Your behaviors as a teacher play a large part in determining your success managing your classroom and all three parts are essential to changing both teacher and student behaviors.

You direct the rider logically by helping students grow in their self-awareness and social-emotional literacy. You motivate the elephant by reinforcing desired behaviors through differential social attention. But to begin with, we'll look at clearing the path by anticipating ruts in the road and false paths that might cause the elephant to stumble or wander off.

This section of the book will sound very familiar to many veteran teachers or those that were heavily influenced by Harry and Rosemary Wong's *The First Days of School* (1997). When administrators and veteran teachers are asked for classroom management advice, there's a reason why so many answer with, "Procedures, procedures, procedures." By anticipating situations in which students might struggle or not know the best way to get something accomplished, strong teachers teach and practice procedures.

The strange thing about procedures is that though they are scripted and structured, they don't diminish autonomy but rather enhance it.

Procedures provide the guardrails to give students boundaries and comfort as they cross the chasm from ignorance into productive learning. In structure there is freedom.

Additionally, teachers can anticipate and avoid traps by maximizing productivity. While many teachers are quick to blame poor behavior on student deficiencies, quite a few wayward actions can be traced back to a poor use of time. When the transitions between activities drag and nothing is provided for early finishers, teachers have only themselves to blame when mischievousness erupts.

In structure there is freedom.

Finally, some teachers inadvertently cause chaos because of poor or nonexistent planning. Materials aren't ready so students are left to their own devices while the teacher scrambles to gather supplies or scrounges for extra copies of the assignment. Many administrative tasks within the classroom can actually be accomplished by the students themselves, keeping things moving at a fast clip while introducing them to the concept of stewardship.

If you examine the moments in your day in which you find that student behavior starts to go sideways, you might find some common themes. Students might not know how to accomplish the task in the desired way so they would benefit from additional practice with classroom procedures. Maybe disorder emerges between activities because the transitions lag and students become bored. Or perhaps your classroom looks like it could be featured on a reality TV show called *Teacher Hoarders* and you take longer looking for supplies than the students' ability to wait patiently.

Anticipate

When you clear the path for your students, you don't guarantee good behavior but do make it remarkably easier. Instead of succeeding in spite of you, they can succeed as a direct result of your planning, procedures, and productivity. When the clearest and most direct path is the one straight toward your desired destination, behavioral change will pull at them with the force of gravity, funneling them toward success.

No one can teach riding so well as a horse.

- C. S. Lewis

3 – 2 Procedures (Anticipate)

Procedures will save your life one day.

Veteran teachers know that building structures and routines into their classrooms is a key to successful classroom management even if they cannot clearly articulate why.

While it might seem incongruous, structures and routines are not diametrically opposed to agency and responsibility. You don't have to choose between building relationships with students or showing them your preferred way to enter the classroom.

It isn't either/or but both/and.

Any misconceptions about procedures typically arise from a misunderstanding of what they are designed to produce. They aren't there to control children, because control is illusory. Any compliance that students offer is of their own volition, not forced from them by rules and regulations. Procedures don't restrict but liberate. Rather than chaos and uncertainty, procedures are designed to create order and provide structure to the structure-less.

Procedures provide something that all children desperately need – safety.

Consistency

When teachers change the lens through which they view procedures, their understanding of them will crystalize. The primary function of teachers in the classroom is to teach. While this might seem obvious to you, the scope of the teaching is sometimes limited by a lack of vision. More than simply teaching students how to read, solve multi-step problems, or execute the quadratic equation, teachers also have the privilege of teaching behaviors.

Routines are merely those – expected behaviors. Whether it be how to enter the classroom, where to find missing work, or how to ask for permission to use the restroom, there are many behaviors that students engage in every day or even multiple times a day. While these sound simple, they can vary greatly from classroom to classroom.

Procedures don't restrict but liberate.

Some teachers have no expectation for how students should enter the classroom, so students can enter quietly and noisily as long as they are in their seats before the bell rings. Others want students to line up in the hall and wait until the teacher has signaled for them to enter. Some teachers have work on the board and expect students to come in and get started right away while others have a series of prescribed actions to perform, such as hanging up backpacks, turning in assignments, and sharpening pencils.

The scary part comes when all of these varying expectations exist within the same classroom and shift from day to day. Some teachers are fickle and their lack of procedures creates wildly changing expectations. When students don't know what is expected of them, they feel insecure and untethered. Behavior that was acceptable yesterday brings a strong reprimand today. This lack of clarity creates anxiety and tension.

Routines, then, are not restrictive but expansive. They teach expected behaviors in the classroom and the school. This, in turn, provides consistency and predictability. These are two qualities that students need in abundance because it helps to answer a fundamental question they ask subconsciously every day, "Am I safe?"

Rules and routines

Some of you might be thinking that you have your classroom rules already posted and the students don't follow them. What you might not know, however, is there is a world of difference between a rule and a routine. Rules are made to stop misbehavior. They are generally enforced with consequences and come from a negative viewpoint (e.g., Do not...).

Routines, on the other hand, are simply the way things should be done. They are behaviors, habits, or a sequence of events that students are expected to follow when accomplishing certain things. There might be a routine for entering the classroom, a routine for lining up for recess, and a routine for asking permission to use the restroom. These predictable routines create a felt sense of safety because students know what is expected of them.

Rules, as they are traditionally written, do not tell students what to do. Instead, they tell them what not to do. Keep your hands and feet to yourself. Do not talk without permission. These parameters attempt to exclude misbehavior while never explicitly telling or showing students what to do. When expectations are made clear through routines, students can maintain and even regain their composure during times of stress.

Many war movies, in an attempt to capture the chaos of the battlefield, will use a handheld camera, sometimes without stabilization (i.e., shaky cam), to put viewers into the action. With bullets whizzing, mortars exploding, and dirt flying everywhere, the deafening sound and fog of war help viewers experience the anarchy of combat.

When you don't establish and practice procedures on a daily basis, this is how some students will view your classroom. They walk in and it seems like a jailhouse riot. Kids are scattered everywhere, some are talking while some are working, and there's no clear order. When students can't see the pattern, their anxiety rises and their sense of safety disappears. Routines for common actions like starting the day or transitioning between activities will help them find the order in the seeming chaos.

Many students fail in school because they simply do not know what to do. True, their lack of academic knowledge shows up as poor performance on tests and assessments, but many of them fail long before the test. If they do not know what to do, if they do not have a clear understanding of what their roles are in the academic environment, learning becomes difficult. Without a strong sense of order and safety, their brains are more concerned with survival than taking in knowledge. Safety that comes through predictable routines is a precursor to learning.

Provides structure

If you were to peer closely at the students that cause you the most trouble year after year, a trend would begin to emerge. These students, for the most part, have home lives that are less structured than your more well-behaved students. They might have to deal with domestic violence, financial worries, lack of adult supervision, and a whole host of other concerns that young children should not have to worry about.

When their lives are filled with unpredictability, their insecurity begins to mount. They don't know what will happen next or whether or not their home will be safe to return to when they leave school. Students, believe it or not, want to know exactly what will be happening every moment of the day. They don't crave surprises or thrive in disorganization. Their brains are pattern-seeking devices and many of these students fail simply because they don't know what to do and when it's appropriate to do it.

Students who grow up and live in homes without adequate boundaries often have less impulse control and less developed self-regulation than their peers. These students are also typically more self-centered, less socially-competent, have lower achievement, and show decreased cognitive performance. In some cases, students do not have even one parent who is clearly the leader in the home, which causes them to feel uncontained, unheld, less safe, and more out of control. All of this directly translates into misbehavior in the classroom.

Many students fail in school because they simply do not know what to do.

But what can you do? You can't solve the world's problems or wave a magic wand and fix your students' broken homes. Think of your students as a river. If the river has well-defined banks on either side, the river flows serenely and predictably. These banks are the rituals and routines that you design for your classroom. They provide the structure and predictability that students need to enjoy the flow. If these banks are missing, however, the river's energy is diffused as it overflows its banks and spreads across the land. Consistent routines provide students with a strong sense of competence and control while lessening your workload at the same time.

While you can never repair your students' stressful home situation, a Herculean task out of your sphere of influence, you can make your classroom a safe haven. While school is in session, your students sometimes spend more waking hours in your classroom than in their own homes. This offers a huge opportunity to make a difference in the lives of your students.

Visual routines

Routines can be communicated visually in addition to orally (Bailey, 2015). Teachers know that if they relied solely on lecture as their method of lesson delivery, many students would be left out of the learning process. While some best gather information through the spoken word, others need to see it while still others need to touch it and experience something viscerally before it sticks. Routines are the same way.

Young children's brains especially are dependent on mental models and images while their expressive and receptive language abilities are still developing. Visual routines are essential for helping students govern their behavior. When students can see what is expected of them, in addition to hearing verbal directions, their chances of success skyrocket.

There are two primary methods for using visuals to support the development of routines, either of which can be used separately or jointly. First, you can take pictures and display them in prominent places, showing students exactly what is expected of them. This would be highly beneficial for procedures that involve cleaning up and arranging inanimate objects.

Anticipate

How many times have you asked students to clean up a center or the library area only to find that your definition of *clean* differs greatly from theirs? Take out the guesswork by taking a picture of the area looking immaculate and post it nearby. Now, rather than trying to figure out what *clean* really means, students have a visual reminder of how things ought to look or be arranged.

Visual routines are essential for helping students govern their behavior.

The second method is through physically practicing the routine. For some events like entering the classroom or walking to the carpet, students need to not only see it done but have attention drawn to key elements. What is clear to you might be obscure to them as they can't see the difference between their running pell-mell across the room while more placid students walk serenely. Have a few students practice while the rest of the class observes. As the students watch the procedure being done correctly, act like a play-by-play announcer and commentate on the action. Draw attention to the important elements of the procedure that students are watching unfold before their very eyes.

Children's brains encode information primarily pictorially rather than semantically. Showing these routines visually, then, provides information to students in a form that their brains can readily use and store. This simple switch, from verbally describing to visually showing, helps students integrate the desired procedures into their regular behavior.

Students with anxiety

For students that suffer from high anxiety, whether diagnosed or undiagnosed, the times of the school day with the least structure are particularly stressful for them. Since these students need structure even more than others, the predictability of routines can help calm their nerves and provide them a safe path forward.

Even though you cannot alter what students face at home every day, you can give them the structure and safety needed to regulate their brains and continue to learn in the midst of domestic chaos. For these students, transition times are going to be the most important to target.

Think about what students are expected to do when they enter into your classroom each morning. Do they wander around and talk to their friends until the bell rings or is something specific ready for them? Do they have a series of tasks required of them or should they simply chat until the teacher gets up in the front of the class? Even these simple moments can cause stress for students that do not have strong guidelines at home.

Increase efficiency

I know what some of you are thinking at this point. You were hired to teach math, not teach students how to behave. You have a state test to worry about and can't afford to lose time having students practice lining up or transitioning between stations.

To answer that, I would say you can't afford *not* to teach procedures. The amount of time you save on the back end of well-taught structures will be more than compensated for the time you have to put in on the front end teaching them to students. When children know what's expected of them, when they can navigate their daily tasks with routines and procedures that have been taught and practiced, they have predictable

Anticipate

patterns to follow. These patterns free up mental space for students to focus on other items like meaningful instruction and rigorous learning.

Think about your drive to work. The first time you took that route, it was new and exciting. You noticed all the trees, the signals, and probably tried to keep a mental map in your mind of where you were in relation to what was already known to you. As you continued to drive into work, it took less and less mental energy to make the trip. You no longer needed to input the destination into your phone's GPS because you could make the trip in your sleep. Instead of struggling to find the correct turn off the highway, your brain can now daydream or listen to podcasts. In fact, it probably seems like it takes little to no mental energy at all for you to drive into work each morning.

That's the power of predictability.

If students are familiar enough with your classroom routines, if they know what's expected of them and can function without explicit instructions, their brain space is freed from the mental demands of trying to figure out what to do next. Instead, their brains can turn to more important matters like the content you are so desperately trying to teach. If you want students to focus on your lessons, you first have to give them the mental space needed to pay attention. That comes from the safety, structure, and predictability of well-established routines.

What can you do tomorrow?

Reinforce routines. Consider the procedures you already have in place. Commit to practicing them a few times this week and explaining to students why they are important. If there are some procedures you'd like to put in place, it's never too late to start.

Make them visible. Provide visual support for students by taking and printing a picture of the completed procedure. This might be a picture of students lined up quietly and placed above the door or a picture of a neat and orderly library center placed on the library bookshelf.

What does this look like in the classroom?

The teacher establishes and consistently practices **routines** that are:

- Clearly structured and explained;
- Visually depicted for easy reference; and
- Reinforced and revisited when correct execution begins to diminish.

How can you reflect on your learning?

Why are procedures so important?

_____

_____

Why are rules inferior to routines for classroom management?

_____

_____

Safe place

Procedures do many helpful things in the classroom. They automate responses and actions in common situations. They provide structure for the seeming chaos of many classrooms. Additionally, they teach students responsibility and empower them to act with agency.

So where should you start?

While there are many procedures that are helpful for students to master, there is one vital procedure that is not obvious to many teachers but central to the social and emotional development of students. As students struggle with big emotions every day, not sure of how to process them or the best way to navigate treacherous social situations, they often feel overwhelmed. When their emotions boil over, outbursts and acts of defiance quickly follow.

Unfortunately for students, many are not given the proper tools to handle the emotions that seem to rise out of nowhere. They have no strong models to watch to see how to handle their hurt and anger when someone says something unkind to them. While students do need to know how to sharpen their pencils, enter the classroom, and ask for permission to use the restroom, all of those procedures pale in comparison to giving students the tools necessary to handle their emotions.

Students need a safe place.

I first learned about safe places when reading *Conscious Discipline* (Bailey, 2015). This procedure is actually five separate actions all rolled up into one. And even before teaching students the steps to use when they need to regulate themselves, teachers have to first create a physical safe place for students to use when upset.

The safe place is the hub of taking charge in the classroom. If students don't learn to regulate themselves, you as the teacher are left to constantly chase after them, attempting to calm and soothe them in-between lessons and small group intervention sessions. Teaching students that they can affect their own emotional states with conscious action is the key that unlocks their limitless potential. The first step in helping students achieve this goal is to provide a physical anchor for them and to teach them how to use it.

The safe place is the hub of taking charge in the classroom.

Typically, safe places have some type of comfortable seating, such as a cushy chair, beanbag, throw rug, or even a few pillows. Instead of being a punishment, safe places should be viewed as welcoming areas that help students tackle their inner feelings. In addition to a location to sit, safe places should have tools to use for the calming process. These vary from classroom to classroom but typically include some type of poster or visual to help identify emotions, glitter jars, and other tactile objects, even stuffed animals.

The first step in using the safe place is for students to go there voluntarily when they feel upset or overwhelmed. To keep the safe place safe, it should never be used as a time-out or any type of punishment. Once it becomes associated with these negative feelings students will not want to go there on their own. At the beginning of the year, introduce the safe place to students and discuss its function. It's not a part of the regular station rotation and it's not a secondary library or reading center. It has one use and one use only, to give students an area to think about and change their emotional states when upset.

The second step in the safe place procedure is another routine all in itself. It doesn't really do students a whole lot of good to simply sit on a beanbag when they're upset. This changes their physical location without doing much to their internal reality. When arriving at the safe place, students should begin using a breathing technique of their choice to begin transforming their emotional state. Obviously, this step is a non-starter if breathing practices are not a regular part of the classroom.

There are many resources available to teach both teachers and students a variety of breathing exercises. Rather than list them here, I will rely on your ability to judiciously use Google and YouTube to search for them. Instead, I'd like to take a moment to share the benefits of regular deep breathing exercises for children (and adults). When students practice deep breathing, it decreases their stress, reduces their anxiety, helps them to remain calm, and lowers their blood pressure. Academically, it strengthens sustained attention, sharpens their ability to focus and learn, and helps them control their emotions.

Convinced yet?

Regularly practicing breathing takes no more than one or two minutes a day and can help save innumerable minutes in the long run. When students engage in this practice daily, they can easily choose a breathing technique to use when going to the safe place. If students only use breathing exercises infrequently, then their use in the safe place will seem inaccessible.

To sum up the first steps in using the safe place strategy, an adequate space must first be set aside for a safe place in the classroom. Students must be familiar with its purpose and comfortable using it voluntarily when upset. Instead of seeing it as a punishment, students should welcome going there as the first step in regulating their emotions. Once there, students should choose a breathing exercise or two to use to begin the calming process. After all that is complete, the real work begins.

Identify emotions

After students use a self-selected breathing strategy and have begun the process of self-regulation, the next step is to identify what emotions are present. This is typically aided by something available to students in the safe place, such as a mood meter or feelings poster. Depending on the age of your students, it can be as wordy or pictorial as fits their developmental level. The key idea is not to mull over the synonyms of *distressed* to find the perfect one to fit the occasion. Instead, the very act of trying to identify emotions helps students take the first step toward recovery.

For many students, emotions are wild, chaotic things that come upon them unsuspectingly with no rhyme or reason. Captive to the rampages of their feelings, many have difficulty even naming their emotions when under the spell of strong sensations. Naming, recognizing, and even honoring their emotions, however, takes a big bite out of their power.

Things that are unknown and unrecognizable are mysterious and frightening. When angry or hurt or anxious, however, those emotions become more manageable when named. Labeling emotions without judgment brings down the level of trepidation because to name is to hold power over. Instead of feeling a sense of shame or embarrassment over their feelings, students can simply name them to tame them.

Next, after breathing and naming their emotions, students can choose to engage in a calming activity, again selecting from items available in the safe place. Whether it be blowing on a pinwheel, playing with a glitter jar, or rubbing some type of tactile implement like a sequined pillow, students need a few minutes for their nervous systems to calm down enough to rejoin the class.

Yet just because the students are more visibly calm at this point does not mean that the crisis has passed. Waiting for children outside of the safe place is the same problem that drove them there in the first place. It is here where adults can step in and help children solve their problems. If thrust back into the classroom immediately, another meltdown might occur without some type of teacher intervention. Helping students solve the initial problem is the final step in this intricate yet life-altering procedure.

Giving students the tools to be able to regulate, calm, and name their emotions is a super power they'll need to get through adolescence and thrive in adulthood. While teachers spend countless hours teaching their students how to line up and put a proper heading on their papers, how often do they give them a series of steps that can be used to work around the number one cause of classroom disruptions, strong emotions?

Talk structures

Talk structures are another set of routines that often get overlooked. Most students grow up in households with a high degree of variance from their classmates. Some students are raised as only children, used to being able to speak whenever they please. Others live in crowded homes with siblings and cousins, learning at a young age that the only way to be heard is with a raised voice.

Students make meaning by talking and doing. When they sit and passively listen, their brains are not wrestling with the concept being presented. Instead, their minds are usually wandering to other topics. If you want them to learn something, they need to experience it and discuss it. This means noise and movement. This is where teachers begin to panic.

Rather than turning them loose to (hopefully) talk about the topic, teachers can employ a specific structure to draw order from the chaos. As most are familiar with the common arrangements, such as think-pair-share, let's discuss a few unique procedures that you can use to supercharge your discussions and decrease off-task behavior.

Students make meaning by talking and doing.

A snowball discussion starts small but quickly grows (or snowballs) to encompass the entire classroom. Students respond to a question in pairs, discussing their answer with a partner (either self-selected or random). After a signal, each pair joins another pair to compare responses and come up with a new consensus. After sufficient time, the groups of four find another group of four and the size doubles until the entire class is one large group.

For situations that warrant a more organized talk structure, students can answer a series of questions in a group of four to six. At a signal, two or three students can move to the next group while the other half remains behind. The next question is discussed but with the new group of students, keeping the conversation fresh as students are continually moved to keep the groups from growing stale.

Another talk structure that gets kids moving but requires a bit more planning involves the use of answer stems. Students should each have a series of response stems on a paper or on sentence strips held together on a ring. They find a partner and listen to the question asked by the teacher.

ANTICIPATE

To begin their response, each student can choose an answer stem from the ones provided to them and then elaborate as needed. After a minute, students find a new partner and answer another question with a self-selected answer stem.

Essential procedures

But what about sharpening pencils? Should students be taught the correct way to title a paper?

Calm down, Harry Wong devotees. Those procedures are important too but most likely ones you've already tried. Novice teachers can usually deduce from their college education and limited experience that students need to be shown the desired way to ask for permission to use the restroom or where to find makeup work. The use of a safe place and talk structures are typically hidden from newer teachers and that's why I chose to emphasize them here.

That does not mean, however, that students don't need to be shown the typical, run-of-the-mill procedures. Procedures are the banks that keep the river of student energy flowing in the right direction. Without them the water's energy is wasted as it floods outward rather than downstream. Likewise, showing students how to complete simple tasks provides them a strong foundation so they can focus their mental energy on important things like learning your content. Here are a few essential procedures to think about and employ.

- Bell ringer: What should students be doing when they first enter the classroom? Misbehavior often follows close behind unstructured time.
- Getting attention: Is there a particular method students should use to signal that they need your attention? Do they shout out or

raise their hands? Does it depend on the situation?
- Dismissing class: Does everyone leave when the bell rings, even if you're still teaching? Should they wait for a signal? This seemingly inconsequential procedure can make a world of difference.
- Tardiness: When students arrive late, do they need to do anything in particular, like sign a book or present you with a tardy slip? How will they get the information they missed?
- Collecting homework: Should homework be turned into a designated place, such as a tray or the teacher's desk? Does it have to be there by a certain time (e.g., before the tardy bell rings)?
- Unfinished classwork: What happens when students don't finish classwork before the end of the period? Do they automatically finish it for homework or do they turn it in unfinished? How will that affect their grade?
- Bathroom break: This procedure can also save you a lot of frustration. How do students signal they need to use the restroom? Are they limited in the number of times they can go during class? What if they just need a drink of water? How many students can be out of the class at once? Is there a log they should sign so you can keep track of who went where and when?
- Replacing pencils: Alongside bathroom breaks, sharpening pencils is another favorite reason for students to be up and out of their seats. I've seen one too many students break their pencil tip just to get up and sharpen it again. Are there certain times students should not sharpen their pencils (e.g., during direct instruction)? If there is an electric sharpener, is it restricted for teacher use only or can everyone use it? How long can the line for the pencil sharpener be? If you don't address the last question, you'll get a

line wrapped around the classroom that rivals those seen on Black Friday outside of a retail store.

These procedures are relatively simple and straightforward. Though many more opportunities exist to implement procedures, answering the questions above with your preferred method of doing things will provide much needed structure for your students. Remember, the less brain space required to navigating these common classroom actions, the more they'll have for learning and applying new knowledge.

What can you do tomorrow?

Create safety. If you have not done so already, create and share the safe place location and procedure with your students. Ensure that you have a specific location with comfortable seating and a visual guide for identifying emotions.

Personalize it. Provide tactile soothing objects and begin to practice breathing techniques with students daily so they can use them in the safe place when needed. Students are more likely to use the safe place if they feel welcomed there.

What does this look like in the classroom?

The teacher helps students **regulate their emotions** by:
- Teaching a safe place routine;
- Leading/participating in daily breathing exercises; and
- Helping students resolve problems.

How can you reflect on your learning?

How can a safe place procedure impact your classroom environment?

_____

_____

Which essential procedures listed at the end of the section will you implement first?

_____

_____

Immediate impact: Go to 4 – 2 Attention (Reinforce) – pg. 263

Lost time is never found again.

- Benjamin Franklin

3 – 3 Productivity (Anticipate)

Benjamin Franklin said that idle hands are the devil's playthings.

He must have been a teacher.

Sometimes classroom management comes down to emotionally disturbed students, who might need to be contained to a behavior unit, causing havoc on unsuspecting educators. Other times, however, students act out simply because they're bored. It's hard to fault children for becoming restless when the pace of instruction is slower than molasses on a frozen Christmas morning.

For others, the pace is fine but they just happen to finish quickly and don't know of productive ways to manage their unstructured time. Sometimes everything seems to go well until it comes to basic management tasks like collecting homework or passing out supplies for an art project. Then your idyllic classroom turns into the opening of *The Hunger Games* in which students mob toward the cornucopia scavenging for supplies.

With all that being said, there are some tips and tricks for making your classroom more productive. With less wasted time comes more opportunities for teaching and learning. Three areas to consider when looking to maximize learning time are early finishers, management tasks, and overall pacing.

Early finishers

I remember when I first felt like a real teacher. In my rookie year in the classroom in 2000 I got my first lesson planner. A simple calendar-type book, it contained neat little boxes for multiple subjects. Each five-day teaching span was spread across two pages. Fill in the boxes and your lessons were done.

It didn't take me long to figure out that teaching (and life in general) does not fit into neat little boxes.

One thing that immediately became apparent was that some students finished earlier than others. Knowing that they needed something to do, I tried what most teachers have used at one time or another for students who regularly finish early. Through a little bit of trial and a whole lot of error, I also learned that my initial ideas weren't always the best.

I first had early finishers help other students. While this seemed like an obvious win, it quickly devolved into chaos. Peer teaching, when done with purpose and guidance, can be a powerful teaching technique for both students involved. However, it assumes a lot of things that are not always true. Just because your brighter students know enough to finish early doesn't mean they have the patience or depth of pedagogical tools to teach something to another student. There's a reason it takes a four-year degree to become a certified teacher.

When that didn't work out, I tried having my early finishers help me with basic administrative tasks. While this was highly motivating to a few students, many weren't nearly as excited as I was about the prospect of cleaning erasers outside or sharpening pencils. Running errands might keep some students busy but it does nothing to impact their learning.

Something that I never tried but many teachers have is adding extra tasks for those who finish early. Nothing sucks the life out of students faster than being rewarded with a job well done with more work to do. This approach is de-motivating but does teach students time management skills. Trust me, students will figure out a way to make an 8-minute task take 15 minutes if they know that finishing early will be rewarded with more work.

With less wasted time comes more opportunities for teaching and learning.

So, if those approaches don't work, what can teachers do for early finishers that doesn't waste their time and keeps them out of trouble simultaneously?

Some students would enjoy working on activity packets if finished early. These shouldn't be filled with coloring sheets or mazes but instead target skills that are aligned with the curriculum but presented as either a series of challenges or in inventive ways. Some of these might be logic puzzles, more open-ended word problems, or a series of problems of the day. Activity packets should be rather lengthy so they last for up to a month at a time (you don't want to have to create new ones weekly). They should also be optional.

Many curriculum programs now come with online components that reinforce and extend the core textbook. Students finishing early can jump on a computer, Chromebook, or iPad to play some of the learning games available to them. While this seems like an easy solution, and it is, it should also come with guidelines. Some students will fly through their work, providing incorrect or incomplete answers to race others for the computer. If you have limited technology available, you'll have to create some type of rotation system so everyone gets a chance to play. You might want to check students' work before they jump on an electronic device to ensure it meets your high-quality standards.

Finally, reading is a favorite pastime of many students. Instead of jumping through hoops trying to manage your limited number of iPads or create endless activity packets, simply let students read when finished early. For some, this will be all the incentive they need. For others, they might need the deal sweetened a bit. Perhaps you can open up the library center and let early finishers sit on a beanbag or spread out on the carpet. Some students might simply enjoy reading if it means they can sit on the floor under their desks. It wouldn't hurt to keep your classroom library stocked with fresh books from the school library.

Not sure which of these would appeal most to your students? Don't make the decision for them! Let them pick from these options and the very act of choosing will be both motivating and calming.

Management tasks

There are many activities or tasks that must be handled daily in order to keep the wheels turning in a classroom. While some of these must be completed by the teacher, it's amazing how many of them can be automated by enlisting the help of students. This not only keeps things moving along because you've multiplied your effort, this also provides an

ANTICIPATE

opportunity for students to practice and gain responsibility.

Attendance needs to be taken every day but not necessarily by you. Students can be shown how to click a few buttons on your computer and keep up with who's here and who's not. Most attendance programs are now online so my suggestion would be to log in yourself first and then let your student take attendance. If you teach in the primary grades, your attendance might be reflected in a pocket chart that students place name cards in with categories such as *At Home* and *At School*. The information can then be transferred to your computer program. This same principle applies to any other logistical tasks, such as getting a daily lunch count for the cafeteria.

For many classroom activities, supplies are needed. Instead of slowly walking around with glue sticks or bags of markers, automate the process. Designate table captains or materials managers at each group and ask them to come get enough materials for their tables. Rather than inviting misbehavior because students are waiting too long for supplies, speed things up by utilizing their help.

Collecting homework and even tabulating it is something that students can also do for you. One simple way to do this is to train your students to put a number next to their name on any classwork or homework. Each number (e.g., 1 – 20) corresponds to the roster so that someone else, like one of your students, can quickly order the assignments without having to memorize all the names. For example, if homework is due in a certain tray or location by 8:00 a.m., a student can be trained to go to the tray at a few minutes after 8:00 a.m. and put the homework in numerical order. If any numbers are missing, you can then immediately go to those students and ask them about their homework.

The opportunities are endless and only limited by your imagination.

While these are just a few ideas, I'm sure you have many more that you've already thought of. The key to making this tip work for you is reflection. Think about the management tasks you complete every day in your classroom. Ask yourself, "Can a student do this?" If so, train your students to do it and let them carry some of the management burden. This frees up your time and helps them feel ownership in the classroom.

Pacing

Some. Lessons. Move. So. Slow. Orsofast!

Here's the ugly truth that many teachers avoid at all costs. They create many behavior problems themselves because they do not properly pace the lesson. When lessons move too slowly, students start to act out from sheer boredom. They finish early or wait interminably between portions of teaching, finding nothing better to do than to cause havoc. Other lessons move at a breakneck pace, leaving educational debris in their dust and generally causing confusion and resentment.

So, what's the Goldilocks solution? How can you find the happy medium and pace your lessons vigorously without losing anyone in the process? Here are a few ideas to get you going. Realize that these suggestions are general and must match your current teaching situation to be effective.

Make the learning goals clear and personal. I know that many of you already have one of my least favorite acronyms on your board because of school requirements – SWBAT. This ominous acronym stands for *student will be able to* and is usually followed by a skills or content objective, such as SWBAT multiply 2-digit numbers using partial products. While the acronym does save space, it can sometimes leave students in the dark. While you know what it means, and you probably told your students once or twice, most of them don't connect it to themselves. It's a statement on the board for you and your administrator, who is liable to walk in at any time. If written in this format, it's not meant for students to reference. Why not make learning goals both clear and personal?

One simple way to do this is to change the point of view of the typical statement. When lesson objectives begin with SWBAT it points to some disinterested third party, a student somewhere who is interested in learning this rigmarole. Instead, use first person language to make it more personal. *I can use partial products to multiply numbers.* When students see themselves in the lesson objective, they're more likely to know what it is they are supposed to do.

Think about the management tasks you complete every day in your classroom. Ask yourself, "Can a student do this?"

And for too many students, the objective is written but never truly made clear or elaborated on. A good habit to get into is to write the lesson objective in first person language and use it both to open the lesson and close it. For your opener, have a student read the objective aloud and then you can expand upon it to begin teaching. To close the lesson, have a different student read the objective aloud and ask for a thumbs up or thumbs down to show their agreement with the statement. This gives you a quick informal assessment on the effectiveness of the lesson and keeps everyone on the same page.

Another common miss in lesson delivery is an over reliance on oral instructions. How many times have you given a set of directions for students and then moments later had five hands shoot up, all wanting to ask a question about something you just explained? It's not purposeful forgetfulness but varying learning strengths. Your verbal instructions make sense to you but that's because you've already thought through the lesson and activity. Students process things differently and many need to read directions rather than simply hear them. Even if they listen just fine, you can forestall many questions by having your directions available for reference on the board, projector, or even on pieces of paper that can be passed out.

Check for understanding

Checking for understanding can also help moderate the pace. Remember, everything you're teaching makes perfect sense to you because you're the teacher – it should make sense! Your students, on the other hand, need ample time to process what they are learning. Within your lesson you should plan stopping points for students to stop and think about or discuss what's happening. These don't need to be extravagant, time-consuming, or taken for a grade. Instead, they should be planned, purposeful, and thought-provoking.

A common technique that teachers use is called think-pair-share. This strategy asks a question, gives students time to think about a response, and then lets them talk about the answer with a partner. A simple adjustment to this tried and true method replaces the first step with some movement. Called mingle-pair-share, students stand up and walk around the room quietly, thinking about their answer while soft music plays. When the music stops, students find the person closest to them to talk with.

Another quick and easy idea to check for understanding is called sage and scribe. Stop during a lesson and have students partner up. One student acts as the teacher (the sage) and the other acts as the student (the scribe). The sage explains what was just learned or discussed and the scribe records the sage's thinking on paper. After a short amount of time, the roles switch with either the same prompt or a new one.

One of my favorite strategies is called inside-outside circle. Have the students make one large circle in the front of the class. Have them count off 1-2-1-2 and the *ones* take a step into the middle of the circle and turn around. Now you have two concentric circles and the students are paired up. Ask a question and direct which student (inside or outside) will answer first. When both have responded, ask either the inside or outside circle to move a certain number of spots to the right or left. This technique provides you with a super simple method of partnering students again and again while keeping things fresh and moving at a fast clip.

There are more techniques but hopefully you found the pattern. Let students talk! That's all they want to do, just talk. They'll talk whether you allow them or not, so why fight it? Talking is how students make sense of what they're learning. They process information by talking things out so don't stifle student discussion, structure it. If you give students opportunities to talk (about the lesson objective, perhaps), they'll be more engaged and less likely to disrupt your classroom.

What can you do tomorrow?

Plan out learning. Think about an upcoming lesson and consider it's pacing and structure. Write a student-friendly objective on the board to guide students, opening and closing with it. If there are any administrative tasks involved with the lesson (e.g., passing out materials), plan to have a student or two take care of them for you.

Encourage student discussion. Plan a talking opportunity for students to process for every five to ten minutes of instruction.

What does this look like in the classroom?

Students' **learning time** is maximized, as evidenced by:
- Clear and worthwhile options for early finishers;
- Management tasks being completed swiftly with the aid of students, when possible; and
- Stopping points built into the lesson to check for understanding.

How can you reflect on your learning?

How can you use students to speed up processes and reduce idle time?

_____

_____

How does utilizing a student friendly learning objective keep the lesson on track?

_____

_____

Anticipate

Transitions

Sometimes the best way to learn what you need to know is to go back to the very beginning. There's a saying going around that you learn everything you need to know in kindergarten. While I don't disagree with that adage, I'd take it one step further. If you want to learn how to really manage your classroom, you need to go back to pre-K.

They don't mess around in pre-K.

I learned this truth early in my second year as an instructional coach. After many years as an administrator in a charter school network, I transitioned to a large urban district in the Dallas/Fort Worth metroplex. I worked in the early childhood department as a district instructional coach for kindergarten through second grade teachers.

In my teaching career I had never taught below third grade, though as a campus and district administrator I worked with kindergarten through eighth grade. While I enjoyed the stretch assignment of now coaching teachers in grade levels I had never actually taught myself, I always kept one eye on the pre-K instructional coaches. To me, they seemed to come from another universe, skilled in mystic arts much like the Jedi in the Star Wars films.

It wasn't until my second year in the department that I had the privilege (and the courage) to coach pre-K teachers. What seemed like voodoo magic before turned out to be a series of highly coordinated moves and routines that pre-K teachers master quickly if they want to survive past September.

With the exception of pre-K (and oftentimes kindergarten), every other grade level teaches students that have typically benefited from past schooling. Someone else has taught the students how to line up, to sit quietly, to raise their hands, and what is generally expected in an academic environment. If kindergarten is considered ground zero for education, then pre-K must be at minus one.

They take the raw, unfiltered versions of potential students and spend a year molding them into something resembling pupils. Without the benefit of previous schooling, these children come in like a pack of feral wolves released into the wild after months of captivity. From these raw materials pre-K teachers create systems and structures that set their students up for over a decade of future success in public school. During the COVID-19 pandemic the term *essential worker* came to the forefront, those whom society could not afford to stay home.

In education, all teachers are essential workers. Pre-K teachers, however, are *essentially* essential.

Of the many areas that pre-K teachers stand out in, one that is pertinent for anyone reading this text is transitions. A transition is simply how a student or a classroom moves from one activity to the next. This could be as simple as closing one textbook and getting out another or as complex as everyone moving from their desks to a whole group area quickly and quietly.

In the grand scheme of things, misbehavior often crops up during these unstructured times. While waiting for instructions or because of someone else's poor choices, students invariably lose their way (behaviorally) when not receiving explicit instructions on how to move from one activity to the next. Something as seemingly simple as closing your textbook and taking out your homework folder can turn a well-mannered class into a set piece for a zombie apocalypse movie.

While *closing your textbook* is innocuous in itself, it doesn't provide enough parameters for many students. Some students will close their books by slamming it shut, competing with each other to see who can make the loudest noise. Others will quietly close their book as they begin chatting with their neighbors. Still others aren't too pressured by the timeliness of the command and fail to close it altogether, instead waiting for another minute or two before complying.

A transition is simply how a student or a classroom moves from one activity to the next.

What pre-K teachers know is that each move must be scripted, choreographed, and practiced multiple times before it's ready to be implemented. Instead of merely telling students what to do verbally and expecting immediate compliance, pre-K teachers take it step by step. They do a wonderful job of breaking down each transition move into bite-sized chunks and practicing them again and again.

If you find that disruptive behavior tends to crop up during transitions or in-between activities, you might want to take a page from the pre-K teacher's playbook.

Hard-wired

But many of you might say at this point, "I tried that already! We practiced how to enter the classroom quietly and it worked for a day or two but then students forgot."

And why exactly does that surprise you?

Are you surprised when your dog begins barking at a random kid walking down the street?

Forgetting is a natural process. Our brains get so much sensory data every moment of every day that we cannot possibly store it all. The brain automatically filters out and recycles unimportant information so as not to overburden its memory system. When students forget what to do during a transition, that simply means it hasn't been practiced enough for automaticity.

When actions are performed again and again, the series of neurons that connect in your brain to make that highly complex maneuver possible begins to become coated in a fatty, insulating myelin layer. This myelin sheath allows electrical impulses to transmit quickly and effectively along the nerve cells. In other words, these actions become hard-wired.

This phenomenon is easily understood when thinking about riding a bicycle. The balance required to stay upright, the coordination of feet, hands, and arms, and the continued pumping of blood while analyzing reams of sensory data to maintain forward momentum takes an incredible amount of cognitive capacity. At first glance, this set of skills seems insurmountable for many children. Yet with repetition and practice, children learn how to not only ride bicycles but can do so years later even if they haven't ridden one for over a decade. Though not used, that network of neurons has a strong myelin sheath that keeps it ready for use again even if dormant for an extended period.

So how can we hardwire routines into students' brains?

Feedback

Think about how you were taught to ride a bicycle or how you taught your own child to ride one. You received constant feedback, whether through your skinned knees or your encouraging parent, as to how you were doing. Someone held on to the back of the seat or maybe even your shoulders until you were steady enough to try it on your own. With constant words of reassurance and helpful tips on maintaining your balance, you eventually learned to do it on your own.

It's this type of feedback that pre-K teachers have mastered and use in their classrooms. If it works for them, why can't it work for you?

When students forget what to do during a transition, that simply means it hasn't been practiced enough for automaticity.

When students fail to meet your expectation for transitioning smoothly and quickly, or for anything else for that matter, you don't yell at them, lash out angrily, or demean them in any way. No, instead you calmly show them a better way. You practice it again and again until everyone does it right.

While the picture of a smooth transition might be clear in your mind, it might be murky for everyone else. If your instructions weren't effective the first or second time, repeating them again a little louder and a little slower won't do you any good. Show them what it looks like yourself or take a coaching approach.

For pre-K students to learn how to navigate their classrooms within the parameters of the teacher's expectations, they must learn a lot of separate procedures and routines. With the oral language receptive abilities of the students varying greatly, they can't rely on verbal directions alone. Instead, students act out the desired routine or transition. As the others watch the display, the teacher can give a running commentary describing the correct actions that the students are taking.

Sports coaches do the same thing when working with their teams. Instead of merely telling them how to execute a play, they demonstrate it themselves or have a few players perform it while everyone watches. As the coach describes the correct actions, the players connect the words with the visual in front of them and the teaching becomes real. If the team still doesn't execute the play or skill correctly, practice is halted and start over. Again and again they practice until it becomes second nature.

If your students aren't moving swiftly or efficiently enough between activities, or if they are taking those opportunities to misbehave, that simply means they need more practice. You don't give up on your child learning to ride a bike after the fifth time she's fallen. You pick her up gently, possibly adjust your support, and try again. Your students need the same type of structured practice without shaming if they are going to ever get better.

Cognitive transitions

Let's assume that your transitions are running smoothly. You can move through the class period quickly and efficiently, not losing any instructional time to redirecting misbehavior or any other tomfoolery.

What's next?

Quick and easy transitions that keep students focused on academic tasks is the penultimate, but not the final, level you can take your students to. If you want to push your students and embed learning into every moment of every day, the next step involves cognitive transitions. Building learning and review into every transition moment works to not only decrease behavior problems that much more, it also looks good for evaluative purposes because it's so rare.

This is a trick I learned from a rookie first grade teacher, one I was supposed to be coaching (go figure).

She had four table groups of students, as is common for lower elementary classrooms. As I looked around the room, I noticed that each table group had a thin wire stand in the middle, similar to those you might use at a fast-food restaurant to hold a plastic card with your order number. Instead of numbers, however, each wire stand had a picture of an historical figure, such as Abraham Lincoln or Martin Luther King, Jr.

After a brief activity that had students at their tables, she wanted to bring them to the carpet for a whole group literacy lesson. Experienced teachers know that one simply does not tell the class to come to the carpet all at once. To do so would recreate the yearly street scene of Pamplona, Spain in which crazy denizens and tourists from around the world run in front of stampeding bulls. No, that is a transition activity and should not take more than 30 seconds.

This transition, however, was different because the rookie teacher had embedded learning into it. Though I had not been in the class during the previous social studies lessons in which she spoke about the famous historical figures and what they contributed to the world, the fact that she had so quickly became evident. Instead of dismissing the students table by table using a table number, she instead gave clues as to which group should be dismissed.

"I need the table group to come to the carpet that has the picture of the person who led the civil rights movement," she said. The Martin Luther King, Jr. table group quietly pushed in their chairs and moved to the carpet. The other students waited expectantly for their table to be called.

"Next I'd like the table group that has the picture of the person who freed the slaves during the Civil War," she stated. Three of the four students at the Abraham Lincoln table quickly got up and pushed in their chairs. When they noticed that their tablemate was still sitting quietly, they started gesturing emphatically for him to join them. The teacher noticed this and offered, "Remember that Abraham Lincoln was president during the Civil War. He wrote the Emancipation Proclamation that freed the slaves in the Southern states."

The litany continued until all the students were quietly seated at the carpet and instruction began. Though the students could have quietly moved to the carpet one at a time or in groups as they did, those moments would have been void of learning. The teacher took the opportunity to embed review of previous material into the transition and made it that much more meaningful.

The opportunities to apply cognitive transitions are almost boundless. One caution, however, is that these cognitive transitions should be short and sweet. They are meant as a review or a focusing task, not a full-blown lesson. If the students are not familiar with the material or it involves a lot of steps, it might bog down the transition.

To prepare for it, one thing you'll need is some way to identify the groups or the answers to the questions you'll ask. The students in this class had pictures of historical figures on their desks and knew enough information about them to answer basic factual questions. Sometimes the identifying traits might be personal (e.g., if you have brown hair) or related to academic vocabulary (e.g., if your geometric solid has 6 faces).

Learning to transition and transition well is a key feature of taking charge of your classroom. Adding cognitive transitions will take that to the next level.

ANTICIPATE

What can you do tomorrow?

Transition well. Evaluate your most useful transitions and dedicate extra time this week to practice them. Practice at least once a week for transitions that are already established.

Never stop teaching. Add a cognitive transition to an everyday movement such as lining up or coming to the carpet. Decide on the vocabulary or descriptor to be used and make sure students are familiar with it so the transition remains brief.

What does this look like in the classroom?

Students **transition** effectively between tasks, as evidenced by:
- Quick execution of the desired actions;
- Corrective feedback and practice opportunities being offered, as needed; and
- Learning opportunities embedded within.

How can you reflect on your learning?

Which transitions need some additional work? How can you add a cognitive component to them?

_____

_____

Why is corrective feedback an important part of productivity?

_____

_____

Immediate impact: Go to 4 – 3 Action (Reinforce) – pg. 285

If you fail to plan, you are planning to fail!

- Benjamin Franklin

3 – 4 Planning (Anticipate)

She had the job before she ever walked in for the interview. She knew it and it didn't take long for me to know it either.

The year was 2011 and I was fresh out of the classroom. In my first administrative position, I served as the assistant principal of a brand-new campus in a successful charter school district. My task, along with the principal's, was to fully staff a new campus by hiring over 30 teachers. We made some really good hires during that time and only missed on a few. The easiest hire, by far, was Amanda.

She interviewed for the elementary art teacher position and the principal and I weren't sure as to what kind of interview we were going to get. Our practice had been to ask each candidate to come in and walk us through a lesson of their choice before we got down to the standard set of interview questions. While most people know how to answer correctly when asked about being a team player and what their greatest weaknesses were, that's not the type of information we were hoping to glean from the interview process.

We wanted to see their level of planning and thoroughness. Did they come in with a detailed lesson plan, complete with standards, lesson objectives, openers, and extensions? Did they write in scaffolds for struggling learners or supports for English language learners? Or did they walk in with a folded piece of paper or a lesson plan hastily scribbled on the back of a Denny's placemat?

This interviewing strategy worked well for us that year. I firmly believe that we hired as well as we did because of the lesson component. We learned so much about lesson preparation, teaching style, and temperament from that portion of the interview that we usually knew our hiring decision before the interview questions actually began.

Thus our dilemma when hiring an art teacher. That position was one of the last ones we hired simply because we didn't know how someone would walk through an art lesson. What did an elementary art lesson even look like?

Amanda quickly showed us.

Preparation

I remember her walking in with a tub of what looked like supplies under her arm. Not sure of what to make of it, we told her that we would begin with her lesson demonstration. She nodded and opened up the tub to reveal some smaller baggies filled with clay and some folded wax paper. As she began to speak about the lesson objective, she unfolded the wax paper squares (already cut and sized for individual use) and placed one before me and one before the principal. That morning we would be working with clay and using it to represent an animal of our choice.

To no one's surprise, she already had sticks of modeling clay ready for us to use as we began to follow her directions throughout the lesson. With no fear, she directed us as she would her students and the principal and I quickly became absorbed in playing with the clay and trying to make an animal (neither of us were very successful). We both snapped out of our reverie as the lesson came to an abrupt end, Amanda consciously keeping within the 10 minutes allotted for the lesson sample.

The principal and I looked at each other and communicated nonverbally that Amanda was a go, a shorthand series of looks we had developed over the course of countless interviews to signal our thoughts on the current candidate. We then both looked at our hands, brown and dirty after an aborted attempt to form life from clay. Before we could say anything, though, Amanda had reached into her magical tub and provided two wet wipes, prepackaged in plastic baggies of course, and ready for us to use to clean off our hands. She had thought of everything and her total preparation impressed us more than she could have ever imagined.

Really, we only had one interview question for her at that point.

"When can you start?"

You see, her preparation and attention to detail showed us everything we needed to know about her. We had found, over the course of interviewing and hiring an entire staff for our new school, that some candidates naturally rose to the top of the list. More than energy and charisma, we valued planning and meticulous preparation. We knew that the level of detail put into preparing lessons would serve as a guidepost for how much effort and planning went into their daily instruction.

And as disconnected as the two might seem, we discovered an interesting connection. A teacher's level of preparation has a direct inverse relationship with the amount of misbehavior in the classroom.

Materials ready

Sometimes teachers aren't ready to teach when the children arrive. Perhaps they didn't lay out their materials ahead of time. Maybe they had every intention of arriving early to make copies only to find a line 10 people deep at the copying machine upon arrival. When you are scrambling to get things together, your students are left to their own devices.

Trust me, they'll find something to do.

Often when teachers complain about the behavior issues they face on a daily basis, they don't take time to examine their ownership of the problem. When there is downtime in the classroom due to disorganization and lack of preparation, that flows right back to the teacher. If you want to minimize the behavior problems you face on a daily basis, a good starting point would be to consistently have your materials ready.

A teacher's level of preparation has a direct inverse relationship with the amount of misbehavior in the classroom.

Before you leave each day, take five or ten minutes to look over your plans for the next day. Yes, it's 4:00 and you want to leave. However, an ounce of prevention is worth a pound of cure. Make sure you have enough copies, your materials and assignments are organized and either obvious or labeled, and your lesson plans are visible in a prominent location.

Why go through all this trouble, you might ask? Why should you bother laying everything out if you can just do it tomorrow morning?

What if you can't?

Anticipate

Any teacher who has taught for more than a few months has had this scenario play out, either for them or for a colleague. Late in the evening, or early in the morning, their child becomes sick. Maybe it's one of their parents who fell and is now going to the hospital. It could even be a personal emergency or car trouble. However it happens, you have to call for a substitute teacher at the last minute. The problem is, you're not ready.

You didn't get the sub plans ready or you didn't make copies. Maybe you left materials to be prepped the morning of the lesson but now you won't be there. However it happened, you're running up to the school on a day you're taking off because you aren't fully prepared. You might even have to leave your sick child at home alone for 30 minutes while you run up to the school to hastily put together some plans for the sub.

Sometimes the plans might be ready but the materials are not. You had planned on using some math manipulatives but they are still in their packages and you need to divide them up into table groups. An activity needs glue sticks but you haven't used any yet this year and they are in a supply closet hidden behind tissue boxes. Whatever the situation, you aren't ready and you have to come in even when you're off.

Having your materials ready at the end of each day won't save you daily from these doomsday scenarios because they only happen infrequently. Yet small benefits can be reaped daily from this level of preparation. Your mind will be more at ease knowing that everything is ready for tomorrow. You have more flexibility to adapt the lessons to meet individual needs because you aren't frantically looking for items. And, most importantly, your students aren't wandering aimlessly or left to their own devices while you struggle to pull together everything you need for the lesson.

And, speaking of lessons…

Lesson preparation

Teacher staff development is notoriously boring. While some speakers and sessions can be engaging, for better or worse they are typically dreaded. Nothing generates apathy faster than sitting through an hour-long presentation in which the speaker reads word for word off the PowerPoint. Think about the level of disengagement you've felt at a boring in-service and then multiply it by 100.

That's what your students feel when you don't know your lesson.

Think about it. Students are in your classroom not out of burning desire but compulsory attendance laws. They are asked to sit quietly in rows and listen to an adult ramble on about things that might not interest them. To top it all off, sometimes it's all too obvious that the teacher isn't familiar with the lesson.

Whether it be reading straight from the teacher's edition, speaking in disconnected sentences and vague generalities, or simply not gauging the audience (students) to track their understanding, many teachers don't know the lesson well enough to teach it. They figure, incorrectly I might add, that they can just get up in front of students and wing it for 10 or 15 minutes and no one will be the wiser.

More than simply laying out your materials ahead of time, teachers that want to take charge of their classrooms must also take time to learn the lesson material diligently. It is alright to reference the teacher's manual on occasion, especially when teaching something new for the first time, but it should never be used as a crutch or a long-term solution. Not being confident in the content signals to students that what is being discussed or taught is not that important.

Think about the times you've had bad experiences with professional development and contrast those with your best experiences. In the latter, the speaker refers sparingly to the slides, instead talking to you (the audience) directly. The presenter obviously knows the content because he or she speaks confidently and rapidly rather than haltingly while referring to notes constantly.

Your students deserve that same level of preparation.

Not being confident in the content signals to students that what is being discussed or taught is not that important.

Take time to go over the lesson the day before presenting it to students. Work through the language of the key points, the ones that you want to drive home. If the first time you've ever verbalized them is in front of students during the lesson, chances are you will miss something important or stumble during a crucial moment.

Performance

The easiest way to think about lesson preparation in this light is that of a performance. You are the main act and you have a captive audience that will either cheer you on or start throwing things if you bomb. You would never go on stage without memorizing your lines or rehearsing thoroughly. Why would you teach a lesson with any less preparation?

Teaching is a dance between two partners, the teacher and the students. In this particular dance, you are leading because you are the only one that knows the steps. How much stumbling will there be, then, if you aren't even sure of all the dance moves? The students don't know what's going on, their job is mainly to show up. When you invite them onto the dance floor, can they follow your lead? Preparing your lessons, both in materials and rehearsal, is a key factor in student engagement.

And there's the secret about engaging students. When they are interested in the lesson, when the material is exciting or the teacher captures their attention, they are completely focused on what's being taught. They don't have time to flick their neighbor's ear or throw a paper wad at the trash can from all the way across the room. Instead, they are focused on what's going on because they don't want to miss anything.

Classroom management should be seen as a series of moves that work in lock step. Decreasing misbehavior is only half of the equation. The other half, student engagement, will be looked at in depth in the last section of the Take CHARGE model. Suffice it to say, however, a large part of engaging students revolves around teacher preparation and presentation. Students will have a hard time engaging with a lesson that seems haphazard and shoddy. Just as you would never go on stage without first memorizing all your lines, teachers must completely learn the material and have the key points of the lesson memorized for maximum effectiveness.

This level of preparation frees you up in the middle of the performance (teaching the lesson) to riff, to adapt, and respond in the moment. A teachable moment might suddenly emerge in the middle of the lesson that's too good to pass up. If you have your nose buried in your teacher's edition, trying to figure out what to say next, both you and your students will lose out.

ANTICIPATE

What can you do tomorrow?

Get ready. Commit to focusing on preparation for the next few days and note how it impacts your students. Make sure your materials are set out the day before and go over the lesson to become familiar with the key ideas.

Be a star. Treat instruction as a part in a stage play in which you perform your role for (and with) the students. Be sure of your content and the key moves of each lesson so you can execute them comfortably and adapt mid-lesson as needed.

What does this look like in the classroom?

Classroom tasks are **well-planned**, as evidenced by:

- Necessary supplies being readily accessible to students who are comfortable using them;
- Materials (e.g., manipulatives, activity cards, handouts) being prepared in advance; and
- The teacher giving directions effortlessly with minimal errors.

How can you reflect on your learning?

How does preparation relate to student behavior?

_____

_____

What are the benefits of viewing your lesson as a performance?

_____

_____

Third wheel

You never forget the moment you realize that you're not needed anymore.

While a district administrator at the same charter school network in Arlington, TX, one day my duties took me into a fourth grade classroom. The teacher needed to go to a meeting of one kind or another during the day and I was called to step into the classroom for coverage. Since the meeting would only last 45 minutes or so, it was decided that I would cover the class rather than calling for a substitute teacher.

Walking in, I didn't know quite what to expect. The students were working quietly on a task as the teacher and I exchanged places. Yet I also knew that sharks liked to circle a few times before coming in for a nip.

Before I could even ask what was going on, a girl came up and gave me the lay of the land. "I'm the class helper this week. That means I help the teacher pass out the assignments and make sure everyone is working if she has to step out of the room."

Interested and slightly amused, I went with it. "That sounds like an important job," I replied. "So, what's everyone doing right now?"

"We're finishing our poetry units. We've been working on cinquains this week and everyone needs to have one by tomorrow. I've already finished mine," the class helper noted.

"Thanks, you're doing a good job," I said and she went back to her seat.

I wandered around the room for the next few minutes, looking over the shoulders of the children but, for the most part, just trying to stay out of the way. A young boy came up a few minutes later and asked for a bandage. He held out his index finger and, perhaps with a powerful microscope and a fistful of imagination, you might be able to make out a paper cut.

Knowing that it's typically easier to simply give students a bandage even when a cut is not visible, I turned toward the teacher's desk.

As if by magic, my class helper was back. She saw me rummaging around in a few drawers and almost sighed in exasperation. "The bandages aren't in the drawers, Mr. Daffern," she said with a verbal eye roll. "There on that table," she said pointing.

I turned around and was met with a neatnik's paradise. There was a massive container with various sized drawers, each one neatly labeled with the inventory inside, such as glue sticks, paper clips, and erasers. The class helper reached past me and got out a bandage from the third drawer from the bottom, neatly labeled with the word *bandages*. She looked at me in all sincerity and asked, "Do you want to put it on or should I?"

That's when I knew I wasn't really needed. That class, with the assistance of its intrepid class helper, could run itself. I was just the third wheel.

Roles and responsibilities

I quickly learned, in that classroom at least, that it wasn't just the teacher that was in charge. The students had been given meaningful roles and responsibilities that put the classroom in their care as much as the teacher's. They took their duties seriously and, because of that responsibility, felt a sense of propriety over the classroom.

Students are much less likely to vandalize their own property than someone else's. They're not going to deface something they treasure nearly as quickly as they might something that has no meaning for them. If students are not caring properly for your classroom, whether through their behavior or through their treatment of your classroom's tools and supplies, that might just be your problem – it's your classroom.

Taking charge of the classroom, we've already found out, is highly oxymoronic. The more power you give away, the less your students struggle with you. In the same way, the best way to take care of your classroom is to make it everyone's job to take care of it, not just yours.

Think about it. Your classroom is a shared learning space, an area that students will inhabit for 180 school days over the course of ten months. If they don't feel any sense of belonging or responsibility, that's a long time for them to be cooped up together without starting to pick at the carpet or draw on their desks. If you can extend the responsibility for the classroom maintenance and success to the students, you have a much better chance of making it through the year in one piece.

There are some standard jobs that you can utilize, like board eraser, homework collector, or pencil sharpener. These and others like it will help keep things running smoothly and increase the feeling of ownership that students have. More than simply assigning them, however, a real opportunity exists to take these roles and responsibilities to the next level by bringing the students themselves into the conversation.

It would be well worth your time to hold a class meeting or two to discuss how everyone is responsible for maintaining a clean and orderly learning environment. Let them brainstorm which tasks need to be done and how often. Instead of simply jotting down everything they suggest without comment, push back on some of their ideas to make them justify why each one is needed.

Start by accepting just a few proposals, letting students know that you want to see how they do with these jobs before adding new ones. By taking it slow and leaving the addition of more jobs up to them, you put the students in charge and place the burden of responsibility back on them.

Supervisory duties

I know what some of you are thinking at this point. Giving students jobs to do is way too much work. You barely have enough time to write lessons and grade papers. How are you going to find the time to make sure your students are doing the jobs they signed up for?

Good questions. The simple answer is that you don't have to take on any extra tasks if you don't want to. All you need to do is find one student and let him or her do the rest.

You need a supervisor.

The more power you give away, the less your students struggle with you.

Every class in every school in every city across the country is blessed with at least one supervisor on the roster. These students are born to be in charge. They are the ones who organize the playground games, run errands for the teacher, and volunteer to keep watch over the classroom while the teacher runs across the hall.

If you can find a good supervisor, that student can take the burden of maintaining the classroom jobs. This student can create a roster of students and their tasks, check to make sure things are done correctly, and report back to you at a certain time each day on progress. They can even take on the hiring and firing duties.

Rather than simply letting students sign up for a classroom job without any kind of accountability, they can apply for it and even interview with the supervisor. The supervisor can set a time to meet with the applicant, go over the duties, and set a schedule for evaluations and monitoring checks. If you play your cards right, your classroom can become highly self-sufficient without a large amount of effort on your part.

Thinking ahead, however, would be wise to build in some automatic checks and balances to the system. While some students might flourish with the added responsibilities, you also have the potential for creating miniature despots in a social experiment gone wrong. If you need to remove students for lack of performance or becoming drunk with power, it helps when you've already built that mechanism into the system.

Rather than being designated supervisor for life, let that role have firm time limits such as two to four weeks. Once the term has run its course, the position becomes open to anyone willing to apply for it. If the previous supervisor is doing splendidly, he or she can continue. If not, however, you can find a replacement without causing much fuss and use it as a growth opportunity for that student.

Visualization

One final word on anticipating problems in the classroom. Many, though not all, of the issues that arise are avoidable. With a little bit of planning and foresight, you can avoid quite a few of the pitfalls that are on the teaching path before you. Though it will take some of your time, what you lose on the front end will be more than compensated for on the back end.

The first key to visualization is to know what you want. What are you looking for? Do you want to increase time on task? Are you trying to anticipate pockets of disengagement when the lesson might lag? Are you simply trying to predict if you have all your materials ready?

As you get ready to leave at the end of the day, pick a focus and begin to visualize the lesson planned for the next day. If it would help, close your door, turn out your lights, put on some ambient music, and close your eyes. Envision the bell ringer activity, the lesson opener, and your direct instruction. Look for gaps or blank spots in the material, areas that you might not be confident in. Those would be some items to look through tonight and rehearse.

Think about all the handouts, materials, and supplies you need for tomorrow. Is everything ready to go? Are your lesson plans laid out just in case you get sick and have to call in a substitute? Thinking of the activities you have planned, what are some groupings that might need to be rethought? Are there some partners that are starting to get on each other's nerves who would benefit from being moved? These questions and more, if given just a bit of your mental real estate at the end of each day, will save you a world of time and help you dodge some preventable mistakes.

One thing to remember when practicing visualization is that your gut reactions have a lot to tell you as long as you're listening. When thinking through tomorrow's lesson, pay close attention to your emotions. Your emotions lie to you far less often than your conscious mind does. Many times we ignore internally-generated warning signals simply because they don't agree with how we want things to be.

For example, let's say that you're taking three minutes before heading home to mentally walk through your lessons for the next day. As you do, you get a slight twinge of uneasiness about the processing activity you have planned. It requires students to follow a set of five instructions precisely in order to apply what they've just learned. Your mind, wanting to leave, begins to list all the reasons why the activity will work fine. This justification and explanation reaction, however, typically only pops up when something is amiss.

As you pause and really think about the activity you have planned, it suddenly dawns on you that the reason you are concerned about it is that it's all oral. You don't have the instructions written down anywhere for students to reference later as they apply them. As the puzzle piece finally fits in place you can imagine yourself tomorrow, hurriedly writing the instructions on the board because students are confused. You see the lesson derailing while they (im)patiently wait for you to finish scrawling directions on the board.

Your eyes snap open and you grab your laptop. Reaching over, you take an extra four minutes to type and print two copies of the directions for the activity. They now lie next to your open lesson plan book and the second copy is labeled with a child's name on it. Thinking about it, Jose has been squinting a lot when looking at the board. It wouldn't hurt to print up an extra copy for him since his mom isn't taking him to the eye doctor until next week.

Your emotions lie to you far less often than your conscious mind does.

If you will faithfully practice visualization, mentally rehearsing your lesson for the next day, you can solve many problems before they even arise. You can catch any copies you forgot to run off or materials you forgot to prepare. You can think about student groupings and if they'll need to be changed before the lesson. You can also picture how various students will act during the lesson, imagining them participating and deciding if another scaffold might be appropriate. Your English language learners might benefit from some picture vocabulary cards or a struggling student might need a manipulative to make the lesson more concrete.

More than that, your emotions, if you allow them, will send you warning flags for things that your conscious mind missed. If you find yourself beginning to justify a part of the lesson, working hard to explain to yourself why it will work and why your preparation is sufficient, stop and get curious. Your defensiveness could be hiding a deficiency and taking care of it ahead of time might just make the difference between a stellar lesson and a substandard one.

While student misbehavior isn't completely solved by planning and preparation, a lack of readiness definitely exacerbates it. As a professional educator, part of your duties include adequately preparing for each day's lessons. Some jobs might let you roll in five minutes before the bell rings and *ad lib* the lessons. Teaching is definitely not that profession. When student misbehavior emerges and the teacher is not prepared to teach, you'll never eliminate the former until you improve the latter.

What can you do tomorrow?

Employ your students. Use classroom jobs to build buy-in. Explain the functions, set up systems to check for faithful execution of duties, and even take student suggestions for new classroom jobs as long as they can justify them.

Visualize. Take five minutes at the end of a day to consider the next day's lesson. Walk through the sequence in your mind, noting areas that need to be tightened up or materials that still need to be prepared.

What does this look like in the classroom?

Classroom tasks encourage **student responsibility**, including:
- Helpers assigned to daily managerial tasks;
- Classroom roles being updated and turned over according to an understood and equitable system; and
- One or more students serving as classroom supervisors.

How can you reflect on your learning?

How can you use roles and responsibilities to streamline your classroom functions?

_____

_____

What are some of the benefits of visualizing your lesson?

_____

_____

Immediate impact: Go to 4 – 4 Attitude (Reinforce) – pg. 307

3 – 5 Conclusion (Anticipate)

Too many teachers make classroom management harder than it needs to be.

Without even taking into account the emotional and behavioral challenges that students bring in with them, sometimes we shoot ourselves in the foot simply because we don't anticipate problem situations and try to eliminate as many as possible before falling headfirst into them.

Procedures are the backbone of any well-run classroom. They clearly and easily describe the preferred method for accomplishing myriad daily tasks, such as lining up to leave the room or turning in homework. Without teaching, explaining, and practicing procedures on a consistent basis, students are left to try to figure out the best method for completing these routines. While some might be able to do so just fine, many students will feel unbound and exposed without strong procedures.

We can never guarantee what type of home life our students will have. If they have stable relationships with one or both parents, if they have ample food, clothing, and shelter, and if they do not suffer from emotional, physical, or sexual abuse, then they'll probably manage just fine in your classroom without procedures.

Yet how many of your students can confidently check off all those boxes?

You might be one of the only stable forces in your students' lives. For seven hours a day, you could be the most nurturing and well-balanced adult in their world. Don't add to their stress by having a chaotic, unstructured classroom. Building in procedures, and explaining their use and rationale, can be a balm to students' stormy souls.

Additionally, you can only expect students to wait so long if instruction lags or transitions take too long. While you might be able to sit for one whole minute without fidgeting (which is actually a lot harder than it seems), asking students to patiently wait for upwards of five minutes to switch activities requires them to have the patience of Job. It's not going to happen.

Procedures are the backbone of any well-run classroom.

Like weeds along a sidewalk, misbehavior sprouts up in the cracks in between each chunk of instruction. Close the gaps and you slowly start to choke out the opportunities that present themselves to your students as golden opportunities to goof off.

If you don't believe me, take your phone out the next time you transition between subjects or activities. Transitions also include how long it takes upon entering the classroom (e.g., returning from lunch, changing classes) until instruction actually begins. Time yourself and see how long it takes. What might seem like a quick transition to you might be lasting over two and a half minutes. Work on whittling down transition times and see how that affects classroom disruptions.

Finally, lesson planning is a lot more than filling in a box in a lesson planner. It's more than submitting a template to your school principal or uploading a file to a shared drive. Being prepared for your lesson means that you can deliver the entire lesson, if required, blindfolded and without any textbook assistance.

Too often, this is not the problem of new teachers, who diligently study the lesson for the next day, trying to keep one step ahead of their students. No, it's the teacher that has a few years under her belt that typically falls into the vice of not planning.

You glance at the next section of the textbook that you'll cover tomorrow and think to yourself, "Oh yeah, chapter 11, we did that last year. No problem," and give it nary a second thought. Then, in the middle of the lesson the next day, you realize that you aren't as prepared as you ought to be. A few vocabulary words pop up in the book that weren't highlighted in the chapter introduction. It would have been helpful if you had frontloaded those words because now you have to stop in the middle of your instruction to define them.

You remember now (too late!) that the chapter review questions you thought they could answer as a process activity require a worksheet to be printed and distributed per pair. It's easily accessible on the textbook website but still takes five minutes for you to pull up and print in the middle of class (why did the printer toner have to run out today of all days?).

And rather than preplanning the partners, you let students choose their own and turn your classroom into a rugby scrum as students elbow each other out the way, clawing each other to claim the smartest kid as their partner. If you had thought through the lesson ahead of time, visualizing each component, you would have spent an extra five minutes mentally walking through your instruction. You also would have been rewarded by avoiding several pitfalls that were lurking just beneath the surface, waiting to suck your lesson into anarchy.

Building in procedures, and explaining their use and rationale, can be a balm to students' stormy souls.

When you anticipate problems, you clear the path for the elephant and the rider. You tweak the environment, build productive habits, and rally your students to all work together for the common goal of learning. You do this by making the road to learning the path of least resistance.

Think of anticipation as an informal science experiment you undoubtedly conducted either as a child or with your own children. Students are naturally drawn to puddles and water found outside, on the playground or in the street. Without even fully comprehending the laws of gravity or the properties of liquids, they start to play. And they notice quickly that water flows downhill while following the path of least resistance.

They dig channels, remove rocks and twigs, and watch as the water moves and flows. They quickly ascertain that many things can stop the budding stream and that it won't go up but always down. With a goal in mind, they can change the environmental factors

so that the water ends up flowing right where they want it to.

Make success in your classroom the path of least resistance.

That's what anticipation does. It tweaks the classroom environment, removing obstacles and clearing the path, so that learning always flows toward the goal of student achievement. When you've built in procedures, increased productivity, and supercharged your planning process, the path of least resistance for your students suddenly flows right where you want it to go.

CONFIDENCE

HEART

ANTICIPATE

REINFORCE

GROW

ENGAGE

4 – 1 Introduction (Reinforce)

If you listen to the Rolling Stones, you might know that you can't always get what you want. But if you try sometimes, you might find, you get what you need.

But what if you could?

In the metaphor of the elephant and the rider (Heath & Heath, 2010), managing change is best accomplished by attending to three separate but interwoven components. In the previous section of this book, you learned how to clear the path of obstacles through anticipation, specifically procedures, productivity, and planning. It's easier for the elephant to go where you want when the path toward your goal is free of roadblocks and offers the path of least resistance.

The second part of change management that we'll look at as a tool for taking charge of your classroom is motivating the elephant. The elephant represents our emotional selves and, as much as we like to think that the rational part of our brains (the rider) might be in charge, anyone who has ever ridden an four-ton elephant knows that it's the elephant who's ultimately in control.

Until you, as a teacher, learn to tap into the emotional part of your students and help them feel the need to manage behavior, you'll never get the results you are hoping for. You need to not only shape the path through anticipation, but you also need to tap into students' feelings to motivate the elephant.

That comes from your attention.

The truth is, you have at your disposal the only weapon you'll ever need to wage war against misbehavior. All students crave social approval. They want to fit in, to be a part of something, whether that be a family, a classroom community, or a social group. The need to belong is inherent to all of us and is as fundamental to our well-being as food, water, and shelter.

That's why before looking at this portion of the book, it would be good to remind you of the first and second part of the Take CHARGE model – confidence and heart. The heart of teaching is relationships. If you do not have positive, mutually beneficial relationships with your students, then giving or withholding your attention and social approval won't make any difference. They won't care whether or not they are pleasing you if they don't care about you at all.

Relationships flow from the confidence you bring into the classroom,

Reinforce

specifically your attention to positivity and protection. When students are confident that you are on their side, that you care for them and that your classroom is a safe place, a refuge in a world of chaos, they'll do almost anything to keep that intact. It's from a foundation of positive, protective relationships that you can begin to motivate the elephant by tapping into emotions.

Like American football has three game phases, taking charge can be viewed in three separate parts. The first two sections of the book, confidence and heart, represent playing defense. You, as the professional educator, must get yourself right first, must defend against negativity and aloofness. Once you've got those bases covered, you transition into offense, which the last section (anticipate) and this section (reinforce) focus on. Taking the metaphorical fight to the students, to the classroom, is an integral part of taking charge.

All students crave social approval.

One word of caution, however. This section looks at explicit behavior management. There is a world of difference between noticing and judging. When you notice behavior, whether it be good or bad, you are simply describing it and calling attention to it. If you assign judgment to it, making it right or wrong, good or bad, then you appeal to the lower state of students' brains. This, unfortunately, makes it harder for them to access their executive functioning skills and the rational part of their brain.

To motivate students emotionally, you must refuse the temptation to remain in the emotional parts of both your brain and their brains.

Make sense?

By placing your attention and social approval on positive behaviors, you begin to show students what you value. Whatever you pay attention to has inherent value. If you spend a good portion of your time nagging students for misbehavior, then the message you are sending them is one you probably do not want them to hear. In effect, you are saying to them, "I value misbehavior, that's why I give it so much of my energy. If you need some attention, simply act out and you'll get it right away."

No teacher wants to send that message.

Instead, wield your attention as you would a laser beam. While it might just be a very narrow beam of light, focused light can cut through solid metal.

And here's one of the big secrets of taking charge of your classroom. What you pay attention to gets reinforced. If you focus on good behavior, you'll get more of the same. If you're constantly chasing after kids and chiding them for their misdeeds, they'll never stop.

When you direct your attention toward positive behaviors, you are letting students know that your social approval is reserved for those students who are making positive choices. This is why positive relationships are the foundation of any classroom.

If the students like you and want to please you, then they'll do anything to earn and maintain your social approval.

If you don't have solid relationships with your students, they'll be indifferent to what you want and don't want.

Like a play-by-play announcer for a sports game, you can describe student actions by noticing, not judging, what is being done that meets your approval. As a steady stream of commentary emerges from your lips, the students begin to recognize what it takes to earn your attention. They'll soon figure out that beneficial actions are called out while poor choices are ignored.

Thus, if they want your attention and social approval, they'll need to make their actions and attitudes match those of the ones that you are describing. This allows them to stay in the upper parts of their brains, choosing to make the right decisions of their own volition, while reaping emotional benefits at the same time. Instead of having their misdeeds called out, shaming them and dropping them into the lower regions of their brain, attention-seeking behaviors are ignored.

Whatever you pay attention to has inherent value.

It feels good to get attention. It brings pleasure and a sense of community to be included, to be noticed, to have your actions described positively by someone you care about. Students will come to crave your social approval like they do food and water.

And, with a commitment to only reinforcing positive actions and attitudes, they'll soon figure out that your attention is reserved for students who meet your expectations.

Attention is psychic energy, and like physical energy, unless we allocate some part of it to the task at hand, no work gets done.

- Mihaly Csikszentmihalyi

4 – 2 Attention (Reinforce)

So now we come to it.

After wading through pages and pages about relationships, positivity, and procedures, we finally get to the part of the book that most people want to find immediately.

How do you get children to behave?

The traditional methods of behavior management are most likely not working for you. If they were, you wouldn't be reading this book!

The most common behavior management system that is employed throughout classrooms across the country is destined for failure. A large majority of teachers rely on punishment and reward, the carrot and the stick, to coax and cajole students to behave.

It's exhausting and doesn't work. Let's take a look at why.

Both ends of the spectrum, punishment and reward, target one key emotion in children – fear. For the former, the relationship is fairly obvious. Children should do what they are told or else they'll be punished through an increasing (and typically intricate) system of penalties.

Students who don't want to have their name written on the board, a note sent or a phone call home, or, heaven forbid, a visit to the office will toe the line and do their best to comply.

This fails for two spectacular reasons. First and foremost, it's time-consuming. You suddenly transform from a loving teacher to a behavior cop, sniffing out crime and always on the lookout for trouble. When you focus your attention on spotting misbehavior, that's what you'll always find. I'm not sure about you, but I got into education to transform lives, not to moonlight as a warden. That trajectory of behavior management doesn't let up because it's a never-ending job without completion or fulfillment.

The most common behavior management system that is employed throughout classrooms across the country is destined for failure.

The other reason focusing on punishment fails is known to many of you who have tried it yourself. There is a small subset of students (small being relative, of course) for whom punishment is either desired or laughable.

Call my parents? Good luck with that! My mom never answers the phone. She kicks me out at 6:00 a.m. every morning and won't let me back in until dinner.

Send me to the office? Great! At least I'll get to sit by myself and not have to listen to you prattle on about long division.

Oh, you're going to yell at me? You think that's going to make me cry? My daddy hits me so hard tears come to my eyes but I still don't cry. What are you going to do to me compared to that?

Swearing off punishment as soul-crushing and ultimately futile, both of which are accurate, some teachers swing to the other extreme as the only option left. They go with a reward system and hope that they can bribe students with homework passes, candy, and extra minutes at recess to improve behavior.

This behavior management approach typically doesn't last nearly as long the negative approach because its flaws stand out more clearly. First and foremost, it's just as exhausting as the negative approach. To make it work, you must chase your students around all day catching them doing good things, passing out Class Dojo points or putting marbles in a jar every time they meet your expectations. If you forget, they remind you and you grow resentful as they refuse to comply unless rewarded. The law of diminishing returns also sets in more quickly than you expect. The prizes you pick out for them were wonderfully motivating at first but now are shown to be the cheap dollar store trinkets that they are. You must up your game (and dip deeper into your paycheck) if you want to keep a sufficiently tantalizing carrot in front of the cart.

After teachers have tried both approaches, most will settle into a lackadaisical mishmash of the two that is just as ineffective but not nearly as tiring.

Fussing.

You go back to how you were most likely taught, with the teacher using verbal praise or criticism to keep students in line. It's low key but doable. It doesn't work all the time but neither did anything else. Yet it still relies on fear.

Fear

Punishment and reward both fail for the same reason. They both operate off of fear. As master Yoda told us, "Fear is the path to the dark side. Fear leads to anger. Anger leads to hate. Hate leads to suffering." For those that don't subscribe to the Star Wars mythology and need something closer to neuroscience to convince them, fear activates the survival state in children.

The amygdala is the part of our brains that is especially useful in dangerous situations. It hijacks the higher-order thinking parts of our brains and helps us focus on survival. When confronted with three large shapes moving toward us in a dark alley, the amygdala is what acts for us and pushes us to either fight, freeze, or run like crazy.

The survival state is great for dark alleys and post-apocalyptic survival movies. It's not so useful for the classroom. Leveraging fear, either of being punished or of not receiving a reward, triggers this part of students' brains. Though not as dangerous as a wild animal or scary monster, the continued invoking of children's survival states bypasses the parts of their brains we desperately want them to use.

When in a survival state, students' executive functioning is placed on hold. Their decision-making apparatus is temporarily on hiatus. They can sometimes act like savage beasts because that's exactly what their brains are trying to keep them safe from. As noted before and backed up by neuroscience or Yoda (your choice), the traditional approaches to behavior management that operate off of fear are counterproductive. They are exhausting and ultimately do not work.

So what does?

Judging and noticing

It all begins with a simple, essential shift from judging to noticing. When we judge students' actions, no one is safe. When we notice them, everyone can still be safe (Bailey, 2015).

Judging makes it about us while noticing makes it about our students. Judgment comes from our own emotional state and stimulates the emotional state in our students. When we notice students instead, it comes from our executive state and stimulates the executive state in our students.

Remember that at all times students (and we ourselves) operate in one of three brain states. The lowest is the aforementioned survival state, run by our amygdala and the brain stem, that is designed to keep us from being eaten by wolves. This state is helpful in a dark forest at night but not in a classroom.

Judging makes it about us while noticing makes it about our students.

The middle state is the emotional state. Dominated by our limbic system, this brain state is heavy on emotions and has an overpowering need for love and connection. Your typical fits, outbursts, and flashes of anger come from this part of the brain. Children here need connection and acceptance before they can move to the highest state.

The executive state is where we hope students can stay for the majority of their time at school. It's dominated by the prefrontal cortex and opens up to them problem-solving, integration, creativity, and self-regulation. This is where students learn.

Thus, you can hopefully see the problem with judging students' behaviors rather than simply noticing them. When we assign designations of good and bad, worthy and unworthy, to students' actions, words, and emotions, we come at them from a place of judgment derived from our own emotional state. That emotional state triggers its reflection in the students and we are doomed before we ever start.

Let's look at a simple example. You are passing out papers to your students and, as you are walking up and down the rows, you say, "Please take out your textbooks and open them to chapter three." You happen to glance over and you see Jennifer, a student who gives you constant problems, rolling her eyes and shaking her head. This behavior, rather than being done quietly and covertly, is instead performed within the view of several students who are giggling at her cheekiness.

You now have a choice as to how to respond.

Judging her would flow from her emotional state and sound something like this. "Jennifer, I saw that! Rolling your eyes is disrespectful and rude. We've talked about this before. I expect you to save that type of behavior for home because I'm not having it in here!"

As you can imagine, that type of response, in which you judged Jennifer's actions as disrespectful and reacted in kind, can do nothing but place Jennifer in an emotional state as the fireworks begin.

If you were to notice rather than judge, the response would look different. If Jennifer had rolled her eyes out of the view of a captive audience, you might have knelt down by her desk and asked her (kindly) if something was bothering her. Since she acted on stage, you need to address the actions for the benefit for all. "Jennifer, I noticed that you rolled your eyes and began to shake your head when I was instructing students to take out their books. Let's go up to my desk and discuss the situation privately. I want to be sure to listen to your concerns and answer any questions you might have."

While you might not use this type of formal language, the difference is clear. You didn't ignore Jennifer's behavior (which, to be honest, would be interpreted as disrespectful by most adults) nor did you pour gasoline on the fire. You noticed it and offered her a chance to discuss her concerns out of earshot of her audience.

As you listen, make sure you actually listen. You never know when a student is going to open up and reveal how something else is really bothering them and offer you a chance to support them. Judging makes it you versus them. Noticing places you alongside the student as you both discuss the behavior.

Ultimately, judging disconnects us while noticing connects us.

Attention

Noticing, then, is the filter through which we wield the only behavioral weapon we have in our arsenal.

Our attention.

What you focus on is what you get more of in your life. Sometimes colloquially referred to as the *yellow car syndrome*, our attention and where we place it has a magnifying effect on what we see. For new car owners, a common phenomenon is to suddenly see more of whatever type of car they just bought. If you recently purchased a new yellow convertible, then suddenly you see them everywhere. They haven't in fact multiplied in the last week or so. They've been there all along. The only thing that changed, then, is your attention.

Where you put your focus in the classroom determines your experience. Giving something your attention places an inherent value on it. Our reticular activating system (RAS), a bundle of nerves in our brain stem, serves many functions. One of its chief duties is to filter out unnecessary information. Our senses are constantly pumping data into our brain at a high, nonstop rate. The RAS filters out most of it as unnecessary and helps us keep only the most important items in our consciousness.

Take a moment to test it out. Stop and listen. Can you hear the air conditioning or heating system in the building you are in? Can you hear your own breathing? They've been there the whole time but your RAS, rightly, filtered them out as unnecessary. Our attention is too valuable a commodity to be wasted on obscure and inconsequential sensory data.

Where you put your focus in the classroom determines your experience.

With that little example, I hope you can begin to fathom the power of your attention. What you focus on creates more of the same in your life. When you focus on misbehavior, on behavioral and attitudinal transgressions, you inadvertently give them value and power.

You're creating more of what you don't want in your life and in your classroom.

Noticing children

When we notice children's behaviors and actions, we direct their power of attention in the same way. We facilitate their increasing self-awareness, activate their neuroplasticity, and empower change in their lives. When we notice children, we scaffold their frontal lobes by serving as an external source of power for their attention, directing them and sustaining their own fledgling abilities to focus and persist.

The real question isn't whether or not we're noticing them but what about them are we noticing?

One of our many roles as educators is that of an encourager. When we notice their positive behaviors, we connect with and accept them for who they are. To meet children's developmental needs in optimal ways, an utterly simplistic but life-changing tool is our attention. When we describe their effort and accomplishments through noticing, we help focus their attention on what they are doing right rather than what they are doing wrong.

Feed the positive and starve the negative. What you give your attention to, you get more of. If you think about it from the opposite perspective, you'll see how this is sadly true.

Behavioral science shows that if a behavior continues to occur, it is being reinforced (Sage, 2017). All behavior is communication and has a distinct purpose, even if that purpose isn't clear to the student or teacher. If a negative behavior continues, that behavior is achieving some purpose or gaining some type of desired response.

So many of our students' behaviors are cries for attention. They shout with their actions, "Notice me! See me! Let me know that I'm not alone!" With our fussing, scolding, and constant badgering, we are giving students exactly what they are wanting. Even though the attention is negative, it's what the students are looking for. When we react to students' misbehavior with our attention, we are teaching them that they can get our attention predictably by acting in certain ways.

Remember, your attention is your only offensive weapon in the fight for classroom management. You get to decide where to aim it.

What can you do tomorrow?

Decrease judging. When talking with students about their misbehavior, do so from a noticing rather than a judging approach. Describing a student action as bad or wrong comes from your emotional state and triggers a similar response in students.

Increase noticing. Describe (or notice) the behavior without assigning value to it. Talk with the child about the behavior dispassionately, as an ally, rather than as the judge, jury, and executioner.

What does this look like in the classroom?

The teacher **notices** student behavior, as evidenced by:
- Describing actions rather than judging them;
- Maintaining a calm disposition when discussing actions; and
- Listening fully while still upholding behavioral expectations.

How can you reflect on your learning?

Why aren't classroom management systems based on punishment and reward effective?

_____

_____

Think of a recent interaction with a student. What would it have sounded like if you had noticed rather than judged?

_____

_____

Social approval

Humans need many things to survive.

Most students learn at a young age that people need food, water, clothing, and shelter to survive at a basic level. While this list covers most everything, there is something missing that is key to taking charge of the classroom.

As a part of society, as communal creatures, students also need social approval. Being accepted, being a part of a larger relational unit, is a core emotional need for humans. While there are always exceptions to this rule, such as loners and hermits, they are few and far between.

Think about how this has played out in your own life. Think of a time in which you felt like you were on the outside looking in, like you didn't belong. What feelings went through your mind as you recognized that you were not accepted and not included?

Now examine these experiences from the other end of the spectrum. Bring to mind a memory of feeling included, of being surrounded by loved ones and friends. What made that moment so special? Why does it bring feelings of warmth and acceptance?

In the same way in which we don't often think of our breathing or our heart beating, as they are automated and unconscious processes, our inner desire for social approval often gets overlooked. That doesn't mean it's not powerful, however. Social approval is the only human need that can be leveraged to motivate student behavior in the classroom.

Selective attention

At the end of the book of Ecclesiastes, Solomon (the author) sums up his collected words of wisdom and philosophy by stating, "The end of the matter; all has been heard. Fear God and keep his commandments, for this is the whole duty of man."

I feel that something similar can be said for classroom and behavior management. Though everything else in this book plays a key role in forming the foundation of student success, including positive relationships, procedures, fostering agency, planning, and engaging instruction, the end of the matter is truly this.

The most effective process for teachers to maintain (and release) control in the classroom is for to selectively direct and withhold their attention based on student behavior.

Social approval is the only human need that can be leveraged to motivate student behavior in the classroom.

It might not be as glitzy and glamorous as respect agreements (which are wonderful) or reward systems (which peter out quickly as students reach satiation), but it's the only method that lies completely within teachers' power. You can't control students and you can't make them behave. What you can do is direct your attention where you will. If you want students to stop behaving inappropriately, reduce or eliminate the amount of attention you give to their misbehavior.

What directing your attention and social approval does is provides students with a window into their own success potential. When you focus on how students are succeeding, and narrate that success through your attention and social approval, you reinforce students' desire to succeed. That need for attention and inclusion is fed when they meet your expectations and you can foster a desire for more without ever having to resort to nagging, belittling, or behavior policing.

Ultimately, rigorous learning and application are the final outcomes that teachers are reaching for. Before internalizing a desire to learn, however, students must receive recognition for being successful at learning. It's the small actions and attitudes that students take, from tracking the teacher with their eyes to building stamina to sustaining attention that set the groundwork for deep learning. Teachers, by systematically directing social approval to every student for the advancements they make in these learning behaviors, can transform learning itself into a desire much like the natural hunger for food (Willans & Williams, 2018).

The consistent use of differential social attention subconsciously informs students that they will not be subjected to psychological pain. Trust is built because poor behavior, or behavior that misses the mark, is not called out. Instead, students meeting expectations are praised while attention-seeking misbehavior is ignored. This allows those students a chance to correct their actions and receive much needed praise without going through a cycle of shame and belittlement. This, then, gives them the space to begin regulating their emotions, inhibit inappropriate behavior, and pursue their developmental potential.

For those that wonder how ignoring, or refusing to give social approval, to misbehavior won't result in chaos and pandemonium, the key lies in creating success. When you are alert to the importance of students being successful in nearly every endeavor they undertake, you'll begin to find ways to manufacture success in even the smallest gestures. You can actively generate success by eliminating variables that get in its way, by minimizing emotional dysregulation, and creating a culture of safety. The more success students have, the more they want. There is no satiation point with success – heap it on! This never-ending need comes from our inborn wiring for social approval and a cycle of positive behavior soon follows.

The power of negative attention is in its predictability. For students that crave attention in any form, and have accustomed themselves to the repercussions of receiving it negatively, its constancy is a comfort. All a student has to do is speak out, get out of his seat, or make a rude noise to get a guaranteed, albeit negative, response from a teacher. To combat this, successful teachers learn to make positive attention as fast, predictable, and consistent as negative attention.

One final thought on differential social approval. Ignoring a misbehavior truly means acting as if it was not occurring. Many teachers, while not outwardly responding with a verbal reprimand, still pay attention to the misbehavior with nonverbal attention. Grimaces, frowns, grunts of displeasure, or even the hunch of your shoulders might be enough for students to continue their heinous ways. To truly change their behavior, you cannot merely limit the attention they get for acting out – you must eliminate it altogether.

Tapping on the shoulder

I act as if this is a new discovery but for me it's not. As memories do, one from over 20 years ago sticks in my mind like a splinter just underneath the surface of my skin. I learned that the most effective way to deal with an attention-seeking behavior is to ignore it.

The location was a dollar theater in Corona, CA. They had a double feature (now that was a bargain!) and I was sitting with a group of my college buddies taking up two rows. Before the movie began, I felt a tap on my shoulder. I turned around to see who it was but was instead met by a wall of blank stares.

Suspiciously blank.

As I faced the front again, I heard a few sniggers and muted laughs. Most of us have been here before.

For those of you that have had the pleasure of being on the receiving end of this game, you know it's pretty simple. Someone behind you taps you on the shoulder, trying to get your attention. You turn around expecting to see someone lean forward to speak to you. Instead, you get averted eyes and straight faces. When you ask, "Who tapped my shoulder?", everyone feigns innocence and you become angry. Rinse and repeat as desired.

For whatever reason, I was not in the mood to engage in this type of tomfoolery that day. Quickly, changing tactics, I waited for the inevitable shoulder tap to come again, which it did.

I did nothing.

The power of negative attention is in its predictability.

The tapping came again, this time a little more insistently.

Still nothing. I began to hear some noises behind me as fabric rustled.

There was one final attempt to anger me but I stoically sat in silence, refusing to engage.

I waited for the next round to begin but, to my surprise, nothing else came. It actually worked!

This rather juvenile example (we were in college, cut us some slack!)

illustrates in a nutshell the power of our attention. The shoulder tapping was typical attention-seeking behavior. The reward for that behavior was watching me flail around each time my shoulder was tapped and demand to know who did it. The game turned sour when I stopped giving my tormenter what he wanted. After a while, the one tapping on my shoulder began to look foolish instead of me and that simply wasn't fun anymore.

Much of the behavior that irks teachers in the classroom is attention-seeking. Students want to be recognized, noticed, seen, and attended to. When they don't get enough positive attention, they'll seek it any way they can. Beggars can't be choosers and negative attention is better than nothing. Successful teachers harness the power of their attention and heap loads of it on students for exhibiting the correct actions and attitudes.

To truly take charge of your classroom, you have to know how to praise.

Praise

When focusing on desired behaviors, the validation comes from a constant stream of praise from the teacher. Specific praise statements frequently have a suggestive influence on other students. When you are careful to explain the rationale for the appropriate behavior you are describing, students will slowly begin to understand the importance of everything that is expected of them (Willans & Williams, 2018).

So how much is enough? Remember, there is no satiation effect for positive approval. The more the merrier, but as a rule of thumb, try to manage about two praise statements per minute with zero or one redirection statement for every ten minutes. For many, that's a drastic shift. Some of you might be working with the opposite ratio, two redirection statements every minute and one praise statement every ten minutes.

Reinforce

How's that working for you?

We'll shortly look at what we should be praising, actions and attitudes, but let's first deconstruct a successful praise statement. Using the letters in the word *praise*, our successful behavior descriptions should be personal, recurring, assorted, immediate, specific, and enthusiastic.

Generic statements are like eating a snow cone with no syrup. You're just chomping on some ice. When praising students, make it personal. Include their names, make sure that you are directing it at someone or a few students in particular. If you say, "The class is getting out their textbooks," that's a broad description that's vague and impersonal. If you say, "Jerome has his textbook on his desk and is ready to learn," it's now personal and Jerome is feeling pretty good about himself.

Praise should also be recurring. If you are a sports fan, you know that for every television broadcast, you typically have at least two announcers in the booth. One is the play-by-play caller, producing a steady stream of narration about what's happening on the screen. The other is the color commentator, the analyst that chimes in periodically to offer a contrasting opinion or a different voice. When you're starting out, you need to be a play-by-play praiser. You need a steady, recurring stream of commentary describing positive behaviors. As your class gains a firm foundation in successful behaviors, you can back off (but never stop) and become more of a periodic color commentator.

Patterns are great for math and science but not for praise. Successful praise statements are assorted and varying. Even if personal, students will quickly tune out your praise if you only have three statements that you use repeatedly. Mix things up and keep it fresh or else run the risk of proving the adage that familiarity breeds contempt.

Immediate praise is a critical factor in selective attention. Even if you were to tie a praise statement successfully to something that happened five minutes before, maximum effect comes from an immediate reward. Think of how we train animals to perform a trick. With treats in hand, we help them perform whatever it is we are asking and immediately reward them with a treat when successful. That rapid reward begins to associate the trick with a positive outcome and a habit is born. Too much space between a positive behavior and a praise statement waters down its effect.

Specific statements can sometimes make all the difference in the world. While you might know what it means to get ready to learn, that broad statement has no teeth to it. If you say, "I see that Kaitlyn is ready to learn," students that want to mimic Kaitlyn's behavior are left to their own devices as to how to copy her. If, instead, you specify her behaviors, such as, "Kaitlyn has a pencil out and a piece of paper. I see that she's put her heading on the top and she's facing the board, waiting for instructions," now you've given other students a quick tip as to how to get ready to learn.

Too much space between a positive behavior and a praise statement waters down its effect.

Finally, praise statements must be enthusiastic. So much of what we communicate is not through the words we use but the tone of our voice, our facial expressions, body language, and other non-verbal factors. You can say, "De'Andre is lined up behind Janice with two squares in between," all day long but if it's with a flat tone and neutral expression, students won't know whether you're complimenting him or simply describing what you see. It's the enthusiasm you imbue into the praise statements that give it

REINFORCE

your stamp of approval and make it worthy of your attention.

One final word on praise statements. If you noticed, none of my sample statements included the phrases *I like* or *Thank you* or anything that carries a judgment. One of the hardest habits to break when changing our praise habits is taking our judgment of good or bad behavior out of them. When we color every statement with our own judgment by describing the behavior as something we like or something good, then we bring the behavior back into the realm of good and evil. That takes away power from students and puts us on the throne as supreme judge of the classroom.

Successful praise statements don't embed judgments because, by inference, those not receiving a praise statement are doing something wrong. This can put students back into a gray area of shame and triggers their limbic system and emotional outbursts. When teachers simply describe successful behaviors with praise statements (personal, recurring, assorted, immediate, specific, and enthusiastic), students get from you the one thing they want the most – your attention. Students not meeting your standards, and thus not receiving praise statements, aren't shamed for being bad. Instead, they are given a model as to how to receive your attention and an open opportunity to join in the fun.

What can you do tomorrow?

Praise. Choose a portion of the day and make a concerted effort to be a play-by-play praise announcer. Look for and describe positive actions made by students, keeping up a steady stream of noticing that is personal, recurring, assorted, immediate, specific, and enthusiastic. **Observe.** Watch to see how your descriptions affect the behavior of those students not initially meeting your expectations.

What does this look like in the classroom?

The teacher **praises** positive student choices, reinforcing beneficial behavior by:
- Frequently describing specific actions that meet expectations,
- Using an enthusiastic tone of voice; and
- Providing immediate and personal feedback.

How can you reflect on your learning?

Why is differential social attention so powerful?

_____

_____

Which part of the *praise* acronym is most natural to you? Which part will require the most change for your verbal patterns?

_____

_____

Immediate impact: Go to 1 – 4 Protection (Confidence) – pg. 71

The quality of one's life depends on the quality of attention. Whatever you pay attention to will grow more important in your life.

- Deepak Chopra

4 – 3 Action (Reinforce)

This is where taking charge gets tough.

You're probably still tracking with me when I exhort you to focus on the positive, to heap your attention and praise on the behaviors you want to see more of. All well and good.

But what about misbehaviors? Are you supposed to ignore those?

Yes.

First, don't shoot the messenger. I'm merely relaying what behavioral therapy and neuroscience have to say about attention and social approval. By withholding your attention from inappropriate behavior, the ignored behavior will weaken. If a student is punching another student in the face, that's not something you ignore. You immediately step in and keep all the students safe. But those moments are few and far between.

Here's an example of ignoring behaviors that are counterproductive to the class. Let's say you are an elementary teacher and you want your students to come to the carpet for story time. This is a procedure you've practiced many times and most students come and sit quietly on their assigned spot.

Except for John.

John thinks it's great fun to instead crawl under the kidney table next to the carpet and stare out from there, making faces at the other students. When this happens, you have several options. One, you can fuss at John and demand that he get out from under the table. Maybe he does, maybe he doesn't. Either way, he won't be in a place to learn because his brain will be flooded with negative emotions as he's scolded. Worst case scenario, he defies your authority and you're left with either looking incompetent or dragging him out bodily, neither of which is a good resolution.

By withholding your attention from inappropriate behavior, the ignored behavior will weaken.

Another option, however, is to use differential social attention. Knowing that this is Johns' go-to behavior when he wants attention, you starve him of it. You refuse to acknowledge him and instead heap praise on students who are meeting your expectations. You've already held many conversations with the class as a whole about ignoring students when they are misbehaving so you also praise them for staying focused on you while you read the story.

All of this happens while John is under the table sticking his tongue out at his classmates. After a while, though, John will grow bored because he's not getting the reaction he wants. He might come out and reluctantly join the students on the carpet. If he does, you find every excuse you can to praise him for meeting your expectations. It doesn't matter so much that he did it in his own time but that he did it at all.

In this alternate timeline, the worst-case scenario is that John stays under the table during the entire read aloud. Rather than growing bored and joining the class, he stays and continues to make faces. In this scenario, you can find an opportunity after the students are back at their desks and sit on the floor next to John. Talking calmly, you can explain how his actions did not meet your expectations but you know that he'll make better choices next time. You can even explain that you don't give attention to students misbehaving but instead focus on those making the right choices.

Conversation over, you allow John to choose what he wants to do in his own time. By taking these measures, even though it is a drawn-out approach, you've not thrown him into an amygdala hijack or created a power struggle. He can make the right choice without shame because you never showed him disdain or disapproval.

Short-term vs long-term

But some of you might be thinking, "All that is silliness. I just tell my students what they should be doing when they're misbehaving and they usually do it." True, when you tell students what to do, most will usually change their behavior immediately. In doing so, however, they are teaching you to direct your attention to problem behaviors. This unfortunately will strengthen the inappropriate behaviors and they will occur more often because they are getting what they want – your attention.

Don't confuse short-term gains with long-term wins. If you jump on the carousel of telling students how to behave when they are misbehaving, you'll find it difficult to jump off. Though you will see a lot of compliance, you'll end up going in circles as the students come to depend on and even crave the attention you give them by focusing on correcting their behavior.

If you find yourself going around and around with students about misbehavior, one possible cause is that you are still inadvertently directing your attention to minor irritations, either through comments, facial expressions, or even the teacher look. Most of us have developed the superhuman ability to communicate entire commands to miscreants merely through the intensity of our gaze. While it gives you a short-term win, it's still attention. Focusing on the negative behavior, even silently, will usually be enough to keep it going.

Starve it. Deny it. Let it wither and die.

This is where it really gets tough because it rubs against the grain of everything you've learned and what experience has taught you. Remember, though, that the most common type of misbehavior is attention-seeking behavior. When a child is acting out and you call his name, have the principal talk to him, or simply fuss at him, he's won. He's already received what he wants and anything else that happens will not be enough to deter that behavior from happening again.

Let's go back to the situation with John. In the short-term, it might appear that John has won or achieved his purpose because he was able to defy the teacher and sit under the table rather than on the carpet. That wasn't his goal, however. It wasn't flexible seating that John was after but attention, either from you, his peers, or both. He lost that battle because he didn't get what he wanted. When you approached him afterward, you explained the choice he should have made and why you didn't call attention to him. This was done in a calm, non-judgmental way. In the long-term, you won because he now learned (or was reminded) that your attention is reserved for those who are meeting your expectations.

Predictability

Negative attention-seeking behavior is usually so effective because the attention it receives is typically predictable, consistent, and efficient (Minahan & Rappaport, 2012). It can come quickly when a teacher has had enough and its intensity is also usually high. Nothing screams *attention!* like a teacher going red in the face or raising her voice to chastise a student. The volume and heightened emotion make this a quick fix that's easy and predictable for those students that crave it.

Ignoring negative behavior won't fix this or make it go away. Needs are needs and students need our attention. The answer is to make positive attention as predictable, intense, and efficient as negative attention. If your social approval is intermittent, lackluster, or simply boring, it won't be enough to replace the excitement of your negative attention. Also, if it's reserved for only the best students, your troublemakers won't bother trying to meet your expectations.

John and his classmates must know through experience that they will receive your attention when they meet your expectations, even if their timeline doesn't coincide with yours. If John does decide to make the right choice and come out from under the table to lay on the carpet, that's an action that needs to be acknowledged and praised. It can be something as simple as, "John has joined us on the carpet and is ready to listen to the story."

Two things to keep in mind about what might happen with John. First, his compliance will most likely not be exactly what you want. While everyone is quietly sitting crisscross applesauce in a square, John might lie down on the floor directly behind the carpet. He's moved out from the table but isn't completely ready to join the class. His partial compliance is better than disobedience and he can be acknowledged for (mostly) meeting your expectations.

Also, attention-seeking behavior sometimes ends after an extinction burst. It gets worse before it gets better as students will try one (or two) last-ditch attempts to get the attention they want before deciding it's not worth the effort. If John doesn't get the attention he needs by simply crawling underneath the table, he might raise the ante by making faces or noises. It will most likely increase in intensity before it disappears altogether.

Focusing on the negative behavior, even silently, will usually be enough to keep it going.

By making your attention predictable for students meeting your expectations, you can train your students to inhibit their attention-seeking behaviors. When they know that you'll only respond to their actions if they make good choices, they'll quickly learn that acting out will not give them what they want.

Words are important

Coming back to noticing vs. judging, we can sometimes have the right idea but execute it poorly if we don't carefully choose our words. Teachers should notice (i.e., describe) compliance with expectations with assertive, or straightforward, declarations (Bailey, 2015). For John, this might sound like, "You did it! You came to the carpet!" or simply, "Good for you!" For someone struggling to comply, something a little more energetic might be required to meet their attentional needs. Students that comply naturally might be satisfied with a simple description, such as, "Joanna is on the carpet and ready to learn," but students who struggle require more intensity to combat the potency of negative attention.

A simple slip, however, can undo all your work. If your go-to statements include judgments, then they move from noticing to evaluating. If John decided to eventually come out from under the table, and your response is, "Good job, John," then you have judged his behavior as good. While his behavior is indeed good, the silent judgment is that his previous behavior, that of crawling under the table, was not good. He was a bad boy while he was not complying but is now a good boy because he is.

Traditional praise statements that contain evaluations overlay children's sense of self with judgments about who we think they should be. Instead of developing a moral compass within themselves, their sense of right and wrong continues to remain external. While this can give us some immediate wins, it does little to strengthen students' resolve in the face of difficult choices. We do not want students to be dependent upon us or another adult to judge their actions as right or wrong. Instead, they need to learn how to guide themselves into beneficial behavior patterns because those are the ones that will help them thrive.

When we notice their positive behaviors and ignore the negative ones, we use their biological and sociological need for attention to strengthen this inner drive. Children learn new skills largely through trial and error. In video games, it's called *learning by death*. Students try something in a new game and their character dies. That immediate feedback teaches them that that action is undesirable and they should try something else. In the same way, trial and error can teach students which behaviors get them what they want, namely, social attention.

Trying to motivate students to comply with external praise doesn't build their self-esteem. At best, it requires you to not only continue the positive judgments but also increase them as their need for it grows. At worst, it plants the seed of addiction and ties students' compliance to your verbal approval or some type of token economy. This last possibility is the bane of many elementary teachers' existence.

If you've ever tried using stickers or a prize box in your classroom to encourage good behavior, you've felt the sting of addiction. What started as a simple box of dollar store bric-a-brac morphs into a weekly trip to Walmart to buy increasingly costly and elaborate prizes. After the newness has worn off, or after they've received three or four new pencils, those simply aren't motivating anymore. To get the same level of behavioral compliance, you must slowly increase the value of the items in the prize box. This slow creep will eventually become more than you can sustain.

We do not want students to be dependent upon us or another adult to judge their actions as right or wrong.

The only primary reinforcer that a teacher has control of is social approval which, thankfully, cannot be overdone. No satiation effect! Students will get tired of pencils and stickers but never be too full of praise that is personal, recurring, assorted, immediate, specific, and enthusiastic. When you learn to specify exactly how you want students to behave and you notice (not judge) those behaviors, you give students your attention appropriately. That noticing is the key that unlocks their habit-forming

Reinforce

system as they continue to associate attention with positive behavior. If they want your attention (and most students do), they'll quickly learn that there's only one way to do that.

They'll need to meet your behavioral expectations. Poor behavior will simply be ignored.

What can you do tomorrow?

Focus on the positive. As you increase your positive noticing to make it predictable and recurring, work to reduce or eliminate your attention to poor behavior. While it will take some retraining, both of yourself and your students, the long-term benefits outweigh the short-term discomfort.

Gird your loins. Be prepared for an extinction burst as students addicted to negative attention start showing withdrawal symptoms.

What does this look like in the classroom?

Students learn to **inhibit negative behaviors** through teacher actions, including:

- Receiving positive, enthusiastic attention when meeting expectations,
- Having negative behaviors ignored; and
- Not being shamed for making poor choices.

How can you reflect on your learning?

Why is ignoring negative behavior so hard?

_____

_____

Why is predictability for positive attention the key to breaking the cycle of negative attention?

_____

_____

Reinforce

Differential social attention

So, is it really as simple as that?

All you need to do is notice children doing the right things, give them verbal praise, and all your behavioral problems just disappear?

Yes and no.

In theory, differential social attention is relatively simple. If some students are out of their seats, you need to find a student or two who are in their seats and praise them. When some students are noisy, you need to find other students who are being quiet and notice them verbally. This process will strengthen appropriate behaviors and weaken the inappropriate ones. Your praise will have a suggestive influence on others while keeping misbehaving students from feeling shame and triggering emotional reactions.

But it's going to be harder than that for two reasons.

First and foremost, eliminating inappropriate behavior is not the goal. Students don't actually eliminate behaviors. They don't forget how to misbehave, they only inhibit behaviors in certain situations. Misbehavior is like cancer. You can beat it into remission but you are never truly in the clear. No matter how many good days you can string together, it's still there ready to jump out and catch you unaware.

Second, ignoring attention-seeking misbehavior is hard. It truly is. You were probably a (relatively) good student in school. You studied hard, got good grades, and achieved the goals you set for yourself. That's why you are a teacher. Instilled in you is a sense of right and wrong, of justice and duty. Ignoring blatant misbehavior is like watching someone shoplift at a store without saying a thing.

It goes against everything you believe in. You would never let your own children get away with those types of behaviors, so why should your students?

Because it's your best shot at improving your students' behavior and academic performance.

Two wrongs don't make a right

Here's the funny thing about behavior. Focusing on inappropriate behavior will never fix anything because it does not teach the appropriate actions. At best, you might be able to coerce students into inhibiting their negative urges. But that doesn't teach them what to do instead.

Your praise will have a suggestive influence on others while keeping misbehaving students from feeling shame and triggering emotional reactions.

If you have ever had the pleasure of trying to teach a young child how to play a sport, you probably have already figured this out. Let's say, for example, you are teaching your daughter how to swing a baseball bat. She grips it all wrong, doesn't stand perpendicular to the plate, nor does she know how to keep her elbow up. Instead of pointing out all the things she is doing wrong, which would be counterproductive, you would instead focus on the correct way to do it. You show her again and again the correct body position and technique and exhort her to mimic that.

It's the same principle for behavior. Focusing on what students are doing wrong does not teach them how to do it right. Two wrongs don't

Reinforce

make a right and the only time two negatives make a positive is when you're multiplying numbers.

Correct behavior only gets taught when it happens and then gets reinforced. Catch students doing something right, pour your attention onto it with appropriate praise, and they'll be on their way to repeating the action again and again. Even though it might go against every grain in your body, correcting students when they are misbehaving will, at the most, get that behavior to stop. Mere correction does not contain within it enough potency to teach the correct behavior even if children listen diligently to the reprimand.

The only way to teach students correct behavior is to watch for it to occur and reinforce it with differential social attention. It's extremely difficult to reinforce something that never happened.

Initiation and continuation

There are two types of positive behaviors that you should be on the watch for. The first type of behavior to scan for are initiation behaviors. When students start, or initiate, an action in accordance with your procedures or expectations, that is the moment to praise them. Even simple behaviors are worthy of your notice and should be commented on immediately.

For example, when you ask students to clean up their areas so they can get ready to switch classes, there will be opportunities galore to comment on the students who are initiating the correct action. "Carlos is putting his pencils away in his pencil box. Gabriel has put his books in his desk and is gathering up his supplies. I see that Angel is standing next to his desk with his chair pushed in, ready to switch classes." These behaviors will be transmitted and reinforced in other students as you give them the power of your attention.

An often overlooked type of behavior, but one worthy of your notice, is a continuation behavior. Sometimes students are making the best choice not just by starting an action but continuing it for a certain period of time. If students are supposed to be working with their partners to solve a math problem, they not only need to initiate the correct behaviors (e.g., writing their names on their papers, quietly talking together, showing their work), they also need to continue those behaviors for a set amount of time.

In many situations, misbehavior occurs not because students can't initiate the correct behaviors but because they can't sustain them. To maximize classroom learning, students need to grow their stamina in continuing desired behaviors. Elementary teachers face this difficulty head on as they try to build their students' ability to read silently for increasing amounts of time. If you've ever wondered what it felt like to cram 15 hours into four minutes, try getting a group of first graders to read on their own for an uninterrupted period of time.

In many situations, misbehavior occurs not because students can't initiate the correct behaviors but because they can't continue them.

As you notice behaviors, keep an eye out for students continuing to meet your expectations. This is what takes classroom empowerment to the next level as students get noticed for maintaining focus. For example, "Debbie and Hilda are talking quietly with each other. I see them both working on the math problem, sharing their ideas, and not distracting the partners around them. Yvette and Monica have already solved the problem and are now drawing a picture to represent their solution." While there might be only a certain number of times in the day that students should initiate correct behaviors, the opportunities to notice positive continuation behaviors are endless.

When students fail to finish their work on time, a good portion of the blame can be laid at the feet of poor work-related behaviors. As we've seen, berating or punishing students does not build in them the correct habits. If teachers want more students to finish their work in a timely and satisfactory manner, they must find and reinforce those desired behaviors. Helping students learn to stick with a task and complete their work is not dependent on eliminating unproductive behaviors but instead on developing productive ones.

Management systems

While differential social attention might not seem like a classroom management system, that's exactly what it is. Other systems that include consequences for inappropriate behavior, or warnings to students to change their behavior, will result in students finding ways to distract or disrupt classroom activities. Though it might seem counterintuitive, focusing only on positive behaviors will guide the students toward making better choices and inhibiting their inappropriate urges.

This constant flow of positive interactions will do much more than simply steer students, through the power of your attention, toward appropriate behaviors. This will also do much to strengthen the positive atmosphere in your classroom. If your students know that your room is one of encouragement and not of shame, that if they (or their peers) act poorly they will not be yelled at, you create a bubble of safety in an otherwise chaotic and sometimes negative world.

Remember, though, that your positive noticing, of both continuation and initiation actions, must be more than simple statements like, "You did it," or "Way to go!" Instead, they should specify the beneficial behavior, be directed at a student or students, and immediately follow the action. The power of your attention should be spread evenly amongst your students, not simply reserved for those with the best behavior. In fact, it's the behaviorally-challenged students that will probably need some extra attention to help support them as they try their hardest to inhibit their inappropriate urges.

Peer pressure can either work for you or against you. While often portrayed as a negative influence on young students, peer pressure can work in your favor if you know how to maximize it. Humans are wired for connection and community. We all want to be a part of something, a part of a larger group. When your classroom takes on the mantle of acting appropriately, of making beneficial choices because that's who they are, they begin to integrate these powerful choices into their class identity. Your class is a good class because that's who they are and what they're known for.

That's a powerful state that you can foster through the power of your social approval. For students to fit in, for them to feel a part of the class, your focus on positive behaviors can make that, rather than disruption, the norm. For students that want to fit in, to be a part of the class and accepted by their peers, they'll have no choice but to behave accordingly. Now that's using peer pressure to your advantage!

Safety

Not only does this system of classroom management work to promote

Reinforce

positive behaviors, it does so in a way that creates an atmosphere of trust and safety. Remember that one of your foundational, core ways of being as a teacher needs to revolve around protection. Your task, more than simply teaching students, is to nurture an environment that makes learning possible and probable. That comes from a feeling of safety which is, in turn, buttressed by differential social attention.

When you find positive ways to motivate appropriate behavior, students will have no reason to mistrust you. In the absence of negative consequences, students know that they are not at risk of being shamed in front of their peers. Using verbal praise that reinforces positive behavior continuously reminds students of your expectations (Willans & Williams, 2018). Rather than nagging students to death, your noticing is the simplest way to keep expectations front and center using an indirect method.

If you resort to coercion or disapproval of poor behavior as a way to control students, the feelings you'll elicit will run toward shame or the fear of being shamed. Keeping students in this heightened state of negative emotions will do much more harm than good, as their natural defense mechanisms will spend an extraordinary amount of psychological energy trying to keep them emotionally safe. Instead of promoting an atmosphere of serenity, you'll end up wading through a morass of chaos and fear.

Ultimately your effectiveness as a teacher might be judged, right or wrong, by your students' ability to perform on high-stakes, standardized tests. If they have difficulty showing mastery, your competence as a teacher might be called into question. There are many components to teaching and learning that fall outside of the scope of this book but one area that intersects neatly with classroom empowerment is independent work.

In most lessons, the students are required to work on a task or answer questions related to something you taught. Whether they do this individually, work with a partner, or even engage with a small group, students will daily have to initiate work-related behaviors and continue exhibiting them for the duration of the class period.

This is where things usually go south.

While they might have listened quietly during the direct teaching portion of the lesson (paying attention is quite another matter), they must initiate many positive behaviors and inhibit multiple negative urges to successfully work independently or with others. They must start the task right away and stay on topic. They must gather any needed materials and resist the urge to talk with their friends about the video game they played last night. They must ignore the rather loud conversation happening a few desks over about the pros and cons of Fortnite and PUBG. There are innumerable distractions that can keep students from working individually or with others on their assignment.

When you find positive ways to motivate appropriate behavior, students will have no reason to mistrust you.

When they can ignore those distractions and inhibit their inclinations toward negative behaviors, they set themselves up for success. This self-control, manifested by a wide range of actions, is key to building learning because learning is accelerated by doing. There's only so much that students can grasp by passive listening. Instead, actively participating in lessons is a hallmark of rigorous instruction. This participation hinges on positive behaviors and the suppression of negative actions.

Reinforce

For students to maximize their learning opportunities, they must master the ability to stay focused and diligently work on their learning tasks. If shaming and ridicule are used to keep them in line, the atmosphere will be negatively charged and their emotions will get in the way of their learning. If, however, you successfully employ differential social attention to praise and notice students for positive initiation and continuation behaviors, you'll create and sustain an environment ripe for academic growth.

What can you do tomorrow?

Differentiate. As you continue to use the power of differential social attention, note the opportunities for noticing and praising continuation behaviors.

Notice continuation. Take special notice of students who are staying focused, working independently, or even showing their work. As you describe these actions with praise statements, you'll begin to see more of them in the future.

What does this look like in the classroom?

Students receive **differential social attention** to reinforce good behaviors, such as:

- Noticing by the teacher when correct actions are initiated;
- Positive praise for continuing desired behaviors; and
- Immediate, descriptive feedback that narrates specific actions.

How can you reflect on your learning?

Why is eliminating misbehavior the wrong goal?

_____

_____

How does leaning on positive motivation for appropriate behavior affect the level of trust in your classroom?

_____

_____

Immediate impact: Go to 1 – 3 Positivity (Confidence) – pg. 49

We are all in the gutter, but some of us are looking at the stars.

- Oscar Wilde

4 – 4 Attitude (Reinforce)

I once had what I thought was a good idea.

Those can be dangerous.

At the time, I was the principal of a charter school in Arlington, Texas. It was a good school with relatively well-behaved students. While I didn't face many severe behavioral problems, I did want to promote positive behaviors. I instituted a *Caught Being Good* program amongst my staff and students. Instead of focusing on poor behaviors, I wanted my staff and students to focus on doing good things. If students were caught being good, a staff member or student could submit their name and deed on a slip of paper to the office.

Every Friday during announcements I would read through the slips of paper and celebrate all the students who had been caught being good during the week. I'd read about students helping friends, picking up papers and spilled food, and holding open the door on the way to recess. Some actions were trite and others were thoughtful, but, for the most part, I was pretty proud of my positive behavior program.

Until I wasn't.

I made it my goal as a principal to be in classrooms every day. Fearing losing touch with my teachers and students, I gave every effort to escape my desk and spend time out with the denizens of my learning community. This helped me keep my finger on the pulse of the school, so to speak. As all the students knew me (and I tried my hardest to know all of them), they would naturally speak to me as I encountered them in the hallways and classrooms.

It started slow at first, but then came on suddenly. Peppered into conversational exchanges with students were questions, "Did you see me, Mr. Daffern? I held the door," or, "Was I good Mr. Daffern?" as the child picked up a microscopic speck off the floor and flicked it in the general direction of the nearest trash can. More and more I saw and heard students doing good acts and then immediately asking for recognition, hoping to be highlighted during Friday's announcements.

It got to the point that one day I found myself having an esoteric conversation with a third grader. "Yes, James, I saw you open the door. That was very nice of you. Remember, though, that it's called *caught being good*. That means someone else has to catch you, you can't catch yourself." As both of us walked away confused, I realized that my good intentions had turned sour. While trying to populate the school with random acts of kindness, I had tied to them recognition and public acclaim. This had twisted the *Caught Being Good* program into something grotesque.

With my eyes now opened, I began to surreptitiously watch students and their behaviors in my peripheral vision. I saw them race down the hallway and shove each other in an effort to hold open a door for someone. Sometimes a clear winner was not evident and two or three students would block the doorway as they fought to see who got to hold it open. As students would do something nice for me, I would look them in the eye, call them by name, and tell them, "Thank you." I'd see the spark of hope die within them as they realized all I was going to do was thank them (how ungracious!) and wasn't going to officially catch them being good.

While the core idea behind it was right, focusing on positive behaviors, the implementation was doomed to fail, as it eventually did, because I had tied too much to the recognition. By focusing on positive behaviors, I had increased their value and given them worth by my attention. Yet for many students, the real payoff was in hearing their exploits over the announcements on Friday. If they realized that they weren't going to be recognized, many students lost interest.

Many of you have probably tried something similar on a smaller scale in your classroom at one time or another. Positive behavior systems, or token economies that deal in stickers, points, or stamps, quickly reach a satiation effect. To keep students motivated to earn points or stickers, the payoff must gradually increase. This creates an ever-upward cycle of need that ends in either students dropping out because of a lack of motivation or the teacher throwing in the towel because it's no longer worth the effort.

Attitudes are important

More than just noticing actions in the classroom, the attitudes that students foster play a large part in their success and the overall atmosphere of the classroom. If you can get students to do the right things, like my ill-fated *Caught Being Good* program, but they're done for the wrong reasons, you'll have solved one problem but created two more.

What attitudes do you want to see in your classroom? What mental models, in your opinion, are necessary to be successful? Knowing that using differential social attention, the power of your noticing, is enough to generate and sustain positive behaviors, how can you also use that to support attitudes that foster learning?

One key attitude to watch out for is positivity. Already spoken of in length in the initial section of this book, positivity is the fuel that keeps the classroom going. You, as the teacher, are the largest factor for setting the atmosphere in your class. Yet for all of your latent power, you are just one person. There will be times that even your positivity will falter in the face of circumstances and the baggage that your students bring in with them every day.

While you are noticing the students that are initiating and continuing the actions that best match your expectations, keep an eye out for those that exemplify positivity. As students work together, are they encouraging each other? When playing partner games, do they pout when losing or laugh and have fun?

Students can do all the right things but with all the wrong attitudes. If they reluctantly get out their books but do so while muttering under their breath, they are technically meeting your expectations but doing so with a bad attitude. When students line up to leave the classroom but slam their chairs into their desks, their attitude speaks louder than their compliance. In addition to noticing actions, we must also be on the lookout for attitudes.

Attitudes are not traits

One key to remember, and to bring to the forefront of your students' minds, is that attitudes are not traits. Physical traits are easy to pick out and make for a good analogy. I happen to be tall and skinny with brown hair and brown eyes. Though I could change my hair color with dye and my eye color with contacts, and even put on enough weight to no longer be considered thin, my physical traits are, for the most part, stationary. Students understand this and can easily recognize various parts of them that are outside of their control, like skin color, freckles, and other physical characteristics.

This type of thinking becomes dangerous when students apply this same thinking to their attitudes. When they begin to think that some people are just more naturally positive or negative, more calm or serious, they begin to feel defeated. They don't feel as if they have the power to change their physical traits, so why should they be able to change their dispositions?

Teachers noticing positive attitudes, and narrating them for students, reinforces the fact that everyone can choose their attitude. Bad things might happen to them, and their home lives may not be ideal, but everyone has the ability to focus on positivity rather than negativity. Just as they can choose which shirt to put on in the morning and how to comb their hair, students can choose to be positive even in the harshest circumstances.

Teachers noticing positive attitudes, and narrating them for students, reinforces the fact that everyone can choose their attitude.

When teaching this power, the easiest way is to explicitly talk about how to choose positivity. Using a simple analogy, like deciding whether to wear sneakers or sandals, talk to them about how the attitude they have affects everything they see and do but is ultimately under their control. Use empowering words like *choose* and *decide* to describe how students can make the choice to bring positivity to the classroom.

Also, when noticing students' attitudes, make sure to use descriptive phrases that highlight how students are making the decision to have a certain attitude. If two students are playing together and one student is losing with grace, saying, "I notice that Serena is happy while playing with Joan," sounds as if Serena has some embedded happiness trait that other students might not have. Saying that she *is* happy, like she *is* short or she *is* blond, downplays her choice in attitude.

A better way to phrase her positive attitude would be to include explicit terms that highlight her autonomy. "Serena is choosing to have fun while playing with Joan, even if she isn't winning. She's keeping a playful attitude," does a better job of not only noticing a good attitude for others to mimic but does so in a way that allows others to imitate it.

Attitudes are everywhere

If you presume the best in your students, if you give them the grace to believe that they are predominantly making good choices, you have endless opportunities to provide scaffolding for teaching students about their attitude choices. Let's take some simple situations and see how you can embed noticing both an action and an attitude with the power of your attention.

After you have given a set of instructions, typically after the direct instruction portion of your lesson, you expect students to get started right away. As a hum of activity rises in the room, you are naturally going to notice students who are making good choices. "Carlos has opened up his book and has already started working on the first problem. Genesis is writing her full name on the top of her paper, just like I've shown you, so that I can easily identify her work." This litany of noticing hopefully flows easily from you as you see students initiating actions.

But how can you take that to the next level? Why not attribute some positive attitudes to the students as they are working?

"Carlos has opened up his book and has already started working on the first problem. He knows how to manage his time wisely and is choosing to get as much done as he can before we head out to recess." Whether or not this is true of Carlos' intentions, you've now doubled-down on Carlos' good choice. Not only are you noticing his actions, but you've given them a rationale that promotes good decision-making and attributes intelligence and power to Carlos. He'll certainly keep going now that he thinks, perhaps for the first time, that he *should* get as much done as he can before recess.

"Genesis is writing her full name on the top of her paper, just like I've shown you, so that I can easily identify her work. She's not rushing but is paying attention to make sure everything is done right." This gives Genesis two boosts, one for her action and one for her attitude. This subtle reminder will serve not only her but other students within earshot as they will look over their work to make sure that they've done everything right as well.

Ascribing attitudes and intentions to continuation behaviors also works. "Jennifer is quietly reading in the library center. She works hard at reading because she knows that the best way to improve is to practice every day." Even though she's been quietly reading and might even be oblivious to your comment, other students have begun to fidget. By drawing attention to her persistence in continuing to read, you bring to other students' minds the expectation for sustained silent reading and its importance. The additional commentary about working hard and improving gives Jennifer a morale boost as she is seen (and hopefully sees herself) as studious and hard-working.

There are endless opportunities for you to notice the attitudes behind your students' actions. Sometimes they will truly be there but often they will be latent. The students themselves might not know why they do what they do but that shouldn't keep you from ascribing good intentions and attitudes to them. By naming and noticing positive attitudes, and doing so in a manner that supports their autonomy, you can not only encourage compliance and prosocial behaviors but also build within them the belief that how they approach their work and react to everyday situations is within their control.

What can you do tomorrow?

Notice attitudes. Add attitudes to your growing list of things to notice about children. When noticing their attitudes and intentions, be sure to incorporate language that shows that students can choose their attitudes.

Highlight the choice. Instead of calling a child positive or happy, praise how they are choosing to be positive or selecting a good attitude for the activity. This keeps students from thinking that only certain people can be happy or studious, friendly or comforting.

What does this look like in the classroom?

Classroom tasks build **camaraderie** between students, as evidenced by:
- Positive attitudes between students;
- Interdependence and peer assistance; and
- Embedded supports that allows for successful independent completion of tasks (if desired).

How can you reflect on your learning?

Why is noticing attitudes as important as noticing actions?

_____

_____

When describing attitudes, why is it helpful to highlight how students chose to exemplify that particular attitude?

_____

_____

Self-image

Students need both social and emotional knowledge and skills to navigate the classroom and life (Borba, 2017). One area that falls neatly into this portion of reinforcing certain attitudes and actions is moral identity. When teachers can help students develop prosocial images of themselves, their sense of who they are begins to change.

At the core of who they are, how do children define themselves?

Who are they? Are they, at their foundation, a good kid? A nice one? A sad one?

A child's self-image is shaped by sundry events and influences, many of which are outside of our control. Rather than blank slates, students come to us, regardless of the grade level, filled to the brim with ideas, identity markers, and perceptions about who they are and what kind of person they will become.

The good news is, however, that those self-images are subject to change. They are not set in concrete but instead in dried clay, firm enough on initial observation but pliable once moistened and softened. But why should we give two figs about how students view themselves?

As humans, we generally behave in ways consistent with our self-image. I see myself as a funny, witty guy and often act in situations to support those views. I'm always quick to make a joke and enjoy a good theoretical debate. That's how I view myself because my past is filled with instances in which I have behaved in this manner.

If, on the other hand, I consciously worked on being silent and slow to speak, I could, through concerted effort, change my behavior and how I view myself. For quite a while, I would be acting against my inclinations because that's not how I see myself. I could change, if I really wanted to, but it would be a long and arduous process (and quite frankly, not worth it for me). How I see myself has accustomed me to act in certain ways in any given situation.

What if students saw themselves as kind?

Moral identity

When students define themselves as caring, responsible people who value the thoughts and feelings of others, they'll act in accordance with their self-perception. This positive moral identity will be their default response, so to speak, that guides their reactions throughout each day. Students will still have emotional meltdowns and some bad days, but overall, they'll typically interact with others in alignment with their self-identity.

As humans, we generally behave in ways consistent with our self-image.

This is more than simply another piece of classroom empowerment. Children's moral identity shapes their character and the adults they will eventually grow into. Having a view of oneself as caring, kind, and helpful is critical for raising empathetic children that thrive. Students that don't view themselves in a positive light tend to struggle all throughout school, manifesting a host of social and academic problems. A strong moral identity can serve as a base camp from which they venture out to further explore the world and add layers of complexity to the image they hold of themselves.

For example, students who hold a view of themselves as altruistic will be almost compelled to help others in need. When a classmate is struggling with a math problem, needs to be cheered up, or simply spilled her pencil box all across the floor, students with a *helper* moral identity will be the first ones to assist. They won't need to be told or even coaxed to help because to not help would be as strange as forgetting to breathe. It's simply who they are.

Too much of a good thing

So how can teachers help develop a strong moral identity in their students? The answer is not as obvious as it seems. If you simply use your gut instinct, you might begin to heap praise on students. Rather than building their internal character, the result of this misguided approach will most likely be to create little monsters.

Praise is a good thing and students naturally want (and need) to feel good about themselves. Too much focus on how wonderful students are, however, can lead some to focus too much on themselves. Students overflowing with praise can become self-centered, competitive, and cut-throat. If they become addicted to genuine praise in reaction to what they do or say, they will grow accustomed to it and need it to feel good about themselves.

When a child holds the door open for a classmate or picks up papers that have spilled on the floor, those actions are exactly what we are looking for as educators. Our natural instinct is to praise the student and thank him for being such a good helper. Unbeknownst to us, however, is the seed of addiction this can plant in students if we are not careful.

This is exactly what happened in my aforementioned *Caught Being Good* disaster. The students in my school came to crave the recognition more than the satisfaction of doing the right thing. They competed with each other, shoving others out of the way as they raced for a door to hold for their classmates. As they picked spilled papers off the ground, they looked around to see if an adult was watching and noticing them. They needed the recognition to satisfy the urge within them to be seen.

Even though verbal, this was still a form of extrinsic, or external, rewards and those always peter out. Students need an increasing dosage of the reward to satisfy the same inner urge and eventually the stakes become too high and the system collapses in on itself. While the outward actions are exemplary (for the most part), students caught in this cycle will eventually turn sour to the system and abandon it as a lost cause. Initial reactions will wane as they cease to get the same thrill from being recognized for doing the right thing.

Actions match identity

The solution requires a minor adjustment to how we recognize and praise students for doing the right thing. As they exhibit behaviors and attitudes that are conducive to their own and to others' success, we want to notice them and give them our attention. When a child helps a friend pick up papers that have scattered on the ground, a recommended response simply notices the behavior. "Justine, you're helping Maria pick up her papers. That's very thoughtful!"

While this does give praise according to the *praise* acronym (personal, recurring, assorted, immediate, specific, and enthusiastic), it can be taken to the next level by referencing a moral identity. "Justine, you're helping Maria pick up her papers. You're the kind of person who always lends a hand."

Do you see what that last sentence did? It matched her actions of helping her friend to her moral identity as a student who always lends a hand to others. Now, does Justine see herself as someone who typically lends a hand? Maybe, maybe not. By hearing her teacher ascribe her behavior to her moral identity, however, she's much more likely to do something similar in the future, which is the point of the entire exercise.

Remember that students (and people in general) typically act in alignment with who they see themselves to be. If they are noticed helping a friend and have that action or attitude tied to their moral identity, it strengthens that behavior so that it's more likely to occur again in the future. Another way to use this technique is to use positive nouns when describing children. If they are helping a friend, call them a *helper*. If they are playing nicely with a classmate, call them a *good friend*.

The same principle applies to students exhibiting positive attitudes. If playing a partner game and staying focused on it rather than the noise around them, you can notice the students, their actions, and their attitudes while still tying them to their identities. "You two are focused on the game. You're both showing determination in playing your very best."

When the noticing and praising shift moves from just their behaviors to their moral identities, these traits begin to actualize in their minds. Words are powerful and can cause great harm or provide great comfort. When students hear the praise statements directed toward them describe not only what they do but who they are, they begin to build their inner monologue. These descriptions stay with them as, unknowingly, they will use them as a filter for making future choices.

When someone else needs help picking up items, they'll be just a bit quicker to help because they view themselves as *helpers*. When a classmate is walking alone on the playground, they'll run over to invite them to play that much sooner if they see themselves as *good friends*. Depositing these words of power not only serve as an example in the moment, directing off-task behavior toward those that are meeting your expectations, they also grow interest and will pay hefty dividends in the future.

The power of your attention

Taken altogether, your attention has great power to not only shift the atmosphere in your classroom but also set students up for a lifetime of success. As they naturally seek attention, being the social creatures that they are, choosing to reserve your noticing to positive examples of behavior is a strong tool in your arsenal of empowerment. It is something that not only works but also lies completely within your power.

Too often, methods designed to help you manage classroom behavior are simply various forms of coercion and control. From token economies and reward systems to progressive discipline punishments (who remembers having their name written on the board with a check mark next to it?), you ultimately only have control of one person – you. Any program or intervention system with the understood purpose of controlling students' behavior is doomed to failure.

Not only can you not ever truly control someone else's behavior, even if you force compliance upon them you are damaging their ability to self-regulate in the future. True empowerment comes when students learn to manage their own behavior, when they act from an internal identity aligned with good behavior and empowering choices. Noticing students that act in accordance with the best wishes of the class reinforces these behaviors without shaming those that are missing the mark.

Tying these behaviors into their moral identity is what truly sets them up for future success. When students see themselves as well-behaved, good friends, or helpful students, they will operate and behave from this position even when no one is watching. The effects of how they view themselves will be felt far beyond the one year you have with them.

You have the power to shape their entire future.

Yet how they act and conduct themselves is not the sole aim of differential social attention. We want to build a brighter future by equipping students with the power of empathy and traits of kindness and generosity. To respond to others in an understanding and empathetic manner, students must first see themselves as people who value others' thoughts and feelings. Those that don't already have this innate self-image can have it crafted by noticing their actions and attributing them to their moral identities.

Any program or intervention system with the understood purpose of controlling students' behavior is doomed to failure.

Students will often share things with each other, such as letting a friend borrow a pencil or a sheet of paper. Even this tiny act, played out daily in classrooms across the country, gives you an opportunity to speak into the core of who they are. A typical praise statement would notice the act, such as, "Sharing your pencil was considerate." To add one extra bit of hook to the statement, tie it into who they are as a person, such as, "You shared your pencil. You are a considerate and helpful friend."

Who am I?

When speaking to students about how to reason morally about actions to take or avoid, you can also share with them a simple test they can use to decide on a course of action. When thinking about whether or not to do something, such as throwing their game pieces across the room because they are upset at losing, they can ask themselves, "Does this go against who I am as a person?" While many students might not have the wherewithal to stop on a dime and apply this test before an action, it's a powerful discussion tool after an incident.

After the child has calmed down and you need to discuss a child's behavior and the natural consequences, a typical feeling would be one of shame or anger. Students might not know how to process what just happened and might take any redirection as a further indictment of their poor moral quality. Already feeling overcome with emotions, adults can sometimes add to their distress by tying those actions into the child's nature. In addition to feeling overwhelmed because of the emotions of the moment, they will begin to infuse these negative descriptors into their self-identity. After enough time, they'll begin to act negatively because that's how they see themselves.

Instead, use the Who Am I? test as a tool to separate their actions from their self-identity. "Elena, I know that you're upset because you lost the game. In your frustration, you threw your game pieces across the room. I know that's not who you are, though. You're a good friend and you didn't want to hurt Derek's feelings. How can we make this right?" Now you and Elena are sitting side-by-side, dispassionately examining her actions that are separate from her moral identity. She's a good friend that just made a poor choice in the moment, like we all do. She can now reconcile with Derek and move on without taking a hit to her pride or her self-perception.

That's the power of noticing and moral identity.

What can you do tomorrow?

Spotlight moral identity. When you notice the positive attitudes and intentions of students, you are speaking into their moral identity.

Stay positive. When talking to students about misbehavior, do not attribute their poor choices to who they are. Instead, declare that they are in fact kind, compassionate students who acted out of accordance with who they are.

What does this look like in the classroom?

Classroom responsibilities promote a **positive moral identity** in students by:

- Encouraging students to help and serve one another;
- Allowing students to build positive self-images through their actions; and
- Reinforcing the communal structure and interdependence of the classroom.

How can you reflect on your learning?

How does our self-identity impact our behaviors?

_____

_____

Why is developing a positive moral identity in students so important?

_____

_____

Immediate impact: Go to 1 – 2 Purpose (Confidence) – pg. 29

4 – 5 Conclusion (Reinforce)

There's a popular t-shirt that simply says, "I teach. What's your superpower?"

While that's a nice sentiment, for our purposes I'd like to change it to, "I teach. My attention *is* my superpower."

Remember that in the metaphor for change management (Heath & Heath, 2010), motivating the elephant is one of the three avenues for making a switch. The elephant represents our emotional side and, as much as we like to tell ourselves that we are rational creatures, we're not. We are emotional beings with just a hint of logic desperately hanging on for dear life.

The third section of this book discussed anticipating problems and shaping the path to avoid as many as possible. The next section will discuss directing the rider, in this case our rational sides, and helping students grow their interpersonal, intrapersonal, and intellectual skills. Yet the metaphor of the elephant and the rider is so apt because those two avenues pale in comparison to motivating the elephant.

Helping students switch their behavior patterns is helped greatly by anticipation (shape the path) and growth (direct the rider).

Yet it's impossible without reinforcement (motivating the elephant). Without engaging the emotions, you simply won't reach deep enough into your students to help them regulate their behavior.

Without the power of your attention, you can't take charge of your classroom.

Your attention is your superpower and, unfortunately, most of us have been using that power for evil. By constant badgering, nagging, and fussing, we've trained our students over the years that our attention can be obtained through positive or negative actions. While we would obviously prefer the former, some students are just fine with the latter.

Yet don't beat yourself up over your natural inclination to fuss at students for misbehaviors. It has a perfectly logical origin that has been strengthened over the years. In typical schools of yesteryear, that's how teachers kept order. They got onto the students who transgressed and that usually worked. Veiled threats, a visit to the principal's office, and even a paddling or two was enough to keep students on the straight and narrow.

I don't have to tell you that today's students are not like us when we were in school. Things have changed. It doesn't really matter why they've changed or who's to blame, we just need to accept it.

Twenty years ago, AT&T made their money by providing phone service that included long-distance fees. I'd be willing to bet that you haven't paid long-distance fees in over a decade and that you don't even have a landline. Times changed and AT&T, along with other telecommunications companies, changed with them and now provide high-speed internet and cellular service.

When we were in school, focusing on misbehavior to root it out mostly worked.

Times changed. Have you?

Another reason that you might naturally be drawn to focusing your attention on misbehavior to get it to stop is that it probably worked (and still works) for you personally. Not only was it the prevalent strategy for classroom management in your formative years, it's probably still effective for you today.

Think about getting called out in a faculty meeting for showing up late or not having your attendance in on time. What feelings emerge? What would that do to you?

If you're like me, you have a healthy fear of missing the mark. You would do anything to not be exposed like that. The mere thought of being shown to be deficient in front of your peers is enough to motivate you to do what you're supposed to do. That's fear-based management and it might just work for you. Thus it's natural for you to think, "It works for me so it should work for my students."

Yet we know it doesn't. There are several reasons why.

First, you are an adult. You have enough emotional fortitude, enough self-regulation skills, and enough of a core identity of success that you can weather those negative emotions. They don't make you melt down (unless you actually are called out – heaven forbid!) but instead motivate you to toe the line.

You can't say that of all your students. Without a strong psychological and emotional foundation, the negative attention you heap on them for their transgressions won't be something they can shy away from. If they are attention-deficient, they'll take it however they can get it. Your negative attention won't shame them into acting right because they don't have enough mental dexterity to differentiate between positive and negative attention.

Without engaging the emotions, you simply won't reach deep enough into your students to help them regulate their behavior.

Second, the most negative attention can do is compel students to inhibit their negative urges. They can stop when you yell, "Stop!" and be quiet when you yell, "Shut up!" That type of correction, however, never tells them what to do instead. It's not corrective, nor is it instructive. You don't teach a child to read by screaming at him when he can't sound out a word. You show him the necessary skills and practice until it becomes natural.

Finally, fear-based management doesn't actually work long-term for anyone. If you think to yourself, "Well, I don't know what's wrong with kids these days, but it worked for me," you're fooling yourself. I didn't work for you either. Fear-based management, even if it does stop misbehavior, has many negative side effects that might not be immediately apparent.

REINFORCE

Let's say that you did forget to turn in your attendance on time. The principal calls you out in the faculty meeting and you become embarrassed. One result of the public chastisement is that you would be sure that your attendance was on time from now on, which is probably what the principal was intending.

But you would also be closed to new learning. You'd spend the faculty meeting stewing over the situation, either blaming the principal for being a fascist jerk (I know of two other people who never turn in their attendance, but were they called out?) or beating yourself up with negative self-talk. Either way, everything else is lost to you. When you don't feel safe psychologically, you can't learn.

That's why only reinforcing desired actions and attitudes is so important. By only noticing the positive, you highlight the behaviors you want to see more of without shaming those who aren't meeting your expectations. You sate the students' need for attention by ensuring that the behaviors you want will be repeated, not the ones you don't want.

When you don't feel safe psychologically, you can't learn.

Think about how you'd feel if the principal had instead opened with the following statement.

"I'd like to thank everyone who continues to turn in their attendance on time. As you know, it's due at 10:00 every morning. Kim, Aurora, Viviam, Andrea, Sandra, and Zoe, to just name a few, always turn theirs in every day promptly at 10:00." This would have restated the expectation without shame and caused you to remember that you hadn't turned yours in that day. You would have hurriedly pulled out your laptop to submit it and then focused back on the meeting, ready to learn.

That's the power of using your attention to notice beneficial behaviors.

CONFIDENCE

HEART

ANTICIPATE

REINFORCE

GROW

ENGAGE

5 – 1 Introduction (Grow)

One of several metaphors used in this book to understand how to take charge of the classroom is comparing the entire process to an American football team. The first two sections of the book, charge and anticipate, focus on defense, getting yourself right as the professional educator and guarding against negativity and cynicism. The middle two sections, anticipate and reinforce, focus on offense. In most situations, it's the offense, not the defense, that scores the points. The offense takes the fight to the opposing team and that's what anticipating and reinforcing does.

Now we come to the final two portions of the book, grow and engage. These two components represent the special teams unit of any American football team. These players return kickoffs and punts, attempt field goals, and defend against these as well. While not as glitzy and glamorous as offense or defense, special teams can change the outcome of the game in an instant. They can flip the field, so to speak, and provide their offense with outstanding field position. They can block the game-winning field goal and keep the other team from victory.

That's what these next two sections, grow and engage, can do for your classroom. Though the core of behavior management was discussed in the middle two sections and the core of your classroom environment was looked at in the first two, these last two have the potential of supercharging everything.

After all, while improving classroom management is a great goal, it's not the final goal. Ultimately, everything comes down to student achievement. Can they pass the test? Will they perform on the standardized assessment? Those results typically separate the good teachers from the great teachers.

That's what the next two sections look at. Once you have a positive classroom atmosphere and solid behavioral management skills, you need to go ahead and win the game. It's time to empower your instruction and ensure that every student succeeds at a high level.

Ultimately, everything comes down to student achievement.

This section of the book, grow, looks specifically at three types of skills that successful students have. While it would be great for students to come with these abilities already preinstalled in their behavioral hard drives, most of them don't. Yet the choice of words here, *skills* and *abilities*, show that they can be learned.

Reading is a skill. Students aren't born with it but learn to read fluently with explicit instruction and ample practice. Writing code in JavaScript, playing the tenor sax, throwing a curveball – all are skills that people learn.

True, some might have a natural aptitude for some physical or intellectual skills, but that does not mean that they cannot be learned. Anyone can learn to do anything with a reasonable degree of skill with enough instruction and practice.

If you don't believe that, you might want to skip this entire section.

If you can learn to read, you can learn emotional literacy and empathy. If you can learn to dribble a soccer ball, you can learn to show grit and resilience. If you can develop artistic skill and passion, you can develop a growth mindset. If, through focus and feedback, you can develop a growing ability for chess or golf, why not intellectual skills like curiosity and creativity?

Everything can be learned and developed to a reasonable degree of skill with enough instruction and practice.

Many students, even if they learn to regulate their behavior, are still hampered in their success because of a lack of interpersonal, intrapersonal, or intellectual skills. They might know how to multiply two-digit numbers, derive the quadratic equation, or write a limerick, but they also give up too easily, don't take academic risks, and can't think outside the box. We know that students who succeed beyond high school, those that jump into the world and flourish, have as many soft skills as hard skills.

In the workplace, writing a five paragraph essay isn't nearly as important as understanding the emotions of others. Correctly calculating the velocity of a moving object pales in comparison to being able to work on a team. Identifying the main idea of a paragraph seems useless if students are unable to come up with new and unique solutions.

There is no textbook solution for life.

In this section of taking charge, we'll look at growing three types of skills that you can actively nurture in your students. The first are interpersonal skills. The ability to understand yourself and others, to know how to communicate effectively, and how to read the emotional currents underneath the surface, are skills that can make or break the success of students. While there are entire books dedicated to this topic, we'll focus on two aspects that will serve not as comprehensive summaries but as conversation starters – emotional literacy and empathy.

Everything can be learned and developed to a reasonable degree of skill with enough instruction and practice.

Additionally, students should spend as much time developing intrapersonal skills as they do memorizing math facts or vocabulary terms. After all, most of what is learned in school today is readily accessible through a smartphone. Students can Google when the Treaty of Versailles was signed or ask Siri about the periodic table of elements. What students should internalize, in addition to factual knowledge, are strengths such as grit and mindset. If you embed resilience and feedback that strengthens a growth mindset, your students will be unstoppable.

Finally, not everything that needs to be learned is found in a book, course, or even a classroom. The best and brightest students learn on their own. They inhabit a space of exploration, taking on new challenges and playing with new concepts naturally rather than under compulsion. Curiosity and creativity are two intellectual skills that you can teach and develop in students much like you teach how to subtract across zeros.

Ready to take your classroom to the next level? With a positive classroom environment (confidence and heart) and effective behavior management skills (anticipate and reinforce), the fun can really begin. Growing interpersonal, intrapersonal, and intellectual skills in students can flip the field and make teaching infinitely easier and more enjoyable.

When dealing with people, remember you are not dealing with creatures of logic, but with creatures of emotion.

- Dale Carnegie

5 – 2 Interpersonal (Grow)

It's amazing what a few years' difference can make.

In 2010 my family and I decided to visit my parents in Ypsilanti, Michigan. This trip from our home in Fort Worth, Texas to just outside Ann Arbor, Michigan, is a mere 1,200 miles. One of the highlights of the trip, at least to me, was finding different routes to and from their home.

You see, I love exploring new places. The trip itself is as exciting (or possibly more) than the chance to see my parents and spend time with them. If we wanted to, we could have taken a fairly straight approach by utilizing interstate highways. The straightest route is interstate 30 northeast from Fort Worth to Little Rock. Continue in the same direction on interstate 40 to Memphis and then head north on interstates 55 and 57 to Chicago. From there it's a straight shot east on interstate 94 and you're there.

So boring.

No, I like finding state highways and backroads. Though the iPhone and other GPS devices were available, I hadn't caught on yet. My flip phone and I were doing just fine, thank you very much. No, I had my trusty Rand McNally road atlas detailing the highway systems of each of the fifty states, including insets with more detail of metro areas. What could possibly go wrong?

Long story short, we made it.

Barely.

One instance I remember quite well was somewhere on the state line between Arkansas and Missouri. The route I had highlighted in yellow seemed so clear on paper but it didn't quite translate as nicely to reality. With my wife questioning my sanity and my spatial awareness, and my dogged determination that the next turn was less than an inch away, we painfully made it across the country. Those feelings of being untethered and free, however, are ones that I'm not sure my children will ever experience.

Nowadays, cars integrate Google Maps into visual displays that sync to your smart phone so you can get turn-by-turn directions to the Walmart two miles down the road that you've been to hundreds of times. No matter where you are or where you go, you are never truly lost when you have a smartphone with you.

Our emotions in many ways act as our internal guidance system. Our emotions signal us when things are out of balance (Bailey, 2015). They help us discern right from wrong and, without access to how we feel, we're like travelers without a map or a smartphone. We cannot see the consequences of our behaviors or even change course to avoid obstacles.

RULER

Marc A. Brackett, psychologist, professor, and founder and director of the Yale Center for Emotional Intelligence, detailed the importance of emotional intelligence (Brackett, 2018). Emotions, once thought to be separate from logic and rational thought, are in fact integral to everything we do. When schools and teachers recognize that emotions drive much of how and what students learn, they are able to better take advantage of learning opportunities.

Strengthening the social-emotional skills of students can reduce the harm that difficult and strong feelings can have on learning. These emotions are not only relevant to intelligence but can affect cognition and distort perception. Ignoring the social-emotional intelligence of students and focusing strictly on developing their reading and math skills is foolhardy at best and dangerous at worst. It's akin to ignoring signs on the beach about riptides and deciding to go on a long swim on your own.

Brackett has developed the acronym RULER to detail important components of growing the social-emotional intelligence of students. First, students should be taught how to *recognize* their own emotions by attending to their thoughts and physiology. Along the same lines, students can benefit greatly by recognizing the emotions of others by attending to their facial expressions, body language, and tone of voice. Without this ability to recognize and name emotions, both in themselves and others, their ability to navigate the treacherous waters of social interaction will be greatly diminished.

Next, students should learn to *understand* the causes of emotions. Rather than thinking of emotions as uncontrollable urges that take them over without consent, students can be taught to examine emotions objectively, seeing them as transitory influences rather than permanent states. This knowledge will then help them understand how their emotions affect their decisions, their behavior, and even their learning. With knowledge of emotions comes power and a sense of control.

Along with the ability to recognize and understand emotions, students benefit when they can *label* them, both theirs and others', with a nuanced vocabulary. Most students are familiar with basic terms such as *sad*, *happy*, and *scared*. While these terms are good entry points into emotional literacy, they fail to capture even a hint of the full range of emotions that we are capable of. Instead of naming their current emotional state as *sad*, it would be good for students to have a spectrum of descriptive terms, such as *discouraged*, *sullen*, and *desolate*.

The fourth part of the RULER acronym is the ability to *express* emotions in accordance with cultural norms and the social context. When is it appropriate to laugh? To tell a joke? When should students be silent and serious? Many students struggle socially because they are unsure of the appropriate way to behave in certain situations. Other times, they might not be adept at reading social cues and lack the flexibility needed to navigate through complex social interactions.

With knowledge of emotions comes power and a sense of control.

Finally, students need skills to be able to *regulate* their emotions. This not only gives them the ability to stay even-keeled in the midst of tumultuous feelings, this helps them achieve goals, both academic and personal, and to maintain healthy well-being. Instead of being subject to the whims and vicissitudes of their feelings, students can feel powerful and full of agency when they learn how to manage their emotions.

What's the end result of using a systemic social-emotional learning program like RULER? Students learning about their emotions have the ability to not only transform a classroom but also an entire school. School administrators, teachers, students, and even parents begin to interact with each other more positively. Classroom experiences improve overall and academic achievement soars while problem behavior, bullying, and stress start to drop.

Emotional states

In *Teaching with the Brain in Mind*, Eric Jensen (2005) shares that emotional states are something that we experience. They come and go like waves on a shore and the tides of the ocean. They happen to you but are not you. This distinction is fine but necessary because many students that fail to note the difference can begin to define themselves by their emotional states.

If, for example, you are often happy and gregarious, you will probably see yourself as a cheerful person. This self-identity will be shared by others as they begin to form generalization based on these typical emotional states. While having a positive image is helpful, it's not always true. Sometimes people who are strongly labelled as *cheerful* feel trapped in that role and have difficulty expressing other, more negative emotions, even when they are natural.

Likewise, someone who is more pessimistic and morose can be tagged as a downer and a party pooper. These people begin to see themselves through the lens of these emotions and struggle to shift into more neutral or positive emotional states. If for some reason they are not in a bad mood when interacting with friends, this change of state can sometimes shock others and cause awkward social interactions.

When students learn to become attuned to their emotional states, especially with a nuanced vocabulary, they begin to distance their core identity from these feelings. They can stand aside, so to speak, and observe these emotions and even begin to influence them. They aren't sad, they just feel sad. They aren't angry, they merely feel angry. With this knowledge comes the ability to change their feelings productively.

If I wanted to change my height, I'd be hard pressed to do so. I've been the same height since I reached maturity and I'll only lose height as I begin to hunch over with old age. My height is a fixed quality about me that is, for the most part, out of my control to change. I'm fine with my height, so it's not a problem, but many people wistfully wish they could be a little bit taller or even a little bit shorter.

My weight, on the other hand, is within my control. Though I can't directly affect my metabolism and body structure, I have total control over my diet and my exercise. I can, if I choose, bulk up with protein shakes and massed weightlifting. If I wanted to, I could go on a cardio kick and slim down. How I eat and how I exercise put my weight in my sphere of influence.

How do students view their emotions? Do they see them as fixed feelings that savage them without mercy? If they view their emotions like a fixed physical quality like height, it's easy to see how they can quickly become disheartened. The truth of the matter is our emotions are transient and within our sphere of influence. We cannot turn them off and on like a light switch, but with dedicated attention and discipline, they can be managed much like our weight.

That's powerful!

Emotional literacy

Social-emotional literacy as a key for unlocking empathy (Borba,

2017). Before people can empathize with others, they must first be able to read not only their own but others' emotions in order to tune into their feelings.

I can't feel with you if I don't know what you're feeling.

Writing these words in the midst of the COVID-19 pandemic, I'm disturbed by Borba's assertion that the single best predictor of healthy emotional interactions is face-to-face communication. This personal type of connection, as opposed to phone calls, texts, and social media posts, is the best way to learn emotions and develop human contact skills.

The truth of the matter is our emotions are transient and within our sphere of influence.

In the age of Zoom and Google Meet, video conferencing is a cheap imitation of much needed face-to-face interaction. Although faces are typically seen, so much of our video interactions are one-way. We're raising an entire generation that includes in their social vernacular, "You're on mute," and, "Please mute yourself." Who knows what the long-term effects of extended video-conferencing exposure will be on emotional literacy.

When possible, face-to-face contact is the best way for children to learn how to read emotions and develop empathy. Real, meaningful, emotion-laden, up-close-and-personal experiences work best to help children understand their feelings and others'. They need an emotional vocabulary to discuss feelings and opportunities and guidance for using intricate terms to name and express emotions.

If you were to travel to a foreign country without any knowledge of the native tongue there, you might be able to use hand gestures and pantomime to indicate your basic needs and wants. You could mime pinching your fingers and thumb together to ask for food. You could curl your hands into a semicircle and bring them up to your mouth to show that you're thirsty.

What you'd be unable to do, however, is get into the finer details of your needs. If you were lactose-intolerant, for instance, or vegetarian, your lack of language skills would hamper your communication abilities. In the same way, some children don't have the linguistic adroitness to adequately describe their emotional landscape. If all they have in their semantic toolbox are basic terms like *sad*, *mad*, and *happy*, they will struggle to describe what they are going through and how it is affecting them (Sage, 2017).

A tool that has introduced into the educational arena to build emotional literacy is a mood meter (Brackett, 2018). Based on the two scales of pleasantness and energy, students have 100 terms to choose from to describe what they are feeling. Ranging from *enraged* (high energy, low pleasantness) to *ecstatic* (high energy, high pleasantness) to *serene* (low energy, high pleasantness) to *despair* (low energy, low pleasantness), the mood meter gives students more than enough vocabulary to take emotional literacy to the next level.

A simple exercise to boost the vocabulary and awareness of students would be to take one of the 100 terms each day and spend about five minutes discussing it. Give students an example or two of why someone would feel that way. Ask them to think about if they've ever felt that way and what the circumstances were. To make it even more rigorous, compare the word to those right around it. For example, what are the variations that separate *disappointed* from *discouraged* and *mellow* from *sleepy?* Learning to differentiate the terms adds additional layers of complexity to students' emotional literacy.

Knowing how to name and describe your feelings and the feelings of others is like having a smartphone GPS on a cross-country road trip. With it, you don't have to be anxious because at any time you can reference it and know where you are and how to get to where you are going. Not having strong emotional literacy, simply using basic feeling words, is about as comforting as trying to find the next state highway on the border between Arkansas and Missouri with nothing but a Rand McNally road atlas.

What can you do tomorrow?

Teach emotions. Use the five parts of RULER to begin developing your students' emotional literacy. A good starting point would be to find a mood meter online (many free images exist for download) and begin to use it with students.

Check in daily. You can talk about a different term each day, have kids check in each morning by placing a magnet on it that shows their current mood, or add it to your safe place.

What does this look like in the classroom?

Students develop **emotional literacy** by:
- Recognizing emotions in themselves and others;
- Labeling emotions with and increasingly nuanced vocabulary; and
- Regulating their emotions through breathing, reflection, and other techniques.

How can you reflect on your learning?

What is the importance of emotional literacy?

_____

_____

What are the benefits of viewing emotions as transient rather than fixed?

_____

_____

Braveheart

We all have a movie (or three) that moved us to the point that we can still feel strong emotions decades after first watching it.

For me, it's Mel Gibson's *Braveheart*.

Inspired by true events but with a strong touch of artistic license, Mel Gibson portrays William Wallace, a Scot who lived in the 13th century and came to be one of the main leaders during the First War of Scottish Independence.

But that's not what matters.

The movie does a fantastic job of setting up Wallace as a sympathetic character who just wants to live a quiet life after a traumatic childhood. The first part of the movie details his romantic ventures as he tries to woo a beautiful lass with an overprotective father. Viewers root for Wallace as he outwits her father and wins the heart of the beautiful girl Murron.

And then reality hits like a ton of bricks.

English soldiers sexually assault Wallace's love and she fights back, injuring her attacker. Wallace comes to the rescue, driving off her attackers and seeming to triumph. While Wallace escapes in the guise of an English soldier that he knocked out, she is actually captured. As an example to the populace, with the declaration that an assault on the king's men is the same as an assault on the king himself, her throat is slit to bring Wallace out of hiding. As she awaits her fate, her eyes are seen flitting about in the distance, searching for her lover that would not come. The camera cuts to an empty horizon and we feel her anguish as she vainly hopes that she would be rescued once again.

Wallace never comes and she dies alone and afraid.

The movie cuts to a glorious two minutes of Wallace slowly riding into the town for retribution. The English wait patiently, smug in their invincibility. What could one barbarian do? At the last minute, instead of surrendering himself, Wallace leads an attack on the fort and he and his fellow Scots butcher countless soldiers, ending in the death of the commander that had killed Wallace's bride Murron.

Over two decades later I can still feel the sense of anguish in her eyes and she dies wondering where Wallace was. The righteous anger that leads to a large-scale uprising still feels raw and visceral when I think about how Wallace must have felt.

That's empathy.

That's what students need to have a chance at success, both in and out of the classroom.

Empathy

In *Unselfie*, Michele Borba (2017) details the importance of empathy in the lives of students today. The ability to empathize, or feel what others feel, affects their future health, wealth, authentic happiness, relationship satisfaction, and ability to bounce back from adversity of our students. Strong empathy skills promote kindness, prosocial behavior, and moral courage. As if those benefits were not enough, empathy reduces bullying, aggression, prejudice, and racism.

Academically, empathy is a positive predictor of children's reading and math test scores. It improves critical thinking skills, prepares them for a global world, and even gives them a considerable job market boost.

Empathy rests on the foundation of emotional literacy. Before children can feel what others feel, they must first be able to identify what those feelings are. When they have a deep well of emotional language to draw from that describes what they and others are feeling, they are better equipped to flex their empathetic muscles.

This is why relationships are at the heart of learning. At the core of any empathetic moment is human connection. While I've never tried to woo a 13th century Scottish girl or had the love of my life violently assaulted and murdered, I had the ability to imagine what those feelings would be like. I felt what Mel Gibson's William Wallace felt, I understood the despair that ripped through Murron as she waited hopelessly to be saved. I hadn't ever been in any of those situations but I had enough human experiences to relate to them.

Empathy is what connects us and brings us together. When students can feel what others feel, when they understand how their actions and words affect others, that shared understanding brings them together. Students are much less likely to act out against others, whether it be fellow students or their teachers, when they feel strongly connected to them. Hurting them would be like hurting themselves because of strong empathetic ties.

Empathy rests on the foundation of emotional literacy.

When students strengthen their empathy skills, they grow closer together. When their relationships grow tighter, they are less likely to act in ways that hurt others because to do so would be like a self-inflicted wound.

That's the power of empathy.

Self-regulation

However, developing empathy is just one part of the equation. The next step that you can help students take is to practice empathy in their daily interactions.

It's not as easy as it seems.

A key skill for students to develop alongside empathy is self-regulation. Self-regulation allows children to keep their emotions in check. They need to be able to recognize and feel the feelings of others (empathy) without letting them consume them. Rather, self-regulation helps them calmly consider how to help or act.

This is something that teachers do every day. When a student is angry because someone just bumped into her, a good reaction on their part would be to recognize her anger and help her calmly consider what to do next. A bad reaction would be to get angry alongside the student and begin to yell at the negligent classmate who caused the problem in the first place.

Children need to be able to feel the feelings of others but then also be able to regulate their responses. This allows them to connect with others but still stay in control of how they act and respond. If self-regulation is missing, empathy is jeopardized as students have difficulty knowing where others' feelings end and theirs begin.

STAND

One of the easiest ways to practice empathy in the classroom is also the hardest. The brain can be thought of as having two regions, the upstairs (rational) part and the downstairs (emotional and primal) part (Siegel & Bryson, 2012). Exercising the upstairs brain balances out the downstairs part and is essential for social and emotional intelligence. The more that we can help students exercise responsible decision-making, the more integrated their brains will become.

To that end, one thing that teachers and parents can do to assist this integration is to avoid rescuing and solving problems. When students make minor mistakes and not-so-great choices, our instinct is to immediately jump in and fix it. As the adult in the room, we are charged with keeping order and helping students stay safe at all times.

Sometimes we simply do it too much.

Whenever you can do so responsibly, fight the urge to fly in to save the day. While you might win the immediate battle, too much rescuing can lose you the eventual war as students never gain the ability to solve their own problems. They need real-life opportunities to practice feeling how their actions affect others and taking steps to solve the problem.

Yet to turn children loose without the tools necessary to solve their own problems is unethical. To avoid creating your own version of *The Lord of the Flies*, use a five-part problem-solving process called *stand* that students can use for peer problem-solving (Borba, 2017).

The first step is to *stop*, look, and listen to their feelings. If students are in conflict, they must first cease and recognize not only their own feelings but try to identify the feelings of the other party. They should stay calm, take a deep breath, and analyze what's going on. This initial step, if followed by students, immediately kicks the brains of both students into the higher, upstairs region of the brain that allows for problem-solving.

The second step is to take turns *telling* the problem. Each child speaks in turn using *I* statements, describing how they feel because of whatever transpired. After each child has spoken, they then turn the situation around using *you* statements. This second part is crucial as students work to adequately capture what the other person is feeling and promotes empathy.

The third step is for the two students to brainstorm *alternatives*. Working together, now that they have spoken with each other and summarized the viewpoints of their peer, they begin to seek solutions to whatever caused the initial problem. This brainstorming is truly a wide-open exercise, naming as many solutions as they can think of.

Fourth, the students begin to *narrow* down the ideas generated in the brainstorming. They look for fair solutions that are viable, don't violate any rules or norms, and are supported by both people. This is the hinge point of the entire exercise and the one that teachers do not need to short circuit by jumping in and rescuing students. When teachers too quickly solve the problems of their students, they restrict their problem-solving muscles and keep them stunted. When, on the other hand, they give them the freedom to try to solve their own issues, students' social-emotional literacy and empathy soar.

Empathy is what connects us and brings us together.

Finally, the two students *decide* on the best choice. They shake on it, fist bump each other, or do something formal or informal to note that both parties agree on the solution. This helps them learn that they can solve their own problems and work through issues on their own.

Unfortunately, this will not work in all circumstances. There will be some times that you'll need to step in and guide the discussion or even make the decision. This does not need to happen all the time, however. Give your students the benefit of the doubt and the opportunity to solve the problem on their own first.

Perspective taking

The ability to understand another person's thoughts, feelings, wants, and needs is called perspective taking. It's a gateway to empathy because it helps us step into another's shoes and feel what another person is feeling. More than that, it helps us see the world through the eyes of another and understand life from his or her point of view. When students practice perspective taking, they take a big step toward deepening their caring connection with others.

There are many tips to help students practice perspective taking (Borba, 2017). One trick is to use a do over. When one student says something rude or nasty to another, you can ask them to do it over. "Stefan, your words made Jalen feel sad. Try that again, but this time say it in a way that will make Jalen feel happy."

This simple rebuttal does two things at once. First, it addresses the problem without shame. Instead of getting Stefan in trouble, signing his agenda or planner, or calling his parents, all of which are traditional consequences that make a student feel shame, it calls attention to the behavior and allows for an immediate do over. It's a simple mistake that can be quickly rectified. Second, it takes it out of the theoretical and into the practical. Rather than wondering what he could have said differently, Stefan has a chance to immediately try out a better way to convey his message.

Another way to encourage perspective taking is to role play. Students are used to thinking about characters in stories and maybe even acting out classroom plays, but rarely do they take on the role of someone they just hurt. "Let's do this again, but this time I want you to think about how Desi feels about not being allowed to play with you. I'll pretend to be you. 'Desi, you can't play with us.' Now you be Desi and tell me how she feels and what she thinks about being left out." These mental exercises, so obvious to us as adults, are sometimes not explicit for students. Often, they need a chance to feel how their words affect others by viewing the situation from someone else's perspective.

Similarly, you can use a freeze and think moment to help students interpret someone else's feelings. "Stop – don't go any further. Take a look at Danny's face and ask yourself how you would feel if someone just spoke to you the way you spoke to him. What do you think you might need to say to Danny?" Like the other tips, it asks a student to consider the situation from someone else's perspective.

Some of you might be wondering, "What's the consequence? What's the punishment for these rude things the children are saying?"

Punishment can never teach someone how to act correctly. At the very best, it'll show students what not to do. It can never inform them as to what they should have done instead. Students need someone to show them a better way to act and communicate, not one more person getting onto them about what they are doing wrong.

I'll never forget how Murron felt when hopelessly waiting for William Wallace to rescue her. I'll always remember the rage and vengeance that burned through her lover as he brought the judgment of God down on his enemies. Those feelings are with me because of my ability to empathize, to feel what others are feeling, even if they are fictional characters.

Your students need that same ability today. Though they will never face the same dilemmas that the characters of *Braveheart* faced, they will need emotional literacy to become successful adults. Without empathy and the ability to take another's perspective, their days will be filled with struggle.

What can you do tomorrow?

Teach conflict resolution. There are several different options in this part for building not only the empathy of your students but also helping manage interpersonal conflict. Introduce your students to the *stand* procedure and allow them to use it to work through minor conflicts.

Explore another's point of view. Help students take the perspective of someone else to encourage empathy and resolve issues emerging from hurtful words or actions.

What does this look like in the classroom?

Students practice **empathy** by:
- Actively working to solve relational problems with classmates;
- Taking the perspective of other students; and
- Role playing to understand how their words and actions affect others.

How can you reflect on your learning?

Why is empathy important?

_____

_____

How can a teacher's problem-solving stunt emotional growth?

_____

_____

Immediate impact: Go to 2 – 4 Release (Heart) – pg. 151

Strength does not come from physical capacity, it comes from indomitable will.

- Mahatma Gandhi

5 – 3 Intrapersonal (Grow)

How bad do you want it?

I remember being overtaken by a question during the winter of 2016-2017. At the time, I was a principal of a charter school in the Dallas/Fort Worth metroplex. My students were mostly well-behaved, high-achieving students. While success was not difficult to achieve with such great students, I was having a harder time with my teachers.

As the only administrator at this intermediate (grades 3-5) campus, one of my many duties was to supervise and evaluate over 30 teachers. Some were naturals, able to teach better than I could, and I felt lucky to sit and learn from them. Others needed some help, and that is where I fell short.

From what I could tell, they were doing everything right. They were using the correct curriculum, doing the same activities as their grade-level peers, and yet they were achieving poorer results. To make a long story short, I began to question student engagement.

What made students engaged with learning? Is there a rhythm or pattern to engaging lessons? How could teachers leverage that for higher participation and achievement?

These questions became a personal passion. If I could answer them, I thought, I could better support my struggling teachers. I saw a gap but didn't know how to fill it. So I started researching student motivation and engagement.

And then I felt the grip of grit.

In her book *Grit*, author Angela Duckworth (2016) explores what makes highly successful people achieve so much and how, if possible, it can be replicated on a large scale. The first and largest question she tackled was grit versus talent.

What matters more in the long run – grit, or individual perseverance, effort, and passion for a long-term goal, or natural talent? If the former, then mere mortals are in luck. We might just have a chance at achieving great things and improving our lives. If the latter, then our fates are determined by how we fared in the genetic lottery.

In a series of studies, Duckworth found that grit did a better job than talent or intelligence of predicting which West Point cadets would make it through the infamous Hell Week initiation, which salespeople would stay in a tough job, which students would earn a high school diploma, and which Army Rangers would make it through the extreme Selection Course.

In short, our potential (read: talent, gifts, intelligence) is one thing. What we do with it is something completely different.

That's not to say, however, that natural talent is to be ignored. It's just a distraction.

Distracted by talent

As a society, we are easily distracted by talent. We are quick to anoint someone a natural. When we view a spectacular performance, a feat of athleticism, or an insight of genius, our natural reaction is to attribute it to some type of innate ability. Some people simply have "it" while others don't. Like Athena springing from Zeus' head fully formed, we believe that there are those walking among us gifted by the gods.

This is a cop-out.

While some might have more physical or intellectual advantages over others, it is not pre-programmed attributes that separate the men from the boys. It's dedication, effort, and hard work. To attribute immense achievement to some type of elemental or inborn ability only serves to let us off the hook. Since we weren't born with that talent, we believe, there's no point even trying to match it.

As a society, we are easily distracted by talent.

Duckworth posited two equations in an attempt to explain achievement in relation to effort. According to her work, innate talent remains unfulfilled until combined with effort. Once effort has time to coalesce with talent, skill emerges.

talent x effort = skill

Skill left on its own, however, simply remains as potential. Many people have many skills. To turn that skill into something worth achieving, more effort is required. After hours and hours, sometimes even days and weeks and months, talent matures into achievement.

skill x effort = achievement

Behind the greatest entrepreneurs, musicians, actors, athletes, and scientists, you'll find a relentless pursuit of excellence. Their seedling of natural ability has been honed into something awe-inspiring as a result of their effort.

As a teacher, my brightest students sometimes received average to below average grades. Their awesome potential never panned out when the rubber met the road. On the other hand, the highest grades usually went to the hardest workers, regardless of innate talent.

For anyone who has received a graduate degree, they usually realize sometime during the program that graduation has more to do with effort than intelligence. For those willing to do the work, a masters or even a doctorate is within (strenuous) reach. When I see alphabet soup after someone's name in an email signature, I read that as dedication and perseverance in addition to smarts.

Effort counts twice

Though we each have various degrees of innate abilities and physical characteristics, very little is out of our reach. When we see excellence and ascribe it to that person being a natural, we are in fact denigrating their achievement. Naturals don't get noticed when that ability is divorced from effort. Inborn abilities, forged over time by persistence and determination, is what makes us gape.

The teaching point for children, then, is that everyone can make an effort. Some students might not ever have the body type typical of a professional athlete. They might face dyslexia, a weakness in computational proficiency, or memory retrieval deficiencies. What one achieves, however, has less to do with talent and more to do with effort. And everyone can have effort.

Students today need to understand that it is their effort and persistence, their grit, that will largely determine their future. Those other children that seem to have been dealt a winning hand might in fact flame out in a few years without the required effort. On the other hand, the world is replete with feel-good stories about people who overcame great adversities to fulfill their dreams. As teachers, we must emphasize that inborn abilities, left unattended, amount only to potential.

That's the amazing part of understanding grit. Your effort counts twice and you have complete control over your effort!

Though natural talent is hit-and-miss, it's effort in developing that talent that turns it into skill.

And everyone owns their effort!

Once we've honed a skill through determination and perseverance, the skill morphs into achievement through more effort.

And everyone owns their effort!

Duckworth found that those with the highest raw intelligence but only mild persistence will achieve far less eminence than those with lower intelligence but the greatest degree of persistence.

So how do we develop persistence and grit in students other than simply telling them about it?

Grit needs four factors to grow in your classroom. As you nurture these in concert, your students will naturally grow in grittiness.

Growing grit

The first ingredient for grit is interest (Duckworth, 2016). This cannot be assigned or dictated to students. Instead, grit comes when they pursue their natural interests. What do they like? What keeps them inside from recess so they can finish a task?

Walking alongside interest, but sometimes lurking in the shadows, is autonomy. When students have choices, they will naturally choose what they are interested in. Students will show much more persistence in self-chosen tasks than those that they are given.

We've probably all witnessed this phenomenon in young children. When playing with blocks, small children will inevitably try to build a large tower. They'll work and work, even after multiple failures, to construct the highest tower possible. This natural curiosity is a part of how they learn and they'll stick with the challenge far longer than we think possible when they initiate the play.

Want to shut down this persistence in a moment? Assign the challenge to the student. Make them go over and build the tallest tower possible. Though you might get some decent structures, they'll come from compliance rather than willingness. Once a few failures start to pop up, students will lose interest because it wasn't their choice to engage. That's the power of autonomy in sustaining interest.

In the classroom, you can intentionally nurture interest by building in unstructured play and exploratory time. If every moment of your day is scripted, then students will never have the opportunity to let the seeds of interest sprout. Give students access to interesting books, videos, manipulatives, and even tools and equipment. Let them play with them, unstructured, and how they choose to use their time (autonomy) will spark interest.

Practice and purpose

The next component of developing grit is practice. If a student has an interest in writing, she needs structures and systems to help her develop her emergent skill. Interest will only get you so far, but purposeful practice can take students to the next level in bolstering their perseverance. For those educators that balked at the idea of unstructured play, remember that's best used for sparking interest. Once it's begun, practice makes perfect (almost).

Inherent to practice, but sometimes overlooked, is the desperate need for feedback. To amend the statement at the end of the previous paragraph, *perfect* practice makes perfect. Doing something incorrectly over and over again will not lead to a better result. For students to gain in grit, they need someone to partner with them to give feedback.

This is clear to anyone that has ever played or follows sports. The highest paid and most skilled athletes in the world still seek coaching every day. For talent to turn into skill, athletes know that their effort must be matched by valuable coaching feedback. More than just telling them what they're doing wrong, students need assistance learning how to do it right.

For students to gain in grit, they need someone to partner with them to give feedback.

Running parallel alongside practice is purpose. Why are they persevering? Why should they stick with something? The reason, or purpose, behind a difficult or meaningful task, is the fuel that keeps students going. What's the point of learning their times tables or how to conjugate Spanish verbs? Why should they revise their essay once again?

It's this purpose piece, more than any other, that marks grit in students and separates them from those that fall by the wayside. Many will find something interesting, even for the short-term. That interest will naturally lead to practice as students want to do something more and more. When learning gets tough, however, when the roadblocks start popping up and they travel to that uncomfortable place between what they can do on their own and what's out of their reach, students have a tough choice to make. Do they continue or do they give up?

Purpose, for many students, has to come from within them. As a teacher, you can attempt to shine the light on the inherent value of sticking with a learning task, but that inner drive must originate within. For students that lack perseverance in learning tasks, they need someone to uncover or reveal for them why learning it is important in the first place.

Hope

The final ingredient of growing grit, after interest, practice, and purpose have germinated, is hope. Students must see that the goal is in sight, even if it's very far off. Something that's unattainable will demotivate students and siphon off any stamina they might have.

A quick personal example sums this point up nicely. I am, have been, and always will be extremely thin. String bean, lanky, however you want to describe it, I'm blessed and cursed with a scrawny body type. If I wanted to put all my effort into becoming an offensive lineman for the Dallas Cowboys, for instance, I'd have no hope. I could have all the interest, practice, and purpose in the world but that wouldn't change the fact that I'm six feet tall and 135 pounds dripping wet. No hope means no perseverance toward reaching an unattainable goal.

How do you foster hope in your classroom? How do you paint a picture for your students that learning is possible? If all they see are their failures, they'll quit after a while. Are you focusing on what they can do or on what they can't? Is it their strengths or their weaknesses that they see reflected in their work?

So when I started my writing journey in late 2016, I definitely had interest. Both a personal and professional interest drove me to read research articles, studies, and books about what motivates students to learn and how teachers could leverage that for increased engagement.

I began to write, practicing my craft and attempting to pull from various data streams a coherent theory and structure for understanding student engagement. The very best feedback I received during those early days were the times I sent proofs to publishers and even my parents, asking for their thoughts and affirmation.

Everyone hated what I wrote, though some framed it more kindly than others. It took me several aborted attempts with that first book before I found my voice. I had to make the shift from reading peer-reviewed research journals to writing for novice teachers that didn't know the difference between pedagogy and phonology. Once I found that, I was off to the races.

Throughout the entire writing of my first book, I was buoyed by both purpose and hope. Rather than writing to make money or a name for myself, I was writing to solve a problem. In an extended story I share in section six (engage – motivation) about that book, which I eventually published as *Solving Student Engagement: Designing Instruction to Motivate Every Student*, one of the big drivers was the fact that my oldest son wanted to drop out of high school because of disengagement.

Eventually, I finished the book and have written several more. Grit, a valuable intrapersonal skill that all students should develop, grows when we acknowledge two key truths from Angela Duckworth's book. First, effort counts twice, and everyone owns their level of effort. Second, the seed of grit grows in the soil of interest, practice, purpose, and hope.

What can you do tomorrow?

Focus on effort. Talk to your students about grit and perseverance. Highlight the fact that the most important factor is effort and everyone owns their effort.

Highlight grit. Share a personal story with them about how grit helped you accomplish a goal. Start to integrate grit and perseverance into the attitudes and actions you notice among your students.

What does this look like in the classroom?

The teacher supports the **development of grit** by:
- Highlighting the importance of effort over talent;
- Providing unstructured time for students to develop their interests; and
- Designing practice and feedback sessions to grow students' skills.

How can you reflect on your learning?

Why is grit more important than talent?

_____

_____

How does student choice factor into grit?

_____

_____

Mindset

More than just developing grit, teachers would do well to cultivate a growth mindset in students. Before you close the book and scream in frustration, "Not another growth mindset speech!", indulge me for just a moment.

If you're an educator and have never heard of the growth mindset, I admire the rock you've been living under. I also have some interesting news about this new-fangled contraption called *the internet*.

But I digress.

A growth mindset, and its fixed mindset counterpart, are belief systems that people hold about the nature of intelligence and talent. Those with a growth mindset believe that their abilities are not fixed at birth but constantly evolving. They relish challenges and feedback, taking failures not so much as an admission of ignorance but as information on how to improve. Those with a fixed mindset have a much more static view of intelligence and talent. You're either born with it or you're not, and failure means you are not good enough. Fixed mindset students shy from challenges because they don't want to be shown as deficient (Dweck, 2006).

Many research studies, training programs, slogans, mottos, and mission statements all attest to the desirability of having a growth mindset over a fixed mindset. But how can you cultivate this much needed learning frame of mind? Is it enough to simply slap a few motivational cat posters on the classroom wall and call it a day?

In *Powerful Teaching*, the authors discuss the idea of *desirable difficulty* (Agarwal & Bain, 2019). When things get hard in the classroom, it's not a sign that something is going wrong. It's only when students have to cognitively stretch themselves that they are doing something right.

Forgetting is a natural process. Our brain processes much more information in a day that it can store in long-term memory. Each night, it combs through recent bits of information and decides what's worth keeping and what isn't. If this didn't happen, we would quickly fill up our memory and storage capacity with useless trivia.

What color was the car that passed you on the way to work this morning? You looked, and if you really strain, you might be able to recall that it was a black sedan. Other than that, though, it's not worth remembering. Your brain will weed that information out in order to make room for more important data like your upcoming meeting or how enjoyable your lunch date was.

Normalizing forgetting is an important step in helping students understand how their brains work. If they don't remember something immediately, that doesn't mean it's gone forever. Instead, that just means it's going to take a little bit more effort to recall the needed information.

Desirable difficulty

Effort is not a sign of stupidity.

Those with a fixed mindset believe that if they have to put forth serious effort to remember something or accomplish a task, it means that they must be dumb. If you can create an atmosphere in your classroom that relishes, rather than rejects, difficulty, then students are much more likely to embrace challenges instead of running from them.

To understand this, think about how people exercise and gain muscle mass. Most will recognize that lifting weights is a common practice for bulking up. If I were to use 3 pound dumbbells for curls each day, the weight is so light that I would most likely see no muscle growth unless I performed an insane amount of repetitions.

On the other hand, if I became too ambitious and chose 50 pound weights, I might not be able to perform any reps at all. The sticks attached to my torso (a.k.a. my arms) are much too scraggly to lift that amount of weight. It's only in the middle of that range, around 25 pounds or so, that I'd find the sweet spot needed for lifting weights and growing muscle mass.

Effort is not a sign of stupidity.

This is the same way that students can view learning and how difficulty is something to be desired rather than shunned. When students don't immediately remember something or perform a skill accurately, that should be celebrated! That means that they're right where they need to be, not too hard but not too easy. If this approach to productive struggle is highlighted for students, they'll be much more amenable to adopting a growth mindset.

Fixed mindset feedback

Carol Dweck (2006) shares many stories and facts about growth mindsets and fixed mindsets. One application for us concerns how we give feedback and praise to our students. It's only natural for teachers to praise students for their accuracy and performance. How we do it, however, can influence the type of mindset they cultivate.

Mistakes happen. Learning requires students to stretch themselves beyond what they already know. If students aren't willing to take academic risks, they won't see much growth. How they handle those intellectual bumps in the road, though, will go a long way toward shaping the environment in the classroom. When students embrace errors as informative tools to improve their learning, taking risks isn't that frightening. If students are subconsciously more concerned with maintaining their self-concept than expanding their knowledge, then they'll become risk-averse and avoid taking cognitive leaps.

While we don't have a say in the mindset of our students as they enter the classroom, we do have a strong influence on their mindset as they leave. The words that we use to give students feedback on their work goes a long way toward developing student attitudes. Whether it be written comments on paper or verbal thoughts shared during a discussion, we are constantly giving students feedback on their learning. Intentional or not, students receive messages from us every day.

They hear that they are smart and gifted. We complain about their messiness and laud them for their creativity. Every time that we open our mouths we subliminally share our mindset orientation with our students. One type pushes students to have more of a growth mindset. Another, though, can take students that believe in their ability to grow themselves and inadvertently make them more hesitant to try new things.

One example of feedback to avoid is when we affirm our students' low opinion of themselves. When students struggle with something and we say something like, "Well, maybe math just isn't your thing," it reinforces a fixed mindset. Students already struggling with a subject and those that have a shaky self-concept will find it difficult to push through obstacles if they don't think they have enough ability. Sometimes teachers trying to let students down lightly end up hardening their fixed mindset.

On the other hand, a sneaky type of damaging feedback is one most of us believe to be helpful. When a child succeeds, it's only natural to compliment her intelligence by telling her that she's smart. When we say something like, "Great job, you're so bright," we are in fact pointing her toward an innate ability. Being smart is typically viewed as something one is born with rather than something that develops, and the more intelligence is praised, the more fixed students become.

Growth mindset feedback

How, then, should we talk to our students? When giving them feedback, we should focus more on effort than intelligence. While most students don't believe they have control over how smart they are, they'll agree that they do have a say in how hard they work. When they succeed, praise their strategies, persistence, and resilience. This draws attention to the fact that their success depends on areas they control rather than abilities they are born with.

Learning requires students to stretch themselves beyond what they already know.

When they struggle, growth mindset feedback gives them a path forward. If they are stuck, we can ask questions like, "So that now you know one way that doesn't work, what can you try next?" This highlights the fact that obstacles are meant to be overcome, not debilitating. Remember, difficulty is something to be desired. Continuing to provide them with feedback that showcases effort instead of smarts can provide some students with the spark they need to keep pushing.

Here are some more examples of the two different types of feedback. See if you can capture the difference.

Fixed: "Not everybody is good at math. Just do your best." Growth:

"When you learn how to do a new kind of problem, it grows your math brain!"

Fixed: "That's OK, maybe math is not one of your strengths." Growth: "If you catch yourself saying, 'I'm not a math person,' just add the word 'yet' to the end of the sentence."

Fixed: "Great effort! You tried your best." Growth: "That feeling of math being hard is the feeling of your brain growing."

Fixed: "Don't worry, you'll get it if you keep trying." Growth: "The point isn't to get it all right away. The point is to grow your understanding step by step. What can you try next?"

Before moving on, take a moment to reread the last two fixed mindset statements.

"Great effort! You tried your best. Don't worry, you'll get it if you keep trying."

Are those correctly labeled? The first one even includes the word *effort*. Isn't that what we should be focusing on?

Yes and no.

Effort alone isn't sufficient. At the end of the day, the results will prove whether or not students are successful. Some teachers have misapplied the idea of a growth mindset and believe that simply trying is enough. Don't get sidetracked by focusing on boosting a student's self-esteem when their effort still leaves them short of the mark.

The statement, "Great effort! You tried your best," is a sneaky fixed mindset statement because it will normally come after a failed attempt. In an attempt to make students feel better and blunt the negative emotions associated with failure, we will sometimes try to bolster their (supposedly) fragile self-image by letting them know they at least tried. This, unfortunately, communicates the fact that they tried their best and it still wasn't good enough! Who wants to hear that?

The statement, "Don't worry, you'll get it if you keep trying," is not always accurate. Doing the wrong thing over and over will not result in success. Sometimes the knowledge and skills needed to complete something is missing and will not be discovered simply through blunt force. Trying again and again will sometimes lead students to conclude that they just aren't good enough and shouldn't keep trying, a fixed mindset approach.

More than effort

A growth mindset, at its core, is focused not just on effort but on learning. In a journal article, Carol Dweck (2015) revisited the growth mindset and said that one of her greatest fears is that the growth mindset, which grew up to counter the failed self-esteem movement of the late 20th century, should be used to perpetuate it instead. By emphasizing effort and the fact that everyone is smart and capable, we miss the fact that an achievement gap exists and some students are failing.

When a fourth grader can't read, he doesn't need someone to praise his effort or to tell him to just keep trying.

He needs someone to teach him how to read.

At the same time, Dweck was afraid that having a fixed mindset is being used to excuse students' lack of learning. "He is failing math because he has a fixed mindset."

Having a growth mindset is related to optimism and thinking positively but they are not synonymous. A growth mindset is always focused on one thing – growth. Growth is measured not by happy thoughts but achievement. If we want our students to stay open to learning, they should not only keep an open mind but also increase their knowledge and skills.

As students make mistakes, as they live in the tension of desirable difficulty, encouraging them to keep trying is only one half of the equation. The other part of our feedback should focus on next steps. Here are some sample questions and prompts to consider using to nurture a growth mindset classroom climate.

Effort alone isn't sufficient.

"So, that didn't work so well. What are you going to try next?"

"Is there anything different you can do next time?"

"Mistakes are okay! They let me know how I can help you."

"Look at how much progress you've made so far. Do you remember how hard this was last week?"

"I'm sure you'll get it if you keep trying. Let's break it down into steps."

"Let's think of how to improve [specific skill]."

"Describe the process you used to get this answer."

"Let's practice one together and then you can do the next one alone."

"Let's ask [another student] for advice. S/he may be able to suggest some strategies."

"I can see a difference in this work compared to yesterday's. You've really grown."

"You were working on this for a while and never quit!"

"Do you remember how hard this was when you started? You did it!"

"The next time you have a challenge like this, what will you do?"

"All that persistence finally paid off. Way to go!"

"Congratulations – you used some great strategies to get this done."

What can you do tomorrow?

Encourage a growth mindset. As you notice students' attitudes and academic actions, examine the praise you give them. Using some of the samples above or some of your own, make sure that the feedback you give students supports a growth rather than a fixed mindset.
Praise for effort. Emphasize their effort, the strategies they used, and normalize mistakes.

What does this look like in the classroom?

The teacher encourages a **growth mindset** in students by:
- Modeling a growth mindset himself/herself;
- Normalizing errors and helping students accept the desirable difficulty of tasks; and
- Using feedback statements that encourage effort and the use of strategies over raw talent.

How can you reflect on your learning?

Why is difficulty desirable?

_____

_____

How does feedback affect the mindset of students?

_____

_____

Immediate impact: Go to 2 – 3 Respect (Heart) – pg. 129

The important thing is not to stop questioning. Curiosity has its own reason for existing.

- Albert Einstein

5 – 4 Intellectual (Grow)

Everything's better with curiosity.

When students are curious, they engage with content at a deeper level and for longer periods of time. They make better connections between new knowledge and existing information and they recall what they learned far easier. It's the ambrosia of the classroom, the nectar of the educational gods.

But is curiosity a mere add-on, something pleasant to have but not necessarily essential?

I guess that depends on how important learning is to you.

When students are in high states of curiosity, they have increased memory for material learned in that state. When curiosity is stimulated, learning experiences become much more effective (Gruber, Gelman, & Ranganath, 2014).

Curiosity also has a strong correlation to beneficial behaviors. Students who are curious are more tolerant of anxiety and uncertainty, have more positive emotional expressiveness, initiate humor and playfulness more frequently, and engage in more unconventional thinking (Kashdan, Sherman, Yarbro, & Funder, 2012).

Curiosity, along with conscientiousness, is as important as intelligence when determining how well students do in school (von Stumm, Hell, & Chamorro-Premuzic, 2011).

So, what exactly is this magical elixir called curiosity and how can we get more of it in the classroom?

Curiosity, put simply, is the pursuit and recognition of new information and experiences. And it has a strong foundation in neuroscience.

Curiosity and the brain

The brain's desire and reward system (the producer of the neurotransmitter dopamine) is deeply embedded in our human development (Ostroff, 2016). Since social scientists believe that reward drives all behavior, and behavior creates adaptation, the dopamine system has been critical in our development into the complex beings we are. When students are curious and seek to satisfy their goals and desires, they get a hit of this pleasure-producing chemical.

In other words, when we are curious, our brains' surge in dopamine causes us to take in and remember the entire landscape of experience and information more deeply. This is because dopamine makes the hippocampus (the part of the brain associated with long-term memory) function better.

Curious students learn more and learn better. This does not happen randomly or by chance but because our brains are wired that way. It's something that is designed to happen when the circumstances are ideal. It's how we learn new things and survive in complex and sometimes dangerous environments.

This is one fact that educators sometimes forget. Our brains are designed to learn new things! If we just get out of the way, students will naturally explore and gain new knowledge. It's something that happens naturally if we can create positive conditions for it. All curiosity is not created equal, however. There are four stages of curiosity that build on each other as students develop that inner desire to learn.

In the first stage students are mostly concerned with the process (Heick, 2019). A typical request in this stage will be, "Just tell me what to do," as students are primarily concerned with procedural knowledge. This includes teacher expectations, student expectations, interactions with peers, and the sequence of the task. This is where most learners begin as they try to make sense of any given task or activity. When at this stage, learners need prompting, repetition of instructions, clarification and paraphrasing, and even directions in multiple formats.

If we just get out of the way, students will naturally explore and gain new knowledge.

The second stage, content, finds students more engaged with the content of the task rather than the directions. The topic of study, rather than a series of instructions, is what drives them to continue. To support students at this level, teachers would do well to find materials at appropriate reading levels, compelling content to interest students, tasks that balance consumption of material and production of artifacts, and various methods of providing voice and choice to students.

The third stage of curiosity, transfer, is one in which students begin to connect knowledge, assimilating what they already know with what they are learning. Students here need continued support but growing levels of freedom as they seek to direct their own learning into new contexts, sometimes without the proper frameworks or strategies. Teachers can provide flexible rubrics, open-ended learning models, and scoring guides to support students here.

The fourth stage of curiosity, self, sees the culmination of curiosity result in students making sense of changes and transferring new learning into their own existing schema. This is the most powerful level of curiosity because it can change students' reasons for learning and their role in the learning process. They begin to ask questions unprompted, think of new learning pathways that are not explicitly stated, and continuously seek to reconcile what they do and don't know without prodding. Here students need space, exemplar models, and strategic collaboration.

Cultivating curiosity

Curiosity cannot be coaxed into the open through the use of dangling carrots or flashing lights. Instead, it stems from past experience and current knowledge, working from the inside out, as students seek patterns and are rewarded, through dopamine releasing in the brain, when those connections are sought after and made. Curiosity can be cultivated by sharing with students that it is a natural part of how their brains work on their own to seek understanding and congruence.

Though it is natural, curiosity is an intellectual habit of mind that can still be cultivated through several explicit practices. First and foremost, curiosity should be modeled in its many forms. During a read-aloud, pause and think aloud what you are wondering and what you hope to learn. Rather than moving quickly through the content, purposefully slow down and explain what you are curious about.

You can drive curiosity by making learning personal whenever possible. For example, students can choose a topic to write about to bring in their personal interests rather than having one assigned to them. They can have unstructured time to play with new tools and explore materials. If applicable, allow them to choose topics to study and pursue.

Many subjects can become more enticing if given the proper spin. Rather than passing out a new novel, let students know that it's controversial or possibly on a banned books list. Frame content as a mystery, solved or unsolved, and invite students to learn more about it. Sometimes, just a real-world connection is enough to pique students' interest.

You can drive curiosity by making learning personal whenever possible.

Finally, lead with questions. Instead of declaring knowledge, ask a few leading questions to "prime the pump" in students' brains. Additionally, you can also ask students to generate their own questions about a topic. Though they might not all be answered, the act of questioning gets students ready to explore and make connections.

Notice and reinforce curiosity when you see it in action, not just when it leads to a good grade or desired outcome. Describe how students' questions, explorations, and investigations are contributing to their own or classroom learning. Sometimes students are cultivating this wonderful habit and they aren't even aware of it. Give them language to name and appreciate the natural curiosity that students exhibit.

Notice when students feel puzzled or confused. Rather than rush to ease their cognitive discomfort, take a moment to let the situation percolate. Let students know that not knowing something isn't the worst thing in the world. In fact, it can become the fuel that inspires deeper learning! Flip the uncomfortable feeling into a teachable moment so that students see these situations as mysteries waiting to be solved.

Word play

Encourage students to tinker and construct. Whether it be with essays, science experiments, poems, or new tools, let them play with words! Word play promotes curiosity in children as they develop an appreciation of word study. It's a component of a rich vocabulary program and develops word meanings in multiple domains. Designed to be done with others, word play builds stronger classroom relationships as it engages students in the practice and rehearsal of words. Playing with words develops phonological, morphological, and syntactic awareness in students (Daffern, 2018).

In addition to word play, word consciousness can be described as an overall awareness of words and their meanings, how meanings change and grow, and a motivation to increase word knowledge. It is supported by teachers who love words and show an interest in the power of vocabulary. Word consciousness feeds on word-rich environments that have a variety of literacy materials of both motivational and instructional value.

Word consciousness transcends mere vocabulary. It's more than simply a fun activity or an effective teaching technique. Word consciousness is a frame of mind. It involves thinking metacognitively about word choice and why certain terms work better than others. This heightened sensitivity translates to a cognizance of encounters with new words and improves vocabulary acquisition.

We can influence word consciousness in a variety of ways. First, put an emphasis on word use during everyday classroom discussions and lessons. Students should see that word choice and selection are important at all times, not just during scripted vocabulary activities. As they read, write, listen, and discuss different topics at school, the words they select are an important component of linguistic expression.

You can add to this by being on the lookout for interesting phrases and terms. As a teacher, discuss why you like a certain wording and its effect on meaning. This will provide a metacognitive link between an author's word choice and the response of the reader. It's not only what words are used but how they are interpreted that contribute to the overall understanding of a passage.

Word consciousness is a frame of mind.

For me, the word that I loved to use as a child was *plethora*. Learned from the classic comedy *The Three Amigos*, I endeavored to use that word in as many different contexts as I could, only some of which actually fit. Utilizing this favorite phrase, again and again and again, is my first recollection of having word consciousness. From that moment I first experienced the power of words which, carefully chosen and cultivated, could even be used for comedic effect!

Additionally, challenge students to formulate hypotheses about the meaning of new or complex terms. Rather than quickly coming to the assistance of your students, ask them to use word parts, prior knowledge, and/or context clues to help build a possible definition. When appropriate, students should also take care to note any nuance of meaning and be sensitive to various connotations. This helps develop a curiosity about word meanings and heightens word analysis skills.

Modeling curiosity

More than simply trying to get students to act more curious, we can build curious environments by modeling and encouraging academic risk-taking. What are you learning that is new? Are you trying to do something that you're excited about but that is also slightly anxiety-inducing? Students need to see us falter now and again and they need to feel like it's okay to be unsure of themselves when starting something new.

If you can't answer *yes* to the preceding questions, a simple way to model this vulnerability is to try and integrate new technology into your classroom. When COVID-19 shutdown the world, schools and classrooms everywhere suddenly had to learn what it meant to teach virtually. Zoom, Google Meet, and Microsoft Teams became daily parts of our instruction. More than simply delivering lessons online, entire classrooms had to figure out what synchronous and asynchronous learning looked like.

So we learned how to post assignments in Google Classroom and Seesaw. We became familiar with Nearpod and leaned more heavily on Kahoot! Shifting everything about how we teach could have been taken as an inconvenience or an opportunity. If we spent the global shutdown moaning and complaining about the way things used to be, then we missed a golden opportunity to model curiosity.

Instead of becoming frustrated and scared about how to teach online, some teachers leaned into the newness of the situation. They were curious about how to teach in two environments at once. They investigated methods of engaging students online. More importantly, they showed their students what it means to be curious.

When we normalize fear and anxiety, we show students that being curious (and uncertain) is not something to be avoided. No matter how hard we try to insulate ourselves from unpredictability, we are never truly in control of our lives. Outside influences seemingly conspire to throw us off track but curiosity is a strong antidote to these feelings of distress. If we practice mindfulness and self-compassion, we will learn how to better tolerate the stress of not knowing and how to navigate the frustration, fear, or anxiety associated with trying new things.

Planning curiosity

Finally, you can provide challenging group tasks to build your students' curiosity. Build time into your curriculum to allow students to drive their own learning by asking and researching answers to higher-order thinking questions. Students are always asking good questions that naturally arise during the course of lessons. Rather than stymieing those opportunities because they don't fit into the lesson plan, place these questions on a bulletin board or creative parking lot.

You can build time each week as free exploration time. Students can use that time, as long as they are caught up on their other work, to explore wonderings that might have caught their attention throughout the course of their learning. If desired, they can work with a partner or even a group to research a particular topic or question and try to figure out the answer. Sometimes they might want to do this for its own sake and other times students might enjoy having the opportunity of sharing their learning with the class. Having a potential audience might make all the difference for some students. Everything's better with curiosity.

What can you do tomorrow?

Be curious. Intentionally discuss your own curiosity with students and model how a curious mindset affects how you learn. Look at your daily schedule to see how you can carve out some curiosity time for students to pursue their interests.

Play with words. One way to do this and allow students to participate is to highlight word play. As you and your students encounter new words, guess at their meanings and explore synonyms.

What does this look like in the classroom?

Classroom tasks nurture **curiosity** in students by:
- Including sufficient procedural knowledge to accomplish tasks independently;
- Bridging across content areas and providing a means of exploration; and
- Encouraging students to transfer knowledge into the production of authentic artifacts.

How can you reflect on your learning?

Why is curiosity so important for learning?

_____

_____

How does word consciousness relate to curiosity?

_____

_____

Creativity

A factory worker, newly retired, wanted to start a garden. He'd never done any gardening before but he loved the sight of flowers in bloom. Now that he had extra time on hand, he figured, "Why not start my own garden? It's summer now and it'll give me something to do." So he found some seeds and put them in the ground.

He waited patiently for about a week or so but then couldn't take it anymore. He went down to the local nursery and spoke with one of the employees. "I'm trying to grow daisies. I got some seeds and put them in the ground but nothing's growing. What am I doing wrong?" he asked.

"What kind of seeds are you using?" the employee asked back.

The novice gardener brought his hand out of his pocket and showed him a handful of white, oblong seeds the size of his fingernail.

"Those look more like pumpkin seeds. If you want to grow daisies, try these," the employee responded, taking him over to a display where dozens of seed packets were hanging.

Going home, the gardener dug up a new patch of earth and planted his daisy seeds. He waited three or four days and went back down to the nursery. Finding the same employee, he thrust the empty packet at his chest.

"These don't work. I need ones that work!"

Calmly stepping back, the employee said, "Good morning sir, so nice to see you again. I believe I helped you a few days ago, correct?" The gardener nodded tersely and he continued. "Daisy seeds take about 10 to 20 days to germinate. Why not come back in…"

The gardener left in a huff, not letting the employee even finish his sentence. He stewed impatiently, checking his garden sometimes ten times a day for signs of growth. Finally, after two long weeks, he sped down to the nursery and combed the aisles until he saw the harried employee.

Rushing up to him, he declared in righteous anger, "You don't know what you're talking about! I've planted them and I've waited but nothing has happened. I demand a refund!"

"Certainly sir, we can refund your $0.48. How often have you watered the seeds?" the employee asked, trying to keep his cool.

"Watered?" the novice gardener asked, dumbfounded.

"Yes sir, it's summer. The seeds need about one to two inches of water per week," the employee explained tiredly.

The gardener stormed out and threw his empty packet on the ground.

Creativity gap

Many schools are suffering from a creativity gap (Davis, 2018). If an outside observer were to follow students around 24 hours a day for a week and note the location and context of periods of creativity, they would most likely be found outside of the classroom. While many teachers bemoan the lack of creativity of students and their inability to think outside the box, to generate novel solutions, or even have an approach for tackling large problems, their skill should not be in question.

Students are overflowing with creativity but there's simply no place for it in the typical classroom.

On the playground, students will spend quite a bit of time playing with no formal rules or guidelines. At any given moment, there could be five separate activities happening with overlapping groups of students, some who are chasing, some who are running, and some who are simply having fun. Without boundaries, scoring criteria, or learning objectives, they simply play and make it up as they go along, adapting the play as students enter or leave or as attention shifts. Creativity bursts out of students every single day at school yet it often has to be left on the playground as they line up and return to the law and order of the classroom.

Why is the creativity gap so dire? More and more, our students are preparing to enter a knowledge workforce economy. Tasks are completed by machines and information is available with the click of a button or a swipe of a finger. We don't need to get students ready to work on an assembly line because those jobs are being automated at an astonishing rate. Instead, our focus in education should be to help students grow in something that can never be replaced by a machine, the ability to think creatively.

Students are overflowing with creativity but there's simply no place for it in the typical classroom.

Creativity, to put it simply, is the generation of a new product, either physical, digital, or cognitive, that is both novel and appropriate to the situation. It's a set of skills and attitudes that include tolerating ambiguity, redefining old problems, taking sensible risks, and following an inner passion. When thinking of creativity, we usually first think of art, an invention, or perhaps poetry. For our circumstances, though, we can ask students to be creative every day.

When we ask them to solve open-ended problems that do not have an explicit formula to use, we are tapping into their creativity. Any type of writing product uses creativity, as does responding to higher-order thinking questions. We might not be asking them to reinvent the light bulb, but teachers, unknowingly or not, can ask students to be creative on a consistent basis.

Yet how are we creating the conditions that best help it bloom?

Growing creativity

Creativity cannot be assigned or demanded of students, much like the novice gardener in the opening scenario could not use brute force to grow daisies. Instead, the most he (and you) could do is to create a culture and environment that is optimal for its development. Many teachers are frustrated that they aren't seeing creative solutions from their students yet they are trying to grow daisies from pumpkin seeds. They complain that students can't handle larger, more complex problems but they haven't watered their creativity seeds for over a month.

Creativity, at its core, blooms in the soil of student choice and the ability to pursue self-selected interests. Highly related to curiosity, creativity is not something that can be assigned but must flourish on its own. A solid first step for creating that environment is filling your class with compassion and acceptance. Creativity is messy. It isn't linear and there isn't an algorithm to follow. For every creative success, there will be many aborted attempts that end in failure. If students don't feel safe trying new things and playing with ideas, if they dread shame or penalty for being wrong, then creativity will never flourish.

Additionally, creativity cannot be scripted. It doesn't have its own separate box in your lesson planner nor is it aligned to state standards. It exists outside the district curriculum but can encompass all of it. Have more informal, social conversations with your students. Follow their lead and let them take you into the craziness of their mindscapes.

GROW

Too often when we talk with students it has a functional purpose. We have a standard or a skill in mind and our questions, even if rigorous, are leading toward an intended outcome. For creativity to begin to be evident, there must be a relaxing of the reins and a level of comfort with ambiguity. Enjoy social conversations and let students lead academic discussions according to their interests. Without that, you'll never get creativity to grow no matter how hard you try.

Creativity, at its core, blooms in the soil of student choice and the ability to pursue self-selected interests.

Think of students playing on a playground during recess. If you simply release them, they can spend an extraordinary amount of time in that chaos playing and being creative. They are constantly problem-solving, analyzing and discarding solutions, and gaining feedback on their interactions with others. Want to kill creative play in an instant? Organize it. Begin recess by laying out clear, defined rules and boundaries and watch as their souls wither and die.

Autonomy, some amount of free choice, is also invaluable for creativity. When you judge and give permission for students' creative pursuits in the classroom, you handcuff their will and restrict their imagination. As long as they aren't endangering themselves or others, physically or emotionally, the more you restrain yourself from directing creativity, the better.

Creativity tasks

So you can't assign creativity, but you can practice it. One method is to take a look at your assignments and tasks. Look at the phrasing and see if they can be adapted using more open instructions that include *create, design, invent, imagine,* or *pretend.* For example, instead of simply asking students to solve a math word problem, ask them to find as many different ways as possible to represent the solutions.

Warm up activities are another easy method of introducing creativity practice. Visual riddles, quick writes, or drawing tasks related to the content can inject a little bit of fun and imagination into any lesson. Watch out though! If you take these tasks for a grade, even a completion grade, you will severely limit their potential. Students will naturally shift from finding unique solutions to finding the correct solutions in order to get a good grade.

A warm up activity that students can engage in uses the keyword method for learning vocabulary (Daffern, 2018). Put simply, students consider a term and create a mnemonic related to it. For example, if working with the math term *parallel,* students will search for something they can relate to that sounds similar or uses a part of the term itself. *Parallel* sounds like *pair of elves* so they can draw parallel lines and then draw an elf standing on each line.

Provide students an opportunity to brainstorm with a partner before creating their own drawing. This will assist students unused to this type of thinking and will deepen the final products. If possible, allow students the opportunity to receive feedback, either from you or their peers, before finishing their keyword drawings. If the association between the drawing and the vocabulary term is weak, or the picture is unclear, it should be modified before being finalized.

Students tend to be more creative when working collaboratively in groups (Price-Mitchell, 2015). Even though we typically associate it with individual talent and achievement, students draw inspiration from their peers and even the environment. Many of the greatest breakthroughs in science and technology have come from teams with diverse thinking patterns struggling together. When students work together to solve a problem, you never know what you're going to get, a hallmark of creativity.

Many activities can be transformed from a boring one to a creative one simply by adding an extra challenge (Johnson, 2019). Whether it be for bonus points or simply for the fun of it, layering on a twist to the base assignment is a great way to foster creativity. If studying shapes, ask students to draw a rhombus and then turn it into a kitten. If studying fairy tales, ask students to take out three items from their desk and work with a partner to use those items to create their own fairy tale.

Benefits of creativity

At this point you might be thinking, "That's all well and good. I'm reading this book to learn about classroom management. What does creativity have to do with that?"

I'm glad you asked.

Creativity is highly related to student motivation, deepening understanding, and promoting joy (Davis, 2018). It is closely associated with happiness and well-being. It is also linked to purpose and intrinsic motivation (Price-Mitchell, 2015).

Creativity builds engagement for learning (Cadiergue, 2015). When students develop inquisitiveness, imagination, and collaboration skills, a proportional rise is also seen in classroom behavior, attendance, and academic achievement. It aligns with everything you want from your students.

Another benefit is that creativity, when nurtured and supported, builds resilience (Davis, 2018). It requires effort and its fruits are not easily obtained. Running parallel with creativity is grit and a growth mindset. For every two steps forward in creative endeavors, students often find there are three steps back and even a step or two to the side. When the solution is obtained, it comes from effort and dedication. Even though it may or may not be directly related to academic content, the development of resilience is a valuable outcome of creativity.

Many activities can be transformed from a boring one to a creative one simply by adding an extra challenge.

Creativity is the secret sauce that takes normal classrooms to the next level.

There's a reason that it sits atop Bloom's revised taxonomy. Students who think creatively notice broader patterns and connect ideas and facts. They are better able to facilitate cross-curricular learning because they think outside of the lines, not limiting geometry to math class or physics to science class. Instead, creativity blurs or even erases the lines between disciplines, allowing students to see and generate novel solutions that don't fit easily into a single academic silo.

When students feel creative, they feel alive. They connect with a deep part of themselves because creativity is at the epicenter of human exploration and discovery (Price-Mitchell, 2015). To be creative is to be human. When students connect with this fundamental truth of humanity, they join a larger universe. This interconnectivity surrounds them but too often flows by without them. When they create, they jump into the raging river of human experience.

To bring it back to the playground example yet one more time, think about the sounds of the playground. Close your eyes for a moment the next time you are monitoring your students during recess and let the noise sink in. What you'll hear is pure and unfiltered creativity. It sounds raucous, chaotic, unrestrained, and joyful. Creativity is fun and engages our emotions. Who doesn't want to have fun in the classroom?

To nurture creativity in your own classroom, be sure to plant the seeds of autonomy and freedom and water them with safety and acceptance.

What can you do tomorrow?

Build a creative environment. Consider how you can nurture creativity in your classroom on a large and small scale. For the former, provide students a sense of safety if they take risks. Give them opportunities to leave the scripted lesson and explore new options.

Be creative daily. On a smaller scale, engage creativity daily with brain teasers, quick writes, and collaborative tasks. Add a twist to an assignment as an extra challenge and tweak existing tasks to be more open-ended.

What does this look like in the classroom?

Classroom tasks support **student creativity** by:
- Embedding open-ended and ambiguous elements;
- Resting on a foundation of autonomy and student choice; and
- Encouraging partner or group collaboration.

How can you reflect on your learning?

What are the essential elements for nurturing creativity?

_____

_____

How does creativity affect classroom management?

_____

_____

5 – 5 Conclusion (Grow)

You've almost made it.

If you're reading this, you've presumably made it five-sixths of the way through the book. Before plunging on (and please do keep reading after this!), let's frame where we've been so far through the lens of some of the metaphors we've used.

One way to view classroom management is through the iceberg model. What we see above the surface might seem massive but only pales in comparison with what is below the surface. At the very bottom is our being, who we are and how we show up. Our identity, the version of ourselves that we subscribe to, colors everything

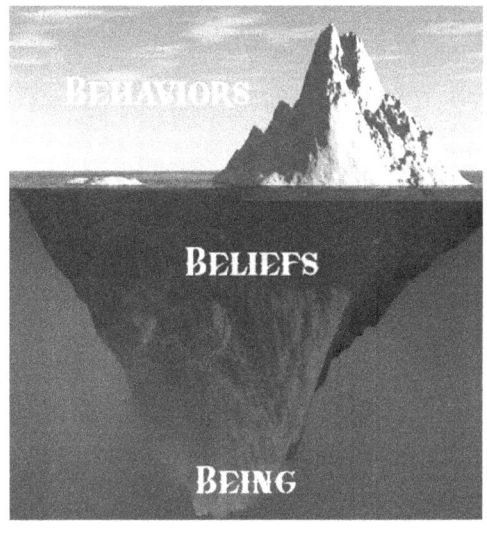

that sits atop it. If you want to take charge of the classroom, make sure you go deep enough to affect your being. This is what the first section, confidence, dealt with.

Above our being in the iceberg model, but still below the surface, are our beliefs. What we believe about the nature and ends of teaching, of the abilities of our students, and how we best instruct them will drive our behaviors. We have many hidden beliefs, instilled in us through our personal experiences, that deserve examination before jumping into teacher behaviors. This is what the second section, heart, looked at.

Finally, in the next three sections, we've looked at actions we can take, or teacher behaviors, that will enable us to take charge. Built on the solid foundation of our being and beliefs, these observable actions lie above the surface and directly impact students. To examine this expanded set of educator moves, we introduced another metaphor.

In the image of the rider and the elephant, change management involves three separate but interrelated factors – logic, emotion, and environment. The third section of the book, anticipate, looked at various ways to clear the path for the elephant and optimize the learning environment for success. The fourth section of the book, reinforce, showed how to use differential social attention to move that

elephant (emotions) along the path toward self-regulation.

It was in this current section, grow, that you began to appeal to the rider himself. In this metaphor, the rider represents our rational and logical selves. Though not nearly as powerful as the elephant (emotions), the rider still has some say in where the elephant will go. It's the rider that has access to vast executive skills and the ability to reason through situations and select the best approach when obstacles block the path or the elephant starts to wander.

Learning happens when the brain is in a relaxed state. Too often our efforts at instructing students to better manage their emotions and behavior fails simply because we choose an inopportune time. Like trying to teach your dog to fetch when he's being attacked by another dog, students aren't receptive to learning how to better regulate themselves in the middle of a meltdown. The approaches in this section are meant to be taught to students outside of behavioral episodes. With enough reinforcement, the lessons learned here will still be accessible within moments of distress.

First we looked at growing emotional literacy. Learning to name our emotions, to normalize those that are sometimes considered negative (e.g., anger, sadness), and the slight variations between them is a huge first step down the path of self-regulation. When students gain the ability to recognize their own emotions and how they affect their attitude and behavior, they've taken a quantum leap toward taking charge of themselves. Integral to emotional literacy is empathy, the ability to feel what others feel. By focusing on the emotions of others, students connect to them and grow closer to them. Acting out against them becomes odious because it feels like they are hurting themselves.

In addition to growing the interpersonal skills of emotional literacy and empathy, teachers and students begin to take charge when they focus on intrapersonal skills. While some negative behaviors are attention-seeking or emerge from peer-related conflicts, some erupt from deep within students. Frustration and disengagement are just two symptoms that alert us when students are struggling with the challenge of learning. For too many of them, when the going gets tough, they simply quit.

Learning happens when the brain is in a relaxed state.

To fight against this, we can focus on developing grit in our students. When they know that effort, more than talent or skill, is the largest factor in their success, it puts them back in the driver's seat. While they cannot change the natural talent they were born with, everyone can affect their effort. Running parallel to grit is a growth mindset. While this framework is known to most in the education and business world, a relevant application for teachers is the type of feedback they give. When their noticing of students focuses on their effort instead of their innate abilities, they strengthen a growth mindset in their students.

Finally, teachers can grow the intellectual skills of their students. Not necessarily content-related, these focus on curiosity and creativity. When students are given opportunities to practice these skills, they develop a frame of mind that will serve them throughout the rest of their education. These abilities, when honored and nurtured, flow right into the final section of the book, engage. When students are engaged in learning, they don't have the time nor are they even inclined to misbehave.

Grow

While it might be one step back for every two steps forward, time spent in growing students' interpersonal, intrapersonal, and intellectual skills is time well spent. When students don't know how to read, we teach them. When they can't multiply two-digits by two-digits, we teach them. When they don't know how to behave, what do you do?

When you invest in the growth of your students, you are depositing skills in them with a long-term focus. Dividends might not appear immediately, but they will come and they will surpass your wildest imagination.

CONFIDENCE

HEART

ANTICIPATE

REINFORCE

GROW

ENGAGE

6 – 1 Introduction (Engage)

Without a strong footing, you'll never be able to take the final leap across the chasm of student indifference from apathy to engagement. That security rests in fully aligning your being, beliefs, and behaviors with student success. When students feel secure, connected, have clear expectations, and are guided toward positive actions and attitudes without shame or coercion, you're finally ready to make the leap.

You can now teach.

If necessary, you could probably close the book at this point and successfully install any instructional program your district throws at you. Taking charge is not meant to serve as an intervention system, a phonics program, or a toolbox for improving student discussions. Instead, it allows all of those things to happen by ensuring that the students and the classroom are ready for rigorous teaching and learning.

That does not mean, however, that there's nothing to be learned about engaging instruction.

In fact, if you do decide to stop reading at this point, you actually run the risk of losing all your hard fought territory in an instant.

If your students misbehave because they are emotionally distraught and are in a reactive state of mind, the first section helped you explore what our brains need to learn and how to build your confidence as a teacher.

If your students act out because they are disconnected, the second section helped you look at the heart of teaching, relationships, and how to develop them through respect and release.

If your students have a lapse in judgment because they don't know what to do or the lesson is poorly paced, the third section assisted you in anticipating these problem areas and avoiding them through procedures, productivity, and planning.

If your students embrace disobedience because they seek attention, whether it be good or bad, the fourth section showed you the power of your noticing and how to direct it through differential social attention.

If you want to take the behavior fight to your students, the fifth section looked at developing prosocial behaviors in students that serve to equip them with necessary skills that also serve to dampen aberrant behavior.

But what if students act out because they're bored?

What if they have the ability to regulate their behavior but don't feel successful and misbehave to hide their frustration?

While it might not be easy to stomach, the truth of the matter is that some of the behavior problems that teachers face in the classroom today are of their own doing. When students are handed a low-level, fill-in-the-blank worksheet to keep them busy or, heaven forbid, be used to teach deep and enduring truths, they often start goofing off simply because they're bored. Though time-filler tasks come in a variety of formats and designs, and the ones available on Teachers Pay Teachers are extremely cute, for our purpose I will refer to them with the derogatory term *worksheets.*

Put simply, worksheets don't work.

They are easy to grade but lousy at promoting deep thinking. Worksheets provide a uniform approach to learning in an academically diverse reality. They relieve the pain of cognitive struggle, both in students and teachers. High doses of worksheets can be harmful to long-term academic growth. They slow the mental demands on students, substituting quick facts for sustained and meaningful learning.

Yet tearing down is easy. Building up is much harder.

Put simply, worksheets don't work.

To that end, this final section of the book will look at three realities about instruction that work with any instructional program or pedagogical practice. They are content-neutral truths that pull from neuroscience, learning theory, and social cognitive research. While the teaching programs and practices that schools and districts implement serve as the skeletal structure for overall instruction, the principles in this section serve as the muscular system, connecting the various parts and giving them the ability to move and interact.

First, engagement is the intersection of instructional design and student motivation. While teachers typically only focus on the first part of the equation, interpreting the textbook and district curricular documents to try and make a coherent learning program, it all is predicated on the assumption that students will engage with the instruction. What if they don't care? What if they are indifferent? When educators become familiar with the five facets of student motivation, they learn secret levers to better involve students in their own learning. Instruction can be designed to help students crave learning when it incorporates competence, relationships, autonomy, value, and emotions.

All the instruction in the world does little good if students can't remember it or apply it. Too often teachers believe their job is done when they've covered the material. In fact, that's only half of it. For learning to have truly occurred, students should remember the information and use it to influence future situations. Research has shown that retrieval practice, paired with interleaving and spacing, increases memory and recall and boosts achievement (Agarwal & Bain, 2019).

The final component is to consider the encoding process that students utilize every day to try and make sense of their world. For learning to stick, something we all yearn for, it has to make sense and connect to prior knowledge. Making sense of knowledge is not something that can be done *for* students. Instead, teachers can help facilitate the process by providing them with opportunities to elaborate on the content and add enough memory anchors that it can later be easily recalled.

The lessons learned in this section work in pre-K and high school. They apply in dual language classrooms and science labs. While the instructional techniques you employ will vary widely from those used in other classrooms across the country, they all have a few things in common.

Every instructional strategy used by schools incorporates student involvement and that is enhanced through the five facets of student motivation.

Every instructional strategy used by schools relies on students' ability to later recall the learned material and that is improved when natural memory systems are leveraged.

Every instructional strategy used by schools hinges on students making

ENGAGE

sense of the content and linking it to prior knowledge.

If you are planning on teaching anything, you need to know how to engage your students through motivation, memory, and making meaning.

Our greatest weakness lies in giving up. The most certain way to succeed is to try just one more time.

- Thomas Edison

6 – 2 Motivation (Engage)

Parenting is eerily similar to a major plot point in the Matrix or Terminator movies. In both series, mankind is doomed because technology became sentient and decided to enslave humanity due to its dangerous tendencies. Something created by people turns on them and becomes their very downfall.

I'm sure you can see the similarities.

The phrase *do as I say, not as I do* has probably been uttered or thought by almost every parent alive. Children are incredibly adept at taking our logic and turning it against us. How can we complain about the amount of time they spend in front of a screen when we can't go five minutes without checking that Facebook notification? Screen time is supposedly rotting our kids' brains but we just have to know how Aunt Claire reacted to the fuzzy panda video we just shared on our timeline.

Personally, motivation never seemed to be a problem for me in school. I always earned good grades because I valued them. I needed the affirmation they provided and worked hard to make sure I brought home all *As*. Truly, my parents did not have to do much to keep me focused in school. The thought of bringing home a *B* repulsed me and I breezed through high school, college, and graduate school. When my wife and I started having children, I figured they'd be like me in that regard. I planned on siring a succession of highly motivated mini-mes that would carry on the Daffern scholastic reputation for another generation. Hah!

The problem is, my wife and I also taught our children to find their own way. We modeled for them the truth that anything they really want to accomplish in life took dedication and perseverance. Rather than enforcing our views on our children, we talked to them about the importance of an education, earning enough money to support a family, and doing something that fulfills them. More than anything, we wanted our children to be their own people. We both watched in chagrin as parents all around us told their children what they should value and forced them to be clones of themselves. Envisioning ourselves as more enlightened, we gave our children room to explore their own desires.

Then the machines took over.

He's working?

You know that feeling you get when you walk into a room and your children are playing together quietly? Suddenly you stop breathing and quickly walk away. You do nothing to shatter the spell and hope they don't realize that instead of playing they are normally fighting with each other. That type of strangeness happened during my oldest son's sophomore year in high school. I came home from work one day and he was hard at work on a PowerPoint presentation on the computer. The scene startled me so much I quickly walked into my bedroom to get my bearings.

You see, my son had a problem completing his work lately. He was failing several classes and had no motivation to do anything. Unless my wife or I constantly nagged him, something we hated doing, he didn't finish his work. It just didn't matter to him. We had gone from hopeful parents of a high schooler with limitless potential to parents of a student struggling to earn high school credits.

The teacher

His *Cs* his freshman year turned into *Ds* and we started contemplating credit recovery and calculating whether or not he would graduate with his class. Take away his phone? Fine with him. Ground him? He never went anywhere. My son embodied the term *disengaged student*. It finally came to a head his sophomore year. He complained about his teacher, as is the God given right of all students, and I listened. Problem is, I listened with my administrator ears (as a former principal). For everything he said, I wondered what the other half of the story was. I know students and I know my son. Most stories of misdeeds are embellished just enough to inflame parents to precipitous action.

Then I realized that it didn't matter what was true. What mattered was what my son perceived to be true. Everyone creates their own reality. Rather than getting into the nitty-gritty about what his teacher was or was not doing, I began to see the effect the teacher had on him. My son was frustrated, angry, insubordinate, and lacked any respect for this teacher. Deserved or not, my son's emotional state was in chaos. He couldn't learn in that class even if we paid him to. That anger spilled over into the rest of his schoolwork.

Perhaps you've taught students like this. You might even think that I've been describing one of your own children. That's why coming home to find him hard at work shocked me so much. I didn't want to do anything to break the spell but alarm bells began to ring in my head. Later that evening my wife told me that my son wanted to speak with me. She prefaced it with, "Now, don't freak out. Listen to his idea before shutting him down."

Great. Now the alarm bells were accompanied by a flashing strobe light and an automated recording telling everyone to stay calm and proceed to the designated shelter area.

Professional gaming

In succinct terms, he pitched this idea to me. He wanted to stop going to high school and instead be homeschooled (later changed to online charter high school). By doing so, he'd have enough time to practice Overwatch, a multiplayer video game, about 4-6 hours a day. He needed to practice in order to get into the top tenth of a percent ranking and have a chance to make it onto one of the competitive teams they are forming up.

You see, Overwatch had just announced that they'd be creating regional teams to play their game full-time. For a living. By paying them salaries. As crazy as it may seem, my son told me, it's no different than paying professional athletes to play sports for a living. He had a point there.

The sucker punch, however, was when he got to the PowerPoint slide with his closing argument. It went something like this:

Dad, imagine that you are stuck in a dead-end job. You hate going to work every day and you don't see the point in anything you do. You know you could do so much more but instead your life is slipping away a day at a time. How would you feel?

That's me every day I go to high school. I don't care about school, I don't want to go to college. It doesn't matter to me. Video games do.

You might be thinking to yourself, sure, dream on kid. Who makes a living playing video games?

Lots of people, actually.

His PowerPoint was thorough. He had a timeline of events showing when he would be good enough for the Overwatch league based on his practice schedule. He had researched how much each part would cost for the gaming computer he wanted to build from scratch. Also, he included his willingness to help out with our newborn son Daniel, something that excited my wife.

Value

Of course my first reaction was to say *No*. Normal kids don't quit school to try and become professional gamers. They go to college and graduate with tens of thousands of dollars in student loan debts and come back to live at home after graduation, right? But my parenting philosophy kicked in and I knew he was right. He was living out everything we had instilled in him for 15 years. What we hadn't figured, though, was that an education wouldn't be valuable to him.

As I began to consider the crazy plan, I thought about the work my son put into this PowerPoint. The reasoning, the research, the presentation. I tried to remember the last time he was excited about something, anything, related to school. I had to go all the way back to his sixth grade year to find something. He had gotten lice and turned his homemade lice removal treatment into a video submitted to the school technology fair, winning him a free iPad mini.

Ever since then, for four years, school didn't interest him. He was going through the motions because that is what we expected but a little of him died every day. The main function of his life, school, had no value for him.

So we said yes.

Ultimately, the gaming didn't work out but it got him through high school. He's now attending a local community college because *he* wants to. He's working part-time at McDonald's because he wants to save enough money to transfer to a four-year college without taking student loans. By letting him find what motivated him to succeed, he was able to chart his own path and find the strength to follow it.

Hidden variable

At the same time that I was going through this parenting crisis with Dave, I was serving as the principal of a charter school and dealing with Jenny from section two (heart – release). These two events, among a few others, resulted in research and writing my first book about student engagement that I mentioned in section five (grow – intrapersonal). What I learned through this experience was that I was missing a key ingredient in the equation of student achievement.

Up to that point I had relied on my own knowledge and skills as an educator to help students succeed. When something didn't go well, I looked to myself for the solution. Perhaps I didn't plan an engaging enough lesson, ask the right questions, or my execution was poor. Something I did obviously didn't work so I'd go back to the drawing board again and again until I figured it out.

While this line of thinking is definitely empowering, it is ultimately flawed. There's a hidden variable in the equation of student achievement. The way I viewed it at the time, curriculum (content) multiplied by pedagogy (execution) equaled achievement.

Curriculum x pedagogy = achievement

If my students weren't successful on the final exam, then I needed to either do a better job of finding a quality curriculum or executing the lesson plan. Through my experience with Dave and Jenny, a formerly missing variable emerged as the mediator of both curriculum and pedagogy.

(Curriculum x pedagogy)motivation = achievement

As hard as I tried to teach and create engaging lessons, the students had to meet me there. All my blood, sweat, and tears were wasted if I couldn't bring the students along with me. If they weren't motivated, I'd never help them be as successful as I wanted them to be.

Student motivation

So, what causes students to engage in learning? For myself, I craved being successful and getting good grades. I didn't really need any outside motivation from teachers because even if they were boring or the subject seemed useless, I'd still work hard to earn *As* because that was important to me.

Obviously that wasn't going to work for either Dave or Jenny. They both sniffed with derision at my antiquated notions of earning good grades because it wasn't valuable or relevant to them. They needed something else to push them to work. When I considered their struggles and the way that the school system was set up, I finally realized why they were never going to succeed in a traditional school environment.

Biology and chemistry, fractions and poetry hold little intrinsic value to some students. They don't think they'll ever use that information in the real world and, if they do, they figure they can simply Google it. Without relevancy, some students will never engage with school no matter how many flashing lights we parade in front of them.

Other students disengage because of a lack of connectedness. They don't feel like they are a part of a larger learning community, whether it be their classroom or even their school. They feel distant, alone, and adrift in a sea of facts and figures. When they don't sense a strong human connection with others, either teachers or peers, many students lose the drive to push through difficult content and learn.

If students aren't thriving in school, and we can reasonably assume that the curriculum is solid and the instructional practices are sound, then we must look elsewhere for solutions. The students themselves hold the key to increased engagement and achievement. If we can figure out how to motivate them, or more accurately, tap into the facet of motivation that most inspires them, then classroom management becomes an afterthought.

Engaged students rarely, if ever, misbehave.

ENGAGE

What can you do tomorrow?

Reflect on your own motivation. Think about what motivates you to succeed in academic tasks. Your default teaching style will cater to this motivational drive.

Expand. Now consider a student that sometimes does not show interest in learning. Think about what they do enjoy and see if you can discover the disconnect. Adjust an upcoming lesson to include what motivates them to learn.

What does this look like in the classroom?

The teacher **motivates** students to engage in learning by:
- Offering students choices and opportunities to lead lessons;
- Highlighting real-word connections within the curriculum; and
- Providing timely feedback to build students' competence.

How can you reflect on your learning?

What kept you engaged as a student?

_____
_____

Think about a disengaged student. Do you think your motivational drives as the same as his/hers? How do you know?

_____
_____

Turning on the TV

Many years ago I was about to leave the house but had a few extra minutes. I decided to turn on the TV quickly to see if there was anything important happening on the news channel. Yet when I picked up the remote to turn the TV on, nothing happened. Utter darkness from the idiot box.

I couldn't figure out why it wasn't working but I assumed one of the kids must have messed with it. I stood stolidly in front of the darkened television, mashing the power button on the remote to no effect. If tenacity and sheer stubbornness could have solved the problem, the matter would have ended there. However, my efforts were useless.

Working through the many possible causes of my conundrum, I began to apply my vast intellectual prowess to the matter at hand. I tried positioning myself directly in front of the sensor, thinking perhaps an object might have obstructed the infrared beam. When that didn't work, I took a cleaning cloth and carefully wiped down the diode at the end of the remote and the plastic covering the receptor on the television unit. Stray fingerprints, however, were not at the root of the problem.

I looked at the remote and came to a sudden realization. It was a multifunction remote that had the capability to not only control the TV but the Blu-ray player, the cable box, and an auxiliary device. I don't know how many times my kids have brought me the remote saying it didn't work or that it needed new batteries when the only problem was that the TV button at the top wasn't selected. Sometimes it's trying to control the Blu-ray player or the cable box and all you have to do is select TV. Satisfied that I had successfully solved the problem, I pressed the TV button on the remote and then the power button to turn the TV on.

Engage

Nothing.

The remote was not the original one that came with the television but instead was a universal remote replacement. I began to suspect that the remote had somehow become uncalibrated with the Sony television. Pulling out the remote's instructions, which I had meticulously dated and filed in my filing cabinet, I ran through the sequence needed for configuring the remote. I held down the setup button on the remote for three seconds until the red light on the remote stayed on. I then punched in the 4-digit sequence designed to work with Sony televisions. A satisfying double blink of the red light let me know that the remote was now correctly configured. With a flourish I pressed the power button on the remote.

Still nothing.

My wife, Heather, found me a few moments later staring numbly at the remote in my hand, not saying a word. "What are you doing?" she asked, wondering why I looked like a garden statue.

"What does it look like I'm doing?!?" I almost yelled back with a manic look in my eyes. "The remote isn't working! I can't figure out why!" I explained everything I had done to that point and was beginning to think we needed to buy an entirely new television.

It took everything within her to not bark out a laugh. She slowly walked over to the wall and stooped down. "I'm sorry, Aaron, it's my fault. I unplugged the TV when I vacuumed the living room earlier and I guess I forgot to plug it back in." She left me standing there with a haunted look in my eyes as the screen came to life. I stared at the remote as if it were an alien object.

Plugged in

Something like this is happening in schools all across the country every day. Teachers and principals are pulling out all the stops trying to engage their students in classroom activities. They are desperate to make learning more fun and to successfully integrate more technology. They are flipping the classrooms and utilizing online learning platforms. Like my situation with the remote, educators are mashing buttons in ridiculous configurations in an attempt to get their students interested in learning.

Teachers know what should work. They took pedagogy classes in college, suffered through student teaching, and have several years of experience under their belts. They attend workshops each summer and participate in yearly book studies. Districts continually pilot and push out new initiatives designed to improve achievement and teacher effectiveness.

But what if the students aren't plugged in?

For me to effectively use the TV remote, two prerequisite conditions must exist. First, I must configure the remote properly. Second, the TV requires power.

For students to engage in learning activities, two prerequisite conditions must likewise exist. First, teachers must design effective instruction that invites students into the learning process. Second, students must be motivated to participate. If students aren't interested, a teacher's plans can quickly become irrelevant in the face of staggering apathy.

Since teachers cannot control student motivation, they must then rely on the only area within their domain: instructional design. Rather than randomly choosing fun activities, however, teachers can purposefully craft instruction that harnesses one or more of the five facets of student motivation – competence, relationships, autonomy, value, and emotions

(Daffern, 2017).

Through their instructional choices, teachers can plug students in.

CRAVE

Some students are highly motivated by competence. When they feel like they are able to accomplish a task, they feel engaged and ready to learn. They love building their proficiency through sequential learning. More importantly, these students need to have an expectancy of success. If they feel like the task is too difficult and out of their reach, they will quickly lose interest.

I like to call these students Bowheads. When I envision predominantly competence-motivated students, I always picture a little girl on the first day of school. She's sitting in the front row with her Easter dress on, she has three pencils sharpened with a pad of paper ready, and she already has her hand up before the bell rings. She greatly enjoys worksheets, multiplication facts, and fill-in-the-blank quizzes. For the most part, the traditional education system is built for students like her. Follow the algorithm, memorize the facts, and success is sure to follow.

Other students get much more out of the classroom when they have built positive relationships with others. Usually the teacher, though sometimes with peers, these students need the connection of other human beings. They thrive on cooperative learning and working with a partner. They best process information by talking things out with a friend and they love to connect their learning to their own lives. Relational learners thrive in the dramatic arts and literature, exploring the human condition and reveling in the stories of others.

I lovingly call these students Stalkers. In elementary school, they are the ones who bring their teacher a flower from recess. Every. Single. Day.

In junior high, they will attempt to add their teacher as a friend on Facebook on their thirteenth birthday. By the time they are in high school, they will know things about their teachers that they have no business knowing. They don't mean to be creepy, they just desperately crave a positive relationship with their teachers.

For some, the key question is not, "What are we learning?" but, "Do I have to?" Autonomy can make all the difference to some students. After being told what to do, what to learn, where to sit, and how to answer questions for their whole life, some students feel the need to break free. A lot of passive-aggressive behavior in the classroom is a result of teachers trying to exert too much control over these students. For every instructor that makes it her mission to keep order in the classroom, there are several students willing to accept that challenge head-on.

If students aren't interested, a teacher's plans can quickly become irrelevant in the face of staggering apathy.

For these students, the term Captain comes to mind. These learners are the ones who like to organize games on the playground, enforce the rules of learning centers, and relish the opportunity to choose their tasks. As long as they are the captain and everyone else acts as a first mate, the world works just fine. When they feel coerced, manipulated, or just plain boxed in, they instinctively try to assert control of their learning and their lives.

If you've ever been asked, "Will this be on the test?" or "Is this for a grade?", you're getting signals that you are instructing a predominantly value-motivated student. For these students, relevancy is everything. If what they are learning somehow connects to them or something important to them (e.g., their grades), then they learn easily. If it seems pointless or useless, however, engagement is elusive. Some students value learning for its own sake while others value learning to accomplish a goal. It might be getting a good grade, helping accomplish a larger aim like getting into college, or getting a good job. Either way, these learners evaluate learning tasks through the filter of value.

These students can be thought of as Real-worlders. They, more than any other type of learner, need to see the relevance in what they are learning. For them, tasks that are not grounded in reality or that fail to help them accomplish a goal are not worth doing. They despise busy work and can quickly check out if they think a teacher or substitute is simply going through the motions. On the other hand, when they work on a task valuable to them, they can quickly become engrossed.

Finally, some students' emotions serve as their primary motivational facet. If the classroom is fun, or an activity is game-like, then they are all-in. If it's a more sterile, factory-like atmosphere, however, they will find it hard to muster enough energy to participate. A key emotion to cultivate in these learners is interest. When their curiosity is piqued, their natural inclination will be to explore and engage. If these students suffer emotional distress, either in or out of the classroom, it will greatly affect their academic behavior.

After seeing Pixar's *Inside Out*, it's hard to think of these students as anything but Rileys. In the movie, Riley is the main character. Personified emotions, such as Joy, Sadness, Anger, and Disgust, influence her actions and wreak all kinds of havoc. Like Riley, emotions-dominant learners can sometimes swing back and forth based on how they are feeling. They feed off of exciting environments but can quickly lose interest if they feel bored.

Designing instruction

As previously stated, these facets of motivation should serve to inform educators rather than typecast students. Knowing what motivates students, teachers can leverage this knowledge to design instruction that engages all learners and increases active learning. Rather than throwing out all of your carefully laid plans, look once again at your lesson plans through the lens of CRAVE to see how motivating the instruction is.

First, does the task support competence? If it's right in the zone of proximal development, the not-too-hard and not-too-easy range for students, then it's well-designed. But how many tasks perfectly fit 25 students? To harness competence, you'll need to build in some supports for struggling students and some extensions for your high flyers. One-size-fits-all activities are lucky if they fit even one-fourth of your class.

Second, how does the task leverage relationships? While the relationships that you build with your students typically happen outside of academic tasks, know that your level of relationship with your students colors everything. They'll be much more likely to work hard for a teacher that cares about them than for a faceless taskmaster. Another aspect of relationships is peer-focused. How does the task build a community of learners? More than simply group or partner work, tasks that help students learn from and rely on each other's knowledge make use of the motivational facet of relationships.

Third, what kind of voice do the students have in the task? Autonomy does not mean choosing whether or not to complete homework. There are myriad opportunities for students to flex their individuality while staying within the lines of your lesson plan. Can they choose which part of the task to start on? Can they choose to work alone or with a partner? Perhaps they have different seating options for the task. Even small, seemingly inconsequential choices give students a sense of power over their own learning.

Fourth, how is the learning relevant? Many students don't see the value in equivalent fractions or subject-verb agreement. Why should they do the task? Why does it matter? For the students that are motivated by grades, simply assigning the task and giving it weight in the grade book will be enough. Yet for those that look for a more personal meaning, they'll need something extra. Find a way to relate the task to a real-world application, previous learning, or even something curious or peculiar. If it isn't very relevant, it won't be very motivating.

Finally, is it fun? Emotions mediate all the other facets of motivation. When students are in depressed moods, or if they are angry about something that just happened at lunch, then they won't be in the right headspace to work on your assignment. Students should at least be emotionally neutral to be able to access their prefrontal cortex and use their critical thinking skills. You can support this by keeping your classroom fun and light-hearted. Some students respond well to competition (who doesn't like a Kahoot! quiz?) but others are turned off by it because they don't think they'll ever win. Whatever your style is, whether it be reading bad puns, showing comic strips from the Sunday paper, or simply having students spend three minutes talking to a partner about their favorite YouTube channel, keep a close eye on the emotional atmosphere in your room.

When troubleshooting situations with students in which you find them unmotivated to participate, run through these five facets. In addition,

CRAVE is a fantastic planning tool for designing engaging instruction for all your students. Considering both the larger unit and each daily lesson, the more facets of motivation you include in your learning, the greater the chance that students will be fully engaged. By harnessing student motivation, you can plug your students into learning.

ENGAGE

What can you do tomorrow?

Evaluate your instruction. Use the five facets of student motivation (competence, relationships, autonomy, value, emotions) as a filter through which you evaluate your instructional design. Look to see which students are sometimes disengaged from learning and whether or not their motivational needs are being met by your normal instructional practices.

Implement your learning. Adjust an upcoming lesson to incorporate all five facets and note the difference in student engagement.

What does this look like in the classroom?

The teacher **designs engaging instruction** that includes:
- Differentiated tasks to meet individual student needs;
- Activities that are fun and light-hearted; and
- Social interactions between the teacher and students and/or between students themselves.

How can you reflect on your learning?

Which facet of motivation do you think is strongest within you?

_____

_____

How can you use the CRAVE model to design engaging instruction?

_____

_____

Immediate impact: Go to 5 – 3 Intrapersonal (Grow) – pg. 363

The human mind is our fundamental resource.

- John F. Kennedy

6 – 3 Memory (Engage)

Imagine that as you drive down the street you hear a pinging noise under the hood. You aren't a mechanic by any stretch of the imagination but you know that that sound cannot be good. Seeing as how you've got some extra time and you don't want to have to replace your entire engine due to negligence, you immediately head to the nearest auto repair shop.

As it happens, there's a repair bay open. You drive the car in and immediately begin talking to the technician, trying your hardest to describe the sound you heard without sounding like a complete fool. As you finish your description, you ask, "So, what do you think it might be?"

The technician looks back at you blankly and says, "Don't look at me, I just work here."

Huh?

That type of response would most likely leave you nonplussed, unsure of the advisability of leaving your car in such incapable hands. In that situation, the least the technician could have done was make some comment about a fan belt or the intake valve. It could have been complete gobbledygook but it would have given you some comfort.

When you go to the auto repair shop, you expect the technicians to know about car engines because that's their job. If you call customer service for your cable company, you expect the representative to be able to talk to you about your account and how to change services. Calling your local State Farm agent should allow you to talk to someone about insurance.

As a teacher, a professional educator, how much can you speak to how the brain learns? What systems are in place to encode and retrieve memories? Which types of learning activities do a better job of creating multiple tags for future recall?

If learning is your business, shouldn't you be able to answer all of those questions?

Learning

First, since learning is our business, we might want to at least come to an agreement as to what it is before we quibble about the best way to impact it. In *Make It Stick* (Brown, Roediger, & McDaniel, 2014), the authors define learning as acquiring knowledge and skills and having them readily available from memory so one can make sense of future problems and opportunities. In other words, learning always has a forward slant. Rather than being merely academic, useful learning enables students to make use of their knowledge and apply it in future settings and situations.

Learning is deeper and more durable when it requires effort. Learning that's easy is like building a sand castle on the water line during low tide – only there for a short time. But probably most often missed in a definition of learning is the requirement of prior knowledge.

When students are skilled at extracting the underlying principles or rules that differentiate types of problems or scenarios, they're more successful at picking the right solutions or strategies in unfamiliar situations. All new learning, however, requires a foundation of prior knowledge. Without something familiar to hook the new learning onto, it won't stick long enough to turn it into long-term memory.

So, we know that when learning is harder, it's stronger and lasts longer. We also know that new learning is built on the foundation of prior knowledge, giving it a hook to latch onto. Learning always builds on a store of existing concepts. We interpret and remember events by building connections to what we already know.

How exactly do we use this information to help students learn better?

Learning is deeper and more durable when it requires effort.

Before we get too far along, let's be clear about what doesn't work. Repetition by itself does not lead to good long-term memory. While drill-and-kill might seem like a viable option for teachers, the results are shallow and fixed. Students who mindlessly repeat the same skill over and over are only successful when they see an identical problem in an identical context.

Learning is not a simple or linear event. It happens in three stages, some of which have their own sub-stages. The first stage is called encoding. We convert sensory information and perceptions into meaningful representations. This initial encoding is held in our short-term working memory before being consolidated into a cohesive representation of knowledge. We teach kindergarteners about the five senses because the majority of our learning begins as a sensory experience.

The second stage is consolidation. The initial representations are strengthened for long-term memories by connecting them to prior knowledge. The memory traces are reorganized and stabilized, given meaning, and connected to past experiences and other knowledge already stored in long-term memory. This stage happens subconsciously and takes some time, typically occurring while we sleep.

The third stage in memory is retrieval. Once information is stored in long-term memory, knowledge is theoretically available but practically out of reach. For us to use our vast stores of facts and figures, we must recall the correct particulars from long-term memory back into our conscious working memory. This allows us to take previously learned information and apply to similar or even unique situations.

Yet retrieval holds a powerful possibility. As we bring information out of storage and into working memory, we can update it and encode it again. Using it in a new situation allows us to encode the information all over again with additional memory tags and layers of meaning. As it gets reconsolidated, it now holds new cues associated with it in addition to the original set. When knowledge gets used again and again, it gains more memory tags through each act of retrieval and reconsolidation. Thus some information, such as multiplication facts, become so robust through constant retrieval that they gain automaticity.

As always, however, the consolidation process, whether it be with brand-new information or knowledge that has been retrieved thousands of times, must be anchored in prior knowledge. Bits of data do not simply float around in our brain but are instead linked and associated with other factoids of knowledge that we are familiar with. The more links the information has, the easier it is to retrieve and apply.

Thus when teachers provide an abundance of shortcuts and hacks to complex skills, they inadvertently hinder the potential for robust learning. Fast and easy strategies lead to short-term learning (Agarwal & Bain, 2019). They can get you through a pinch but won't have enough tags and encoding opportunities to make retrieval from long-term memory viable. Slower and more effortful strategies, such as deriving equations rather than simply memorizing them, lead to better long-term memory. The more work it takes to understand a new concept, the more opportunities for association with prior knowledge and subsequent retrieval.

Retrieval

For information to be useful and applicable once stored in long-term memory, it must be periodically retrieved and examined, much like polishing the family silver every few months. The ideal intervals between retrieval are not set in stone but vary based on the newness of the encoding.

Eric Jensen (2005) shared that we have 24 – 48 hours to revisit, review and apply new learning in order to make it permanent and consolidated in long-term memory. If learning is strengthened enough during this initial encoding, it becomes a part of our skill set, background knowledge, or conceptual understanding.

To keep this new learning retrievable, he recommends practicing with it at regular intervals, with intensity and deliberateness. One way to do that is to repeat key ideas within ten minutes of the original learning, again 48 hours later, and then tie it all together with one more repetition seven days later. An easy procedure to keep a constant stream of ideas in front of students is to open and close each class with important words or concepts of the day. Previous learning can be sprinkled in as well to constantly review material.

One of our most common practices for reviewing material is not nearly as useful as we think. Often, students will reread material in a textbook or from notes when preparing for an exam. Rereading gives us a false sense of security as the material feels familiar and we believe we know it. In fact, this is fool's gold and we would do much better to practice retrieval instead of rereading (Brown, Roediger, & McDaniel, 2014).

So, before your next major test, don't reread the chapter or skim your notes. Instead, sit down and try to write out (retrieve) the major points from the material. This effortful practice of laboriously bringing to mind these buried nuggets is shown by research to be much more effective on exam performance. After retrieving everything you can, then refer to the chapter or your notes to compare the two.

Fast and easy strategies lead to short-term learning.

The act of retrieving information from memory has two profound benefits. First, it gives you a clear picture of what you know and what you don't know, allowing you to focus further studying efforts in the areas that need it most. Second, bringing the memory to mind, or retrieving it, brings it back to your working memory and allows it to be reconsolidated. This strengthens the connections of this information and makes it easier for you to recall it in the future.

The more cognitive effort expended in retrieval, the greater the future retention of the information. The act of retrieving a memory changes it, making it easier to retrieve again. This repeated experience of retrieval and reconsolidation will entrench the memory, ultimately leading to automaticity for those items, like letter-sound correspondence or basic math facts, that are recalled continually.

When students have confidence in themselves and their abilities based on repeated performance with retrieval practice, they learn to lean into it and leverage it. With enough effortful practice, a complex set of interrelated ideas or sequence of motor skills fuse into a meaningful whole. Thus, while you read this passage, you are most likely doing it fluently and without difficulty. You don't have to sound out any words or try to fill in gaps because of unknown words. Instead, the highly complex act of reading has become automatic for many literate children and adults due to continuous effortful practice.

That level of comfortable skill is possible in any content area.

Powerful teaching

Retrieval practice boosts learning by pulling information out of students' heads rather than cramming information in, a key distinction that, when fully applied, will affect many traditional teaching and testing practices (Agarwal & Bain, 2019). The key is the importance of making retrieval practice either no-stakes or very low-stakes. When students can practice recalling information without the fear of a poor grade or failing a task, an atmosphere of growth infuses the classroom. If they struggle, they can focus on filling the gap and learning the missed information without the shame of failure.

Retrieval practice has been found to be more potent than both lecturing and taking notes. While most teachers, though some grudgingly, will admit the inadequacy of lecture as a method for increasing student achievement, some might question note-taking. The flaw in this overused practice comes from the mirage of multitasking. While many people think they can do many things at once, in fact our brains simply cannot. Instead, we constantly shift our attention from one task to the next, sometimes giving the illusion of multitasking while in fact inhibiting performance in both tasks.

While students are writing notes during a lesson, they can either be listening to the content or writing down a note, *but never both at the same time.* Instead, bits of information are overlooked or lost as students attempt to switch back and forth between writing and listening. A simple solution that utilizes retrieval practice would be to pause every few minutes during a lesson and ask students to write down everything they remember about what was just said. This recall from short-term memory is an act of retrieval, an example of effortful recall, and not performed at the expense of listening to the teacher.

The more cognitive effort expended in retrieval, the greater the future retention of the information.

For those that wonder about the complexity of retrieval practice possibilities, it can be mixed with both fact-based and higher-order types of questions. Another benefit is that it isn't something else to be graded. In fact, constant retrieval practice will not only improve performance but doesn't require any data collection, grading, or points.

So the next time you want to know what your students have learned, put away the worksheet or chapter review. Instead, stop in the middle of the lesson and ask students to talk to a partner about two things they've learned so far today. Better yet, ask them to share two things that they learned yesterday or how the lesson relates to something in their own lives.

Remember, the greater the effort expended in the recall, the greater the impact of the action. Retrieval can be fact-based, concept-based, or used with complex questions. It can be multiple choice, short answer, or free recall. Any way you look at it, retrieval helps students better encode the information because when they are retrieving, they're also encoding.

What can you do tomorrow?

Incorporate retrieval. To boost learning and recall, incorporate retrieval practice into your lesson instead of a traditional worksheet. Ask them to recall what was taught last week rather than today.

Retrieve in different ways. Have students write down or discuss what they learned from the lesson. Use retrieval practice to encode and consolidate information in a continuous cycle, robustly linking prior knowledge with new learning.

What does this look like in the classroom?

Students **practice retrieval** regularly, using techniques such as:
- Stopping during instruction to discuss or write notes about what was just learned;
- Purposefully recalling information from past lessons; and
- Writing a short summary of the lesson for homework.

How can you reflect on your learning?

Why is difficult learning better than effortless learning?

_____

_____

How does retrieval practice benefit students?

_____

_____

Engage

Spacing

Retrieval practice is a key weapon in fighting classroom boredom and misbehavior. Remember that the first facet of student motivation is competence. When students feel able and capable, they are more likely to engage and less likely to act out. Many behavior problems stem from the fact that students are frustrated and unable to complete the work. Leaning into retrieval practice boosts their confidence through increased knowledge and skill.

But there are other factors that, when added together with retrieval practice, make it even more powerful. What is most likely understood, but bears mentioning explicitly, is how valuable feedback is to the retrieval practice. Working hard to bring a memory or fact out of long-term storage is only as useful as its validity and the confidence it engenders. If students continuously apply misinformation without correction, then they'll actually be reinforcing the wrong pieces of data.

When engaging in retrieval practice, build in a little bit of feedback time so students can check the accuracy of their recall. This can be done by referring to notes or to a textbook, checking answers with a friend, or briefly giving the correct answers to the class as a whole. Either way, students need to not only practice recalling important information but also get immediate validation of the precision of their recollection.

Yet as powerful as retrieval practice is on its own, it gains more potency when combined with two other techniques, the first of which is spacing. Learning and memory improves when done in shorter sessions with rest intervals rather than constant exposure to new or the same material. Less is more. Too much content in too short of a window will greatly reduce its permanence. Processing time is needed so information can solidify rather than going out as quickly as it goes in (Jensen, 2005).

Another go-to study habit, cramming before an exam, also needs to go the way of the dinosaur. In extensive studies, any gains achieved during massed practice (i.e., cramming) are transitory and melt away quickly (Brown, Roediger, & McDaniel, 2014). Even without research to back this up, most of us understand this truth at a personal level.

In college I used to call it a data dump, but whatever it's called, it worked in the short term. I'd go over my notes again and again before a semester or final exam, memorizing key facts and figures to regurgitate on the test. I'd cram some more while waiting for the exam to begin and, nine times out of ten, it would work. I'd remember just enough to convince my professor that I knew what I was talking about.

Yet none of it lasted. Two days later, let alone two weeks later, over 90% of the information would be gone. That didn't bother me at the time because, in my mind, I had already achieved my purpose. I kept the information in just long enough to spit back out on a test, but don't we want our students to know more than that? Are we okay if our students forget everything they learned two days after the test?

Spacing out the retrieval practice, rather than massing it all together, it allows for some forgetting to occur in between learning sessions. It's this temporary forgetting that leads to stronger long-term retention. Though massed practice and spaced practice can both deliver the goods in the short-term, massed practice also inevitably leads to rapid forgetting. Easy come, easy go (Brown, Roediger, & McDaniel, 2014).

One way to think about it, albeit in an unpleasant manner, is to relate cramming to binge-and-purge eating. A lot can go into our brains in a short amount of time, but most of it will come back out again. For information to transfer into long-term memory (consolidation), it must be chewed slowly and allowed to connect to prior knowledge. If everything is swallowed wholesale, the chances of it sticking around are relatively low.

So when studying, students would be better served to space out their retrieval practice. Though harder to bring to mind in multiple sessions, this effortful reconstruction of learning makes the big ideas more salient and memorable. Additionally, it connects them more securely to other knowledge and more recent learning. In between spaced practice will presumably be additional classroom experiences. As retrieval gets stretched out, it has a greater opportunity for extra connections in this intermittent learning.

Learning and memory improves when done in shorter sessions with rest intervals rather than constant exposure to new or the same material.

Spaced practice allows for continuous retrieval and encoding. Rather than cramming as much learning as possible into the narrowest time period imaginable, spaced practice boosts learning by spreading the retrieval out over time. Every time the knowledge is pulled out of memory, it is briefly interacted with and encoded with additional memory tags, making it that much more robust (Agarwal & Bain, 2019).

Spacing also has the added benefit of decreasing the total amount of time needed to study. When students cram, they forget more over the long term and have to increase the amount of time they study to catch up. With spacing, students learn more in the long-term and actually have to study less before a major exam. They bring their learning with them as they move through the learning unit rather than forgetting it quickly and requiring additional cramming.

Forgetting is a natural process that occurs whether we want it to or not. Spacing takes advantage of this reality and turns it into desirable difficulty. That extra effort required to bring the information back to mind is just the ingredient needed to make it stickier and more resilient. This means that retrieval practice should not always recall what was just learned. Instead, ask students to bring to mind what was covered a day or two ago.

Homework can be viewed in the same way. In a typical classroom, content is delivered and students practice it with teacher guidance before being given a set of problems to do on their own for homework. Spacing, in this context, would continue to deliver lessons and provide students the opportunity to practice the new skill with teacher assistance. The homework, however, would be over something learned the previous week. It would be more strenuous to remember that content but the learning gains would be substantially higher.

As spaced practice flourishes in the classroom, knowledge begins to return more quickly and fluently. Information gets hard-wired into memory as it's recalled over and over in new and unique contexts. Students might first be surprised by their own knowledge after a delay between the initial learning and the retrieval practice, but this builds their confidence. They will grow less fearful of the forgetting process, knowing that what they learn is in their memory banks and can be called upon when needed. This confidence boosts motivation and engagement while driving down misbehavior.

Interleaving

The final ingredient in the secret sauce that makes retrieval practice so potent is interleaving. Instead of continuously practicing with similar problems or recalling information that is nearly identical, interleaving is a deliberate practice that varies the types of problems being recalled or retrieved. Another advantage (or disadvantage, depending on your outlook) is that interleaving is simply more difficult.

If you've ever taught a math class, or can remember taking a math course yourself, you can probably recall the dangers of not varying, or interleaving, practice. Many math assignments focus on one skill at a time and repeat it endlessly in a series of computational and word problems that all look eerily similar except for the values used. When students are faced with a series of ten word problems to complete for a math assignment, they can easily turn their analytical powers off and go into robot mode. If the first four problems they complete require them to multiply the two values, then a pattern emerges and they simply begin to scan and multiply. If the final two problems suddenly ask them to divide rather than multiply, they'll probably miss it and keep on multiplying come hell or high water.

Interleaved practice would mix up the types of problems that students are asked to complete. Instead of mindlessly multiplying, students might see an array of problem types, some asking students to multiply, some to divide, and some to use both operations in a two-step problem. When the practice or recall is varied, it forces students to slow down and really read to understand what is being asked of them.

The learning gained from interleaved practice feels slower than massed practice (Brown, Roediger, & McDaniel, 2014). Though more cumbersome, the learning gains from mixing it up are not transitory like those earned from massed or similar practice. Mastery and long-term retention are much improved from interleaved and spaced practice. This is due largely to the gains made during interleaved practice in recognition and knowledge transfer.

When we are forced to slow down and truly understand a problem situation to recall the pertinent information or skill, rather than blindly applying the same algorithm again and again, it helps us learn to better assess the context of the learning task. This in turn assists us as we practice discriminating between problems, selecting and applying the correct solution from a range of possibilities, and adding additional layers of meaning to known material. Interleaving asks us to apply learning in a variety of situations and contexts, making it richer and more intricately encoded. Knowledge is associated with increasingly versatile cues that make future retrieval that much more simple.

The learning gained from interleaved practice feels slower than massed practice.

If, for example, you are studying for an upcoming history exam over the Russian Revolution, interleave the material with similar but different facts of other revolutions, such as the American Revolution and the French Revolution. Being able to discriminate between similar yet separate events will increase your ability to recall the correct information when called up in a testing situation.

It's this closeness of material that gives interleaving its potency. It boosts learning by mixing up closely related topics and encouraging discrimination (Agarwal & Bain, 2019). If, for example, you interleaved key facts about the Russian Revolution with geometry theorems or atomic masses from the periodic table of elements, those facts are so disparate that you would have no problem keeping them separate. It's when you mix up facts from topics that aren't easily distinguishable, such as data from different revolutions or math word problems that ask for different operations to be performed, that interleaving truly becomes powerful.

An additional facet of interleaving is that it can be implemented without finding similar topics to mix into the review. If you're practicing retrieval with students in preparation for an exam, even rearranging the order of the items without changing the content can increase student learning. Our minds are adept at picking up patterns quickly and sometimes our ability to respond quickly has more to do with remembering the order of questions than our knowledge. Put things in a new order and watch the desirable difficulty rise.

Retrieval, mindset, and relationships

Putting it altogether, retrieval practice that is spaced out, interleaved with other types of learning or simply rearranged, and includes immediate feedback produces higher levels of achievement. Students retain information longer and are more versatile in its application. However, these benefits come at a price. This type of practice is much harder, producing slower gains that do not feel as effortless as massed practice.

This is why none of the components in this book work in isolation. Instead, you must work hard to integrate each part, even if they do not seem related, so that a clear picture of student learning emerges. This is a perfect example of the saying *the whole is greater than the sum of its parts*.

For students to be open to this level of difficulty, they must first feel cared for and connected with you. This type of practice is hard and they won't be open to it if they are emotionally vulnerable and feel unsafe. Relationships and protection are the foundational pieces of the classroom environment on which everything else rests.

Once safety is established, students must be allowed and encouraged to develop a growth mindset. Rather than fighting mistakes and fearing what will happen if they get something wrong, students flourish when they see errors as learning opportunities. If open to correction and reflective of what they know and don't know, they'll be in the ideal position to take full advantage of retrieval practice.

They'll embrace its inherent difficulties as a sign that their brains are getting stronger. Every time they fail to remember something they'll immediately seek the correct answer so they don't make the same mistake twice. Students in the right frame of mind will hunger for learning opportunities and feedback for growth as much as they do for air, food, and water. Putting everything together can create an unstoppable learning machine that is powered and directed by the students, not you.

This is when we see them truly take charge.

What can you do tomorrow?

Space your retrieval. Spread out your practice rather than massing it altogether. Ask students to recall and apply learning from last week instead of always applying something they just learned that day.

Mix things up. Interleave the retrieval practice with similar items. This increases desirable difficulty and gives them an opportunity to grow in their ability to distinguish between problems and apply the correct solution strategy.

What does this look like in the classroom?

Students review material using **memory techniques**, including:
- Immediate feedback to validate the retrieval;
- Spacing out the recall to increase the difficulty; and
- Mixing up the content to encourage recognition and discrimination.

How can you reflect on your learning?

How does spacing take advantage of our natural tendency to forget?
_____
_____

What are the benefits of interleaving?
_____
_____

Immediate impact: Go to 5 – 2 Interpersonal (Grow) – pg. 343

Tell me and I forget. Teach me and I remember. Involve me and I learn.

- Benjamin Franklin

6 – 4 Making meaning (Engage)

We've all had that moment of panic before.

We download a new program off the internet and are excited to give it a test run. We play with the features, edit a new creation, and click the disc icon to save. A window pops up and we select *save* a moment before we realize that it's too late.

We have no idea where the file landed on our computer.

We didn't take the time to examine the file path, change the destination to a known location, such as our desktop, or even write down the file name. It's on our hard drive, somewhere, but we have no idea where. Perhaps we can find it with some searching or tedious examination of that ubiquitous folder conveniently labeled *My Documents*.

Just because we saved it doesn't mean we can easily find it again.

This all too often occurrence is a perfect analogy for how our memory works.

Information comes in through the senses and seemingly lands somewhere in our memory banks. Yes, we heard the lecture and answered the questions, but just because we experience something once (or thrice) doesn't mean we can easily recall the information later upon demand.

To easily locate the knowledge later, it needs to have a certain stickiness to it. Just like finding a random save file is easier when the filename is known, the save location is logical, the file folders are organized, or it's easy to search for, knowledge that students learn also needs a few qualities to make it memorable.

Sticky learning, or learning that is easy to recall and apply in new and unique situations, has multiple memory tags associated with it. We remember it because it links to something else we already know, is connected with different senses and emotions, and is related to a larger narrative or big picture. If we want a document to be found easily on our computer, there are various steps we can take to organize our filing system and naming conventions. If we want students to later recall something we are trying to teach them, there are also multiple tactics we can employ to make learning stickier.

Making meaning

Here's a mind-blowing truth that will change the way you teach forever.

Meaning is generated internally by students, not received from an outside source (i.e., you).

I'll give you a moment to process that.

There are a few staggering implications to this revelation. First, all the planning and thought you put into your lessons pale in comparison to the importance of what students do with the information. In order for learning to stick, the students, not you, have to make meaningful connections and discover unknown facts. It cannot be passively received or transferred like a file from one folder to another on your laptop.

Second, the true result of any lesson comes more from the output than from the input. How students interact with, chew on, process, and digest the content you're delivering will ultimately decide its efficacy. Third, Eric Jenson (2005) reminds us that you can either have your students' attention or they can be making meaning, but never both at the same time.

Do you want to encourage students to make meaning of what you just taught? Be quiet and let them do it. External input conflicts with processing of prior content and thoughtful reflection.

To easily locate the knowledge later, it needs to have a certain stickiness to it.

How do we process information? What we understand is shaped by a hunger for narrative. Our minds naturally want things to make sense and they'll do everything possible to put things together into a logical story. We have a discomfort with ambiguity and arbitrary events (Brown, Roediger, & McDaniel, 2014).

In other words, our brains are designed to learn!

This constant seeking of narrative provides a mental framework for giving future experiences and information meaning and a place in the grand scheme of things. Our brains actually shape and interpret new memories to fit established constructs of ourselves and the world.

Our brains naturally seek patterns to solve problems. Our brains are happiest when they make progress toward finding the solution, discovering the pattern, or completing the activity (Hammond, 2014).

Instead of shying away from ambiguity, we poke around in it to see if we can clear it up and add it to the larger narratives that exist in our memories.

This is why prior knowledge is so powerful and should be the entry point for all new learning. If new content can be related to existing knowledge, it makes for a much easier to hook the new learning to current understanding (Jensen, 2005). When teachers understand, respect, and build on students' prior knowledge, they leverage learning in alignment with how our brains naturally learn.

Rock cycle

Let's say, for instance, that you want to teach your third grade students about the rock cycle. You show a large, detailed diagram that has many multi-colored arrows and rich vocabulary terms, such as weathering, erosion, deposition, compaction, igneous, sedimentary, metamorphic, and transportation. You have vocabulary cards ready to go on your word wall and have a crossword puzzle or two ready for their enjoyment.

The only problem is, your students have never learned about rocks. They think of them as simple potential missiles found on the playground and do not consider that there are myriad types of rocks or how they are interrelated.

I'm sure you can picture the standard science textbook diagram now and realize that it's much too large for students to digest all at once without any previous learning. They need prior knowledge to connect this new information to. One option would be to spend time collecting and examining various rocks, gathering necessary exposure through the five senses and exploration of the intricacies of pumice and obsidian.

On the other hand, you can connect the rock cycle to the life cycle of a frog that you just finished studying. Your students loved learning about tadpoles, froglets, and adult frogs. You know that last year they studied the life cycle of a butterfly and in first grade they learned about the life cycle of grasshoppers. Your students are, relatively speaking, life cycle experts and you see this as an opportunity to tack on some new connections.

Knowing this, you decide to introduce the rock cycle in a much more efficient way. Even though the content of each type of cycle is completely different, your students have sufficient background knowledge in how cycles work in science to add to that understanding. You have your students help you create the life cycle of a frog on half of the board and then next to it you begin drawing a new cycle.

You hold up a piece of limestone, label it as *sedimentary rock*, and explain how it's formed when water containing a certain mineral evaporates (something you've learned about previously during the water cycle). You then hold up a marble sample, label it as *metamorphic rock*, and explain how it forms when limestone is exposed to high temperatures and pressures. Marble, through uplift and erosion, can turn back into sedimentary rock. Or, through melting and cooling, can turn into a third type of rock, *igneous*.

Your arrows are now flying all over the place and you're introducing a gaggle of high-leverage vocabulary words. Your students are tracking with you, though not indefinitely, because you linked new learning to previous learning (life cycle of a frog and the water cycle). That simple connection gives their brains enough of a hook for you to connect a few new pieces of information.

Learning by death

When one of your students gets a brand-new video game, the first thing he'll do won't be to open up the instruction manual. He won't find the instructions on the manufacturer's website, read the cautionary warnings about potential electric shock if the game is playing in the bathtub. He won't even search for a walkthrough video showing how to beat the first level, though that is a valid technique if stuck.

He'll play. And he'll die. And he'll learn.

Our brains naturally seek patterns to solve problems.

This strategy, called *learning by death*, is how most students learn a new video game. Most games are designed to have a tutorial level, either formal or informal, that explains the major functions of gameplay and what each button on the controller does. After enough experience with the controls, students are ready to plunge into the open (video game) world and find treasure, defeat monsters, or collect rare insects. Video game developers learned a while ago how to leverage our brain's natural penchant for learning to teach customers how to use their games. It's high time teachers do the same as well.

Called active learning by many, this type of teaching strategy has many biological advantages. When students are trying something out for the first (or thirtieth) time, there's motion involved and that brings in more neural resources. Active involvement increases attention, focus, and thinking skills. Additionally, our brains recall better what we actively do than what we receive passively (Jensen, 2005).

Active learning allows us to have a larger palette of unique mental, emotional, and physical states, key memory makers that are essential to learning. Each separate state mobilizes additional neurons in more lasting and complex connections than mere semantic, or word-based, lessons, such as lectures or reading from a textbook. Trial and error involves more emotional structures because of the brain's natural tendency to predict what will happen next. The feelings that arise out of successful or even unsuccessful predictions can activate the pleasure centers in the brain far more readily than simple memorization or reading tasks.

Physical activities, like role-playing, conducting a science experiment, or welding something in metal shop class, are very easy to recall. They create wider, more complex, and generally better sources of sensory input than mere cognition activities. However you design your learning experiences, the more active they are, the better. Simply by trying, failing, and trying again, students will better encode knowledge than if they were to passively receive it.

Reflection

Another method for making learning stickier is one that takes virtually no preparation or even grading – cultivating a habit of reflection in the classroom. When students think about what they've learned and the experiences they've had while learning, they tend to craft them into a story or larger narrative. This structure strengthens learning because our minds are designed to crave stories (Brown, Roediger, & McDaniel, 2014).

Reflection works so well because it involves several cognitive activities. First, students retrieve past learning, either from short-term or long-term memory. Second, they elaborate on knowledge, connecting new information to what they've already learned. Third, students generate knowledge by rephrasing key ideas in their own words, oftentimes visualizing and mentally rehearsing what they might do differently next time. Finally, the reflection usually has some type of output, written or oral, that provides yet another opportunity to relate topics to prior knowledge and other disciplines.

Students can stop and think about what went right that day, what went wrong, and how they might try something different the next time. When students take a moment to engage in reflection, either on their own or with a partner, it helps them isolate key ideas, organize them into mental models that make sense, and apply these nuggets of knowledge again in the future with an eye toward improvement and building on what they already know.

Active learning allows us to have a larger palette of unique mental, emotional, and physical states, memory tags that are essential to learning.

At the end of a lesson or while packing up to go for the day, put some reflection questions on the board for students to ponder. What went well today? What could have gone better? What other experiences did it remind you of? What strategies might you try next time?

There are two different types of metacognitive reflection that students can engage in (Agarwal & Bain, 2019). One is a judgment of learning, in which students predict their future learning or ability to recall based on past experience. Having students reflect in this manner might go something like this: Based on what you learned today, how well will you do on the activity tomorrow? Why?

A similar type of reflection asks students to rate their confidence in their knowledge. These types of ratings ask them to predict how confident they'll be on an upcoming task or assessment and to justify their level of confidence. Either way, having students reflect on their knowledge and use it as a tool to predict future performance is, in itself, a powerful learning opportunity.

When learning is done, don't let it end! Ask students to reflect on what they've learned, either on their performance or on their potential future performance. Let them write down or share with a partner what the key ideas are and how it relates to another topic. Give them a chance to think about, chew on, and apply their knowledge and their learning potential will increase exponentially.

What can you do tomorrow?

Make learning active. Think about how you can make an upcoming lesson more active. Reduce the amount of passive listening and increase students' participation in creating their own understanding. **Build in time to reflect.** Have students think about what they learned and use their experience to predict how they will perform in the future.

What does this look like in the classroom?

Classroom tasks include **reflection activities** to stamp learning, such as:

- Thinking about what parts of the lesson went well for the students;
- Judging their level of learning and using that to predict their future success; and
- Evaluating their confidence in their learning and justifying it.

How can you reflect on your learning?

How does the brain's hunger for narrative impact how students learn?

_____

_____

Why is active learning better than passive learning?

_____

_____

Engage

Generation

Easy come, easy go should not be the motto of education.

All too often, unfortunately, this saying aptly describes many class sessions. Students listen to something, perhaps watch a video or participate in guided practice, and then work independently on an assignment. This cycle, natural to so many in education, is comfortable but only mildly effective.

The traditional teaching method, as we'll call it here, has two major drawbacks. First, the content is learned only at a surface level for a short period of time. Hopefully students can remember the facts and figures for the end of unit exam, but most forget the important pieces before the end of year assessment. Second, anything learned is isolated and not easily applied to new situations. Students learn a theorem, equation, or factoid but are not able to later recognize it in a slightly different context or scenario.

For students to truly take charge of their learning, they need access to sticky teaching. How students chew on and process new information plays a large part in determining how much of it becomes consolidated in long-term memory and how easy it is to retrieve when needed. Several different types of cognitive actions can be employed to help students better make meaning of what they are learning.

Though correct answers are usually the aim of a question or activity, how students get there can make a world of difference. One technique, called generation, creates a wonderful learning space for students when learning something new. Generation is simply the act of trying to answer a question or attempting to solve a problem before being shown the answer (Brown, Roediger, & McDaniel, 2014).

While this might sound simple (and it is!), there are layers of complexity here. When students are given something they don't fully understand, they are introduced to difficulty, or a disruption of fluency. Our brains do not like not knowing, and this cognitive dissonance craves resolution. We want to know the answer to the problem, the solution to the mystery, because our minds seek balance and completion.

When students are asked to answer a question they don't know, or solve a problem whose procedure is unknown, it requires quite a bit of effort and causes a little frustration. These feelings are the fertile soil in which new information can be planted. Their effort in trying to solve the problem on their own creates emotions and a cognitive framework in which the answer, when revealed, makes the discovered solution memorable. It's the extra effort of trying to work out the problem ahead of time that increases comprehension and learning.

Generation is simply the act of trying to answer a question or attempting to solve a problem before being shown the answer

---

So, if you are a third grade teacher about to introduce the algorithm for solving two-digit by two-digit multiplication problems, don't withhold the joy of trying to figure it out. You can give students a problem, such as 96 x 36, and also provide the answer of 3,456. The purpose here would not be to try to find a solution, since you provided the answer with the practice problem. The new learning will be the standard algorithm, and their task would be to try and figure out how to come to the given answer without using previously learned strategies such as partial products, breaking apart, or repeated addition.

Whether they discover the trick on their own or not, the effort expended in attempting to figure it out ahead of time is what will make the subsequent learning sticky. Instead of throwing random nuggets of wisdom at students and hoping they remember them, introduce disruptions to fluency, or cognitive dissonance, and give them an opportunity to try and solve the mystery themselves. One way or the other, their brains will thank you when the true answer is revealed.

Error correction and feedback

Although it is implied in generation, let's take a moment to really drill down to the power of error correction. Neural networks become more efficient when a learner tries out several possible options and eliminates the ones that don't work. With every trial and error, the neural framework is being added to that will support a strong connection to the correct answer when discovered or revealed (Jensen, 2005).

Feedback-driven learning helps students make more accurate and complex neurological connections. All the generation in the world will ultimately fall short if any errors expressed along the way are not uncovered and corrected. These connections continue to grow with additional usage and ultimately become more efficient.

To be wholly effective, any type of feedback must, at the minimum, contain two powerful elements. First, it should be positive. When delivered harshly or even received with a negative bias, feedback becomes a psychological attack on the students' intelligence and ability, triggering all kinds of emotions and defense mechanisms against which the feedback will bounce off harmlessly.

Additionally, the feedback must be corrective. Receiving a check mark, a smiley face, a grade, or even a red *x* is not feedback. To correct errors, students have to fill in their gaps with knowledge or skills to be able to produce a better result the next time. Don't merely say, "Good job," or, "Please try again." Instead, be specific. Give students details, missing strategies, or hidden information so they know where they erred and how to improve their performance.

Feedback also provides students a chance to calibrate (Brown, Roediger, & McDaniel, 2014). More than simply correcting errors, students are constantly judging their confidence in their knowledge and skills. Students who do a poor job of calibrating, because they overestimate or underestimate their abilities, are more prone to failure. Feedback allows them to align their judgments of what they know and don't know against objective data to avoid illusions of mastery.

Frequent feedback also strengthens the learning partnership between teachers and students (Hammond, 2014). When students recognize that teachers are committed to helping them improve through instruction and feedback, trust is built. Quality feedback is instructive rather than evaluative, specific and in the right dose, timely, and delivered in a low-stress environment. Missing those components can turn even well-intentioned feedback into criticism.

Ultimately, feedback serves as a barrier between knowledge and ignorance. The adage *practice makes perfect* isn't quite right, as any elementary math teacher can attest to. There's nothing more disheartening that seeing a student's homework filled with a procedural error, such as regrouping incorrectly. Doing the wrong thing over and over again will not improve performance. Instead, it will reinforce the error and it'll take twice the work for the teacher to rid the student of his ingrained bad habits.

When students are aware of what they know and don't know, their learning is more successful both in the classroom and out of the classroom. Feedback improves studying because students can drill themselves on the areas in which they need the most support (Agarwal & Bain, 2019).

One final word on feedback. As teachers, we can sometimes get too caught up in correct answers. We sometimes blindly assume that when students give correct answers, that reflects total and complete understanding. Correct answers might result from educated guesses or random luck. Feedback is just as important for correct answers as it is for incorrect answers. Even if you are reasonably certain that the student has a firm grasp on the content, there will inevitably be some gaps. Explanations following correct answers serve to reinforce key points and might just fill in a few gaps that were hidden by the correct answer.

Mental models

In the Indian parable of the *Blind Men and the Elephant*, a group of blind men come across an elephant for the first time and try to conceptualize what it is like by touching it. The first man touches the trunk and claims that the creature is like a big snake. The second man touches the ear and describes the creature as a kind of fan. The next man touches the elephant's leg and argues that it is a tree trunk. The fourth blind man places his hand on the side and is sure he's touching a rough wall. The man who touched its tail thinks that he's grasped a rope and the final man, grabbing the tusk, states that it's a smooth spear.

Without a larger understanding of the elephant, each man is emphatic in his understanding but far from the whole truth. Another key to making meaning is organizing information into mental models that deepen conceptual understanding. More than just learning new content and not knowing how to sort it, students should constantly be evaluating their existing knowledge for patterns and models so they can make sense of the whole. This attitude then allows new information to more easily be absorbed as it is filed with existing knowledge that already exists in a sensible schema (Jensen, 2005).

Students who learn to extract key ideas from new material and organize them into mental models, and then connect those mental models to prior knowledge, show a distinct advantage in learning complex mastery (Brown, Roediger, & McDaniel, 2014). If the blind men already knew of the existence of elephants, or perhaps of a related animal such as a wooly mammoth, they could have worked together to piece their sensory information together to mentally construct the elephant. Without that prior knowledge, however, they truly were the blind leading the blind.

Feedback-driven learning helps students make more accurate and complex neurological connections.

As educators, we must always keep one eye on the details and another on the big picture. Unless students have the structure in place within their prior knowledge to sort the incoming data, most of it will be lost in translation. As you teach, always tie new learning into prior knowledge, even if it's through the use of analogy. Giving this mental structure to students will allow them to retain the information and excel academically.

Elaborate

If we as teachers can do a better job of supporting students as they encode new information, their engagement will increase alongside their achievement while misbehavior fades away. Students all want to learn and be successful because their brains are designed for it. I share in a previous book, *Worksheets Don't Work* (Daffern, 2020), that elaboration is an important tool that teachers can use to help students link new information to prior knowledge and add memory tags so it is easier to recall. Using the term *elaborate* as an acrostic, there are several thought processes and actions that students can take to make learning sticky – explain, look, associate, build, organize, reflect, analyze, try, and extend.

Explain

Teaching something to someone else requires a high amount of concentration and processing. Though ideas often seem simple when mulling them over in our own minds, putting them into words requires a whole different level of understanding. Students gain deep insights into content when they work to explain it to their peers.

Look

The act of observation helps students gather data about what they are learning. By looking and describing what they see, hear, or feel, students invoke multiple senses to aid the encoding of information. Additionally, sometimes students can get a unique perspective by looking at something from a different point of view. By examining ideas or objects from varying viewpoints, they increase the stickiness factor.

Associate

Our brains are pattern detectors. One of the greatest ways to improve memory and recall is to link new learning to something that is already known. When students purposefully look for associations between what they are studying and their prior knowledge, their ability to recall it later grows mightily.

Build

Abstract concepts can sometimes be difficult to understand without a representation to describe it. Students can work to build examples, diagrams, and frameworks, either physical or pictorial, to help make sense of classroom content. Once these representations are built, students will find it much easier to consider the content conceptually.

Organize

Placing new ideas into a larger structure often helps students see the big picture. By classifying information, finding similarities, and exploring nuances, students can work to organize data into memorable forms. These mental models assist students when not only sorting through existing concepts but also help to easily categorize new learning.

Reflect

Too often students overestimate their understanding of a concept. Reflective students gauge what they think they know against objective data, seeking to find gaps in their knowledge and forming strategies to fill them. Rather than breezing past known content, being lured by its familiarity, students should frequently examine how much they really understand something. Through reflection, they can figure out if they truly know what they think they know.

Analyze

Rarely does learning occur in a straight line with simple relationships. More often than not, inferential thinking, component parts, and complex relationships better describe content systems. Sticky learning requires analysis, asking students to explore connections and understand how

Engage

pieces work together.

Try

One of the simplest ways to make learning stick is to try it out. In video games, it's called *learning by death*, as players slowly acclimate to the functions of a game through various attempts and failures. Trial and error, accompanied by purposeful feedback, is one of the most powerful ways to learn something new.

Extend

Some of the best teaching strategies or activities are not terminal. If so desired, they can be added onto to extend learning in a multitude of ways. When students take something and stretch it to new and unique configurations, they are engaging in robust encoding.

What can you do tomorrow?

Connect learning. Prioritize generation and linking new experiences to previous learning. Allow cognitive dissonance, either natural or planned, to percolate long enough to increase the learning potential. **Make learning sticky.** Create maximized learning opportunities by having students use various processes and actions from *elaborate*.

What does this look like in the classroom?

Classroom tasks promote **active learning** using techniques such as:
- Asking students to solve problems and generate solutions before being shown the correct strategy or algorithm (cognitive dissonance);
- Embedding error correction and instructive feedback; and
- Adding newly learned information to mental models.

How can you reflect on your learning?

Why is feedback so important?

_____

_____

Which part of *elaborate* can you use immediately to increase the stickiness of your teaching?

_____

_____

Immediate impact: Go to 5 – 4 Intellectual (Grow) – pg. 383

6 – 5 Conclusion (Engage)

This has been a long journey but hopefully a fulfilling one. Let us revisit the intention behind this book and how it lines up with other district and curricular initiatives.

The need for taking charge came from my experience as an instructional coach, working alongside teachers to help them improve all aspects of their teaching. While I brought them the components of balanced literacy, the intricacies of the science of teaching reading, and talk structures to improve math instruction, I often found that I couldn't coach on what I was hired to coach on.

Instruction can only occur when a solid foundation of self-management has been laid. When students can regulate their emotions and the teacher can provide rituals and routines to ensure an environment of safety, then instructional techniques can be tweaked. Yet in my work as a classroom coach, I ran into teacher after teacher that couldn't take the time or energy to appreciate the similarities between shared writing and shared reading. When your house is burning down, you don't take time to consider if you should replace your older light fixtures with ones that are more energy efficient.

This need to provide teachers with a mental framework for understanding how they and their students can take charge of their classroom served as the genesis of this work. What resulted started as a simple acronym (CHARGE) yet morphed into the tome you are finishing at this moment.

When looking for answers to the classroom management dilemma, I ran into my own obstacles. Too often, the solutions I found focused on only one or two aspects of successful behavior management. You are forced to choose between neuroscience and behavioral therapy, between social-emotional learning and teaching procedures. Instead of choosing one angle, I've attempted to weave them altogether into a larger narrative that incorporates each of them.

Before you begin the journey toward empowering your students to embrace the power of their own learning, you have to know who you're bringing on the journey. It's hard to take students to a place you've never been to, so the first step in classroom management is actually self-management. Gaining true, not phony, confidence in your role, and learning to not shrink from your own power and potential, comes from examining your purpose, your positivity, and offering protection.

Our identity as humans, and the social connections that identity entails, is key to understanding the power of teaching and learning. At its heart, teaching is about relationships. The impact of your teaching is directly proportional to the quality of the relationships you have with your students. Trying to teach students yet ignoring your relationship to them is like trying to start a campfire and ignoring the fact that it's pouring outside. You understand the true heart of teaching when you center on relationships, respect, and release.

Changing behavior, and empowering students to govern themselves successfully, is a large part of classroom management. To that end, the next three steps in the Take CHARGE model all work together to support change management. You make the path toward improvement clearer when you anticipate problems and seek to minimize them ahead of time. This happens when you practice procedures, increase productivity, and spend extra time planning for upcoming lessons.

Additionally, the power of your attention, and learning how to direct it appropriately, is the most powerful weapon you have in your war against misbehavior. Differential social attention, or choosing to give weight only to behaviors that meet your expectations, reinforces what you want to see more of without resorting to shaming or nagging. Your attention, when focused on positive actions and attitudes, can painlessly train your students that to get your attention they'll need to meet your expectations.

Most students are doing the best they can. When their best isn't good enough, teachers can help grow certain qualities in them to improve their learning and social behaviors. Instructing students in interpersonal skills helps them improve their emotional literacy and gives them better tools to use when interacting with others. Intrapersonal skills help bolster their resilience while intellectual skills encourage them to take a more active part in their learning.

Finally, the entire framework up to this point is doomed to fail if the final piece, engagement, is forgotten. Even the most well-behaved students will find it hard to concentrate if they are bored to death. More than simply keeping students entertained, engaging students drives straight at the heart of every educator's desire, increased student achievement. When student motivation is understood, educators can use it to design instruction that engages all students. As teachers understand memory systems and how students make meaning, they can ensure that students are not just interested in their lessons but remember them and can apply them when needed.

Your attention, when focused on positive actions and attitudes, can painlessly train your students that to get your attention they'll need to meet your expectations.

In short, and as mentioned several times throughout this book, taking charge is two-fold. First, teachers take charge by how they enter their classroom each day and design it to be a safe, structured, and supportive environment. More importantly, students take charge when they learn to not only regulate their emotions and behaviors but also direct their own learning.

When these two conditions are met, the possibilities are endless.

Appendix

Confidence Look Fors

The teacher provides **emotional and psychological protection** by:
- Anticipating potential problems and planning for them accordingly;
- Providing comfort and assistance to students; and
- Showing appropriate affection toward students.

The teacher provides **secure attachment** for students by:
- Being emotionally available for them;
- Attuning to their emotional states; and
- Building trust through fulfilling commitments.

Students and teacher build and sustain a **supportive environment** through:
- Positive expectations for students;
- Demonstrations and/or time set aside for gratitude and thankfulness; and
- Instruction delivered in a warm tone of voice.

Students and teacher maintain **positive communication**, as evidenced by:

- Presuming positive intent regarding student misbehavior;
- Students being open to discussing misbehavior and rectifying it as needed; and
- Students seeking support and guidance from the teacher.

Classroom tasks are **designed with purpose** to support student learning by:

- Reflecting students' cultures and interests;
- Stretching students to reach increasing rigorous goals; and
- Aligning with curriculum standards and assessment tools.

Classroom tasks contain **clear learning objectives** that build student success by:

- Outlining what students are learning;
- Describing how students will know that they've met the objective; and
- Making connections to students' lives and the real world.

Heart Look Fors

The teacher develops and maintains **positive relationships** that are reflected in:

- Social conversations between teacher and students;
- Interactions with students that are relaxed and open; and
- Frequent laughter and nurturing facial expressions.

The teacher develops and maintains **connection rituals**, which can include:

- Greeting students at the door with a smile and handshake;
- Classroom rituals (e.g., walk-and-talks); and
- Using humor (sharing jokes, puns, or comics with students).

APPENDIX

Students are held to **high expectations**, as evidenced by:
- Being assigned rigorous tasks that do not water down the curriculum;
- Receiving thoughtful instruction on how to act; and
- Being spoken to with dignity and respect.

Students' **cultural and linguistic heritage** is valued, as evidenced by:
- Diverse environmental print and a classroom library collection that reflects the student population;
- Engagement strategies that maximize cultural strengths (e.g., movement, call-and-response); and
- Artifacts from students' culture on display.

Classroom tasks **empower** students by:
- Embedding authentic choices within them;
- Providing clear instructions and expectations; and
- Aligning with learning goals and curriculum standards.

Classroom tasks develop **student agency** by:
- Allowing freedom in how students complete them;
- Providing students opportunities to analyze and correct mistakes; and
- Including supports to meet the needs of diverse learners.

Anticipate Look Fors

The teacher establishes and consistently practices **routines** that are:
- Clearly structured and explained;
- Visually depicted for easy reference; and
- Reinforced and revisited when correct execution begins to diminish.

The teacher helps students **regulate their emotions** by:
- Teaching a safe place routine;
- Leading/participating in daily breathing exercises; and
- Helping students resolve problems.

Students' **learning time** is maximized, as evidenced by:
- Clear and worthwhile options for early finishers;
- Management tasks being completed swiftly with the aid of students, when possible; and
- Stopping points built into the lesson to check for understanding.

Students **transition** effectively between tasks, as evidenced by:
- Quick execution of the desired actions;
- Corrective feedback and practice opportunities being offered, as needed; and
- Learning opportunities embedded within.

Classroom tasks are **well-planned**, as evidenced by:
- Necessary supplies being readily accessible to students who are comfortable using them;
- Materials (e.g., manipulatives, activity cards, handouts) being prepared in advance; and
- The teacher giving directions effortlessly with minimal errors.

Classroom tasks encourage **student responsibility**, including:
- Helpers assigned to daily managerial tasks;
- Classroom roles being updated and turned over according to an understood and equitable system; and
- One or more students serving as classroom supervisors.

Reinforce Look Fors

The teacher **notices** student behavior, as evidenced by:
- Describing actions rather than judging them;
- Maintaining a calm disposition when discussing actions; and
- Listening fully while still upholding behavioral expectations.

APPENDIX

The teacher **praises** positive student choices, reinforcing beneficial behavior by:
- Frequently describing specific actions that meet expectations,
- Using an enthusiastic tone of voice; and
- Providing immediate and personal feedback.

Students learn to **inhibit negative behaviors** through teacher actions, including:
- Receiving positive, enthusiastic attention when meeting expectations,
- Having negative behaviors ignored; and
- Not being shamed for making poor choices.

Students receive **differential social attention** to reinforce good behaviors, such as:
- Noticing by the teacher when correct actions are initiated;
- Positive praise for continuing desired behaviors; and
- Immediate, descriptive feedback that narrates specific actions.

Classroom tasks build **camaraderie** between students, as evidenced by:
- Positive attitudes between students;
- Interdependence and peer assistance; and
- Embedded supports that allows for successful independent completion of tasks (if desired).

Classroom responsibilities promote a **positive moral identity** in students by:
- Encouraging students to help and serve one another;
- Allowing students to build positive self-images through their actions; and
- Reinforcing the communal structure and interdependence of the classroom.

Grow Look Fors

The teacher supports the development of **grit** by:

- Highlighting the importance of effort over talent;
- Providing unstructured time for students to develop their interests; and
- Designing practice and feedback sessions to grow students' skills.

The teacher encourages a **growth mindset** in students by:

- Modeling a growth mindset himself/herself;
- Normalizing errors and helping students accept the desirable difficulty of tasks; and
- Using feedback statements that encourage effort and the use of strategies over raw talent.

Students develop **emotional literacy** by:

- Recognizing emotions in themselves and others;
- Labeling emotions with and increasingly nuanced vocabulary; and
- Regulating their emotions through breathing, reflection, and other techniques.

Students practice **empathy** by:

- Actively working to solve relational problems with classmates;
- Taking the perspective of other students; and
- Role playing to understand how their words and actions affect others.

Classroom tasks nurture **curiosity** in students by:

- Including sufficient procedural knowledge to accomplish tasks independently;
- Bridging across content areas and providing a means of exploration; and
- Encouraging students to transfer knowledge into the production of

authentic artifacts.

Classroom tasks support **student creativity** by:

- Embedding open-ended and ambiguous elements;
- Resting on a foundation of autonomy and student choice; and
- Encouraging partner or group collaboration.

Engage Look Fors

The teacher **motivates** students to engage in learning by:

- Offering students choices and opportunities to lead lessons;
- Highlighting real-word connections within the curriculum; and
- Providing timely feedback to build students' competence.

The teacher **designs engaging instruction** that includes:

- Differentiated tasks to meet individual student needs;
- Activities that are fun and light-hearted; and
- Social interactions between the teacher and students and/or between students themselves.

Students **practice retrieval** regularly, using techniques such as:

- Stopping during instruction to discuss or write notes about what was just learned;
- Purposefully recalling information from past lessons; and
- Writing a short summary of the lesson for homework.

Students review material using **memory techniques**, including:

- Immediate feedback to validate the retrieval;
- Spacing out the recall to increase the difficulty; and
- Mixing up the content to encourage recognition and discrimination.

Classroom tasks include **reflection activities** to stamp learning, such as:

- Thinking about what parts of the lesson went well for the students;
- Judging their level of learning and using that to predict their future

success; and

- Evaluating their confidence in their learning and justifying it.

Classroom tasks promote **active learning** using techniques such as:

- Asking students to solve problems and generate solutions before being shown the correct strategy or algorithm (cognitive dissonance);
- Embedding error correction and instructive feedback; and
- Adding newly learned information to mental models.

You can find a PDF version of these Look Fors on my website at *AaronDaffern.com/resources.*

Bibliography

Agarwal, P. K., & Bain, P. M. (2019). *Powerful teaching: Unleash the science of learning.* Jossey-Bass.

Bailey, R. A. (2015). *Conscious discipline: Building resilient classrooms.* Oviedo, FL: Loving Guidance.

Birnie, B. F. (2017). *A teacher's guide to successful classroom management and differentiated instruction.* Lanham: Rowman & Littlefield.

Borba, M. (2017). *Unselfie: Why empathetic kids succeed in our all-about-me world.* Touchstone.

Brackett, M. A. (2018). The emotional intelligence we owe students and educators. *Educational Leadership, 76*(2), 12-18.

Brafman, O., & Brafman, R. (2010). *Click: The magic of instant connections.* Crown Business.

Brown, B. (2018). *Dare to lead: Brave work, tough conversations, whole hearts.* Random House.

Brown, P. C., Roediger, H. L., & McDaniel, M. A. (2014). *Make it stick: The science of successful learning.* Belknap Press: An Imprint of Harvard University Press.

Cadiergue, D. (2015, March 26). *The science (and practice) of creativity.* Retrieved from Edutopia: https://www.edutopia.org/blog/changemakers-science-practice-of-creativity-diane-cadiergue

Covey, S. M., & Merrill, R. R. (2008). *The speed of trust: The one thing that changes everything.* New York: FranklinCovey.

Daffern, A. (2017). *Solving student engagement: Designing instruction to motivate every student.* Aaron Daffern Consulting.

Daffern, A. (2018). *Wrestling with words: The five parts of a powerful vocabulary program.* Aaron Daffern Consulting.

Daffern, A. (2020). *Worksheets don't work: 50 engaging tasks that make learning stick.* Aaron Daffern Consulting.

Davis, L. C. (2018, December 17). *Creative teaching and teaching creativity: How to foster creativity in the classroom.* Retrieved from Psych Learning Curve:

BIBLIOGRAPHY

http://psychlearningcurve.org/creative-teaching-and-teaching-creativity-how-to-foster-creativity-in-the-classroom/

Duckworth, A. (2016). *Grit: The power of passion and perseverance.* Scribner Book Company.

Dweck, C. S. (2006). *Mindset: The new psychology of success.* Random House.

Dweck, C. S. (2015, 22 September). *Carol Dweck revisits the 'growth mindset'.* Retrieved from Education Week: https://www.edweek.org/leadership/opinion-carol-dweck-revisits-the-growth-mindset/2015/09

Gruber, M. J., Gelman, B. D., & Ranganath, C. (2014). States of curiosity modulate hippocampus-dependent learning via the dopaminergic circuit. *Neuron, 84*(2), 486-496. doi:https://doi.org/10.1016/j.neuron.2014.08.060

Hagopian, L. P., Fisher, W. W., & Legacy, S. M. (1994). Schedule effects of noncontingent reinforcement on attention-maintained destructive behavior in identical quadruplets. *Journal of Applied Behavior Analysis, 27*(2), 317-325.

Hammond, Z. (2014). *Culturally responsive teaching and the brain: Promoting authentic engagement and rigor among culturally and linguistically diverse students.* Thousand Oaks, CA: Corwin.

Heath, C., & Heath, D. (2010). *Switch: How to change things when change is hard.* Crown Business.

Heick, T. (2019, October 7). *From procedural knowledge to self knowledge: The 4 stages of curiosity.* Retrieved from Teachthought: https://www.teachthought.com/learning/4-stages-of-curiosity/

Jensen, E. (2005). *Teaching with the brain in mind.* ASCD.

Johnson, B. (2019, January 16). *4 ways to develop creativity in students.* Retrieved from Edutopia: https://www.edutopia.org/article/4-ways-develop-creativity-students

Kashdan, T. B., Sherman, R. A., Yarbro, J., & Funder, D. C. (2012). How are curious people viewed and how do they behave in social situations? From the perspectives of self, friends, parents, and unacquainted observers. *Journal of Personality, 81*(2), 142-154. doi:https://doi.org/10.1111/j.1467-6494.2012.00796.x

Minahan, J. (2019). Trauma-informed teaching strategies. *Educational Leadership, 77*(2), 30-35.

Minahan, J., & Rappaport, N. (2012). *The behavior code: A practical guide to understanding and teaching the most challenging students.* Cambridge, MA: Harvard University Press.

Ostroff, W. L. (2016). *Cultivating curiosity in K-12 classrooms: How to promote and sustain deep learning.* ASCD.

Price-Mitchell, M. (2015, August 14). *Cultivating creativity in standards-based classrooms.* Retrieved from Edutopia: https://www.edutopia.org/blog/cultivating-creativity-standards-based-classrooms-marilyn-price-mitchell

Sage, J. (2017). *Happy class: The practical guide to classroom management.* Lanham, MD: Rowman & Littlefield.

Shapiro, S. L., & White, C. (2014). *Mindful discipline: A loving approach to setting limits and raising an emotionally intelligent child.* Oakland, CA: New Harbinger Publications.

Siegel, D. J., & Bryson, T. P. (2012). *The whole-brain child: 12 revolutionary strategies to nurture your child's developing mind.* Bantam.

Siegel, D. J., & Bryson, T. P. (2021). *The power of showing up: How parental presence shapes who our kids become and how their brains get wired.* Ballantine Books.

Srinivasan, M. (2014). *Teach, breathe, learn: Mindfulness in and out of the classroom.* Berkeley, CA: Parallax Press.

von Stumm, S., Hell, B., & Chamorro-Premuzic, T. (2011). The hungry mind: Intellectual curiosity is the third pillar of academic performance. *Perspectives on Psychological Science, 6,* 574-588.

doi:https://doi.org/10.1177/1745691611421204

Vygotsky, L. S. (1978). *Mind in society: The development of higher psychological processes.* Cambridge, MA: Harvard University Press.

Willans, A., & Williams, C. L. (2018). *Freedom to learn: Creating a classroom where every child thrives.* Gabriola Island, BC: New Society Publishers.

Wong, H. K., & Wong, R. T. (1997). *The first days of school: How to be an effective teacher.* Harry K Wong Publishing.

About the author

Aaron lives in Ft. Worth, TX, with his wife Heather, his children Dave, Drew, Desiree, and Daniel. He is an avid disc golfer and sports nut, closely following the Rangers, Cowboys, and Mavericks. He enjoys fantasy novels, watching Star Trek, the Marvel Cinematic Universe, James Bond, and reading peer-reviewed educational psychology research articles.

Before becoming an education consultant, Aaron spent over ten years in the classroom as a 3rd, 4th, and 6th grade teacher. He also spent several years as a campus and district administrator of a charter school in Arlington, TX before becoming an instructional specialist and later manager in a large urban district in the DFW area.

Aaron has written two previous books on the subject of student engagement – *Solving Student Engagement: Designing Instruction to Motivate Every Student* and *Don't Quit Your Day Job: An Educator's Guide to Student Engagement*. He also wrote about best practices in vocabulary instruction – *Wrestling with Words: The Five Parts of a Powerful Vocabulary Program*. His fourth book fights against boredom in the classroom – *Worksheets Don't Work: 50 Engaging Tasks That Make Learning Stick*. In addition to writing profusely, Aaron serves as an instructional, leadership, and executive coach, mentoring educators both on-site and online. He also trains educators across the country in increasing instructional techniques that engage students and maximize learning.

You can connect with Aaron online at AaronDaffern.com, email him at AaronDaffern@gmail.com, and follow him on Twitter @AaronDaffern.

www.ingramcontent.com/pod-product-compliance
Lightning Source LLC
Chambersburg PA
CBHW050117170426
43197CB00011B/1614